A TRANSLATOR'S HANDBOOK
on
THE BOOKS OF NAHUM, HABAKKUK,
and
ZEPHANIAH

Helps for Translators Series

Technical Helps:

Old Testament Quotations in the New Testament
Short Bible Reference System
New Testament Index
The Theory and Practice of Translation
Bible Index
Fauna and Flora of the Bible
Marginal Notes for the Old Testament
Marginal Notes for the New Testament
The Practice of Translating

Handbooks:

A Translator's Handbook on . . .

Leviticus
the Book of Joshua
the Book of Ruth
the Book of Psalms
the Book of Amos
the Books of Obadiah and Micah
the Book of Jonah
the Books of Nahum, Habakkuk, and Zephaniah
the Gospel of Matthew
the Gospel of Mark
the Gospel of Luke
the Gospel of John
the Acts of the Apostles
Paul's Letter to the Romans
Paul's First Letter to the Corinthians
Paul's Letter to the Galatians
Paul's Letter to the Ephesians
Paul's Letter to the Philippians
Paul's Letters to the Colossians and to Philemon
Paul's Letters to the Thessalonians
the Letter to the Hebrews
the First Letter from Peter
the Letters of John

Guides:

A Translator's Guide to . . .

Selections from the First Five Books of the Old Testament
Selected Psalms
the Gospel of Matthew
the Gospel of Mark
the Gospel of Luke
Paul's First Letter to the Corinthians
Paul's Second Letter to the Corinthians
Paul's Letters to Timothy and to Titus
the Letters to James, Peter, and Jude
the Revelation to John

HELPS FOR TRANSLATORS

A TRANSLATOR'S HANDBOOK
on
THE BOOKS OF NAHUM, HABAKKUK,
and
ZEPHANIAH

by
DAVID J. CLARK
and
HOWARD A. HATTON

UNITED BIBLE SOCIETIES

New York

© 1989 by the United Bible Societies

All Rights Reserved

No part of this book may be translated or reproduced in any form without the written permission of the United Bible Societies.

The text of the Revised Standard Version of the Bible used in this publication is copyrighted 1946, 1952, © 1971, 1973 by the Division of Christian Education of the National Council of the Churches of Christ in the U.S.A., and used by permission.

Quotations from Today's English Version are used by permission of the copyright owner, the American Bible Society, © 1966, 1971, 1976.

Illustration on page 56 by Horace Knowles Copyright © The British and Foreign Bible Society, London, England, 1954, 1967, 1972. Illustration on page 26 by Annie Vallotton © 1976 by American Bible Society.

Books in the series of **Helps for Translators** may be ordered from a national Bible Society, or from either of the following centers:

United Bible Societies
European Production Fund
D-7000 Stuttgart 80
Postfach 81 03 40
West Germany

United Bible Societies
1865 Broadway
New York, New York 10023
U.S.A.

L.C. Cataloging-in-Publication Data

Clark, David J., 1937-
   A translator's handbook on the books of Nahum, Habakkuk, and Zephaniah / by David J. Clark and Howard A. Hatton.
        p.   cm. -- (Helps for translators)
   Bibliography: p.
   Includes index.
   ISBN 0-8267-0130-2
   1. Bible. O.T. Nahum--Commentaries. 2. Bible. O.T. Nahum--Translating. 3. Bible. O.T. Habakkuk--Commentaries. 4. Bible. O.T.   Habakkuk--Translating.   5. Bible.   O.T. Zephaniah--Commentaries. 6. Bible. O.T. Zephaniah--Translating. I. Hatton, Howard, 1929- . II. Title. III. Series.
BS1625.3.C55 1989
224'.9406--dc20   89-34150
                                                                CIP

ABS-1991-1,250-CM-2-102694

Contents

Preface vii

Abbreviations used in this volume ix

Nahum
    Translating the Book of Nahum 1
    The Lord's Vengeance against Nineveh (1.1-15) 3
    A Description of the Fall of the City (2.1—3.19) 23

Habakkuk
    Translating the Book of Habakkuk 65
    Questions and Answers (1.1—2.5) 68
        Habakkuk's First Question (1.2-4) 69
        The Lord's First Answer (1.5-11) 72
        Habakkuk's Second Question (1.12-17) 81
        The Lord's Second Answer (2.1-5) 88
    Taunts against the Wicked (2.6-20) 94
        The First Taunt (2.6-8) 94
        The Second Taunt (2.9-11) 100
        The Third Taunt (2.12-14) 103
        The Fourth Taunt (2.15-17) 105
        The Fifth Taunt (2.18-20) 109
    Habakkuk's Prayer: A Psalm of Trust (3.1-19) 113

Zephaniah
    Translating the Book of Zephaniah 141
    The Day of the Lord's Judgment (1.1—2.3) 143
        Introduction (1.1) 143
        The Announcement of the Lord's Punishment
        (1.2-18) 144
        A Call to Repentance (2.1-3) 163
    The Doom of Israel's Neighbors (2.4-15) 166
    Jerusalem's Doom and Redemption (3.1-20) 182

Bibliography 205

Glossary 209

Index 219

Preface

The publication of *A Translator's Handbook on the Books of Nahum, Habakkuk, and Zephaniah* marks another step forward in preparing the much-needed Helps for Translators that cover books of the Old Testament. The authors of this volume have spent many years working with translation teams in a variety of languages from a number of language families. It is out of this experience that they have combined exegetical, linguistic, and cultural information so that other translators from the widest variety of linguistic backgrounds may have access to the data they need for responsible translation of the books of these prophets.

While many who use this Handbook may be thoroughly acquainted with the Hebrew language in which these three books have come down to us, the authors have attempted to address the information to those who do not know Hebrew. And they have done so with the intention of providing them with as much information as possible that is important for translation, so that the readers will be as well equipped as if they did have a knowledge of Hebrew. The Revised Standard Version (RSV) serves as a kind of window through which to explain the Hebrew, and therefore it serves as the base on which the discussion is built. The Today's English Version (TEV) is provided as one of many possible alternative models which may suggest ideas for re-creating the original message in a functional manner in a language of today. Many modern versions, including TEV, occasionally yield some unfortunate models of translation which should be avoided. Therefore there is no substitute for a careful study and analysis of the text prior to any attempt at rendering it in the receptor language.

RSV and TEV are displayed in small print and without footnotes at the beginning of each larger section of text. Certain aspects of the discourse structure of the section will be made more apparent in this way, and the translator can see how these two versions have divided the text into paragraphs or into poetic lines. The two texts are then displayed again in parallel columns, in boldface, footnotes included, prior to the discussion of individual verses. Quotations from RSV in the verse under discussion are in **<u>underlined boldface</u>**, while those from TEV are in "**boldface within quotation marks**." Quotations from other portions of RSV or of TEV are displayed in the same way as quotations from other versions of the Scriptures, namely, in ordinary print and within quotation marks.

This Handbook, like others in the series, concentrates on exegetical information important for translators, and it attempts to indicate possible solutions for translational problems related to language or culture. The authors do not consciously attempt to provide help that other theologians and scholars may seek but which is not directly related to the translation task. Such information is normally sought elsewhere.

A limited Bibliography is included for the benefit of those interested in further study. The Glossary explains technical terms according to their usage in this volume. The translator may find it useful to read through the Glossary in order to become aware of the specialized way in which certain terms are used.

PREFACE

An Index give the location by page number of some of the important words and subjects discussed in the Handbook, especially where the Handbook provides the translator with help in rendering these concepts into the receptor language.

Several colleagues from within the United Bible Societies' family of translation personnel have provided important comments and help, based on earlier drafts of the manuscript. But the authors and editorial staff wish to include a special word of thanks to others who have helped: the Rev. Theo Aerts, MSC, and the Rev. Dr. Theodore N. Swanson, who commented on earlier drafts of the exegetical material, and especially Dr. Katharine Barnwell, Miss Mona Perrin, and Dr. Elaine Thomas, of the Summer Institute of Linguistics, and to their translation teams whom they involved in the project. They did a good exegetical and practical review, relating the material to their work at hand, and provided comments that were very useful to the authors. The editor of Helps for Translators continues to seek comments from translators and others who use these books, so that future volumes may benefit and may better serve the needs of the readers.

Abbreviations Used in This Volume

General Abbreviations, Bible Texts, Versions, and Other Works Cited
(For details see Bibliography)

B.C.	Before Christ	Mft	Moffatt
BJ	*Bible de Jérusalem*	NAB	New American Bible
FrCL	French common language version	NEB	New English Bible
		NIV	New International Version
GeCL	German common language version	NJV	New Jewish Version, *The Prophets*
HOTTP	Hebrew Old Testament Text Project, Preliminary and Interim Report	RSV	Revised Standard Version
		RV	Revised Version
		TEV	Today's English Version
JB	Jerusalem Bible	TOB	*Traduction œcuménique de la Bible*
KJV	King James Version		

Books of the Bible

Gen	Genesis	Dan	Daniel
Exo	Exodus	Hos	Hosea
Lev	Leviticus	Hab	Habakkuk
Num	Numbers	Zeph	Zephaniah
Deut	Deuteronomy	Hag	Haggai
Josh	Joshua	Zech	Zechariah
1,2 Sam	1,2 Samuel	Mal	Malachi
1,2 Kgs	1,2 Kings	Matt	Matthew
Neh	Nehemiah	Rom	Romans
Psa	Psalms	1,2 Cor	1,2 Corinthians
Isa	Isaiah	Gal	Galatians
Jer	Jeremiah	1,2 Tim	1,2 Timothy
Lam	Lamentations	Heb	Hebrews
Ezek	Ezekiel	Rev	Revelation

Translating the Book of Nahum

The short prophecy of Nahum is concerned solely with the fall of Nineveh, the capital of the Assyrian empire. There is no statement within the book about when it was written, but certain limits can be set, based on references to historical events whose dates are known. In 3.8-10 the prophet speaks of the fall of the Egyptian city of Thebes. This took place in 663 B.C., so the Book of Nahum must be dated later than that. The prophet also speaks of the fall of Nineveh as something which was inevitable at the time of writing and could not be long delayed (2.1). Nineveh was actually captured by the Babylonians and Medes in the middle of 612 B.C., so it seems most probable that the Book of Nahum comes from a time shortly before that date, say 613 or early 612. Such a date could also explain the fact noted by many scholars that Nahum, unlike almost all the other prophets, makes no mention of the sins of Judah. Under the godly king Josiah a national reform of religion had been started in 621 B.C., and this continued in effect until Josiah's death in 609. If Nahum was writing in about 613, the social evils spoken about, both by earlier prophets like Zephaniah and by later ones like Habakkuk, were probably being suppressed by Josiah.

Because the theme of Nahum's prophecy is restricted to a single topic, the fall of Nineveh, some scholars have contrasted Nahum with Jeremiah, who lived at the same time and had a much broader range of interests. Some have even said that Nahum seems closer in outlook to such false prophets as Zedekiah (1 Kgs 22) and Hananiah (Jer 28) than to Jeremiah. However, it is rather unrealistic to compare a book of only three chapters with a book of fifty-two chapters like Jeremiah. We simply do not know what views Nahum may have held on topics he does not mention, and it would be rash to jump to conclusions.

Nahum's attitude toward Nineveh may appear to be vindictive, but it must be remembered that for the previous 130 years the Assyrians had been very cruel and oppressive toward all the smaller states that they had conquered or dominated, including Judah. When the prophet rejoices in the fall of such a vicious and arrogant enemy, he is rejoicing in one aspect of the character of the Lord, who "never lets the guilty go unpunished" (1.3, Today's English Version [TEV]). In one sense, the destruction of an empire as brutal as that of the Assyrians is a symbol of the final triumph of the Lord over all the forces of evil. The Book of Nahum is rarely quoted directly in the New Testament, but its spirit and attitudes can be seen in the description of the fall of "Babylon" in Revelation 18, where the theme of the final victory of the Lord is taken up and developed more fully.

Outline

The Book of Nahum is relatively simple in its outline, consisting of only two parts.

       1.1-15:   The LORD's vengeance against Nineveh.
       2.1—3.19: A description of the fall of the city.

The division of these two sections into shorter paragraphs is discussed at the beginning of each section. It is notable that the French common language (FrCL) and German common language (GeCL) versions use more section headings than TEV. Where these may be helpful, they are noted in the main body of the text.

The Poetic Layout of the Book

In the Revised Standard Version (RSV) the entire book is set out in poetic format with the exception of one verse (2.13). Even in TEV, three large sections are set out in poetic format (1.2-10; 2.1,3-12; and 3.1-7). There is no need for translations into other languages to follow these examples unless there is some reason for doing so. Since the linguistic features that distinguish poetry from prose are very different in different languages, it is useless to try to copy the outward features of the original Hebrew poetry. However, if translators think that any parts of the Book of Nahum are appropriate to translate into poetry in their languages, they are of course free to try. For further advice see *A Translator's Handbook on the Book of Amos*, pages 10-19.

Deciding on the Meaning of Difficult Verses

In the comments on the Books of Nahum, Habakkuk, and Zephaniah, there are many places where the meaning of the Hebrew is uncertain. When any of two or more meanings is possible, the comments often make a recommendation about which meaning is more probable. But in some places the evidence is so evenly divided that no clear recommendation can be made. In such cases people who are translating into minority languages will usually be wise to follow the meaning given in the most widely used translation in the national language of their country, or in some other major language of their area. They should of course check that the version they propose to follow does give one of the acceptable meanings and is itself free from errors of translation or printing.

SECTION 1: THE LORD'S VENGEANCE AGAINST NINEVEH
(Chapter 1.1-15)

Chapter 1

Within this section the opening verse serves as a title for the whole book, but there is a wide range of opinion on how best to divide up the remaining verses into paragraphs. Only RSV, TEV, and GeCL have a break in the middle of verse 3, and only TEV, New International Version (NIV), and GeCL have a break after verse 6. However, Jerusalem Bible (JB), New American Bible (NAB), *Traduction œcuménique de la Bible* (TOB), NIV, FrCL, and GeCL have a break after verse 8. The reason for this is that verses 2-8 form part of an incomplete alphabetic poem (see the opening comments on verses 2-8). The structure of this poem cannot be clearly traced beyond verse 8, and that is apparently why these versions have a break there.

TEV implies a major break after verse 10 by dropping at that point the pattern of indented lines which indicates poetry in the Hebrew. In the latter part of the chapter, there is more agreement between versions. All except New English Bible (NEB) place paragraph breaks after verse 13 and after verse 14, and most place one also after verse 15.

In the light of all these different views, it is impossible to give firm advice to translators. They should always consider the needs of their own readers and the natural patterns of their own languages. However, in this section they should consider having paragraph breaks at least after verses 8, 10, 13, and 14.

1.1 REVISED STANDARD VERSION | TODAY'S ENGLISH VERSION

An oracle concerning Nineveh. The book of the vision of Nahum of Elkosh. | This is a message about Nineveh, the account of a vision seen by Nahum, who was from Elkosh.

This verse is a title to the book and is actually in two parts, as shown by RSV with two separate sentences. The first part gives the content of the prophecy, **An oracle concerning Nineveh**.

Oracle is a technical term for a message given by a prophet ("**message**" in TEV) and occurs frequently in the Old Testament, for instance in Isaiah 13.1; 14.28; 15.1. If translators have in their languages a technical term for a message given through spiritual insight, they may be able to use it here, but only if it is not too closely linked with evil spirits. In order to avoid such misunderstandings, some translators may prefer to translate this sentence as "This is a message from God concerning the city of Nineveh."

Nineveh was the capital city of the Assyrian empire. Its site is near the modern town of Mosul in northern Iraq. In some translations it will be helpful to say "the city of Nineveh" or "the city called Nineveh."

The book of the vision of Nahum of Elkosh: the second part of the title speaks about the prophet himself and his experiences. The use of the term **book** here ("account" in TEV) may imply that the prophecy was written down at an early date. Nahum's is the only prophecy which calls itself a **book**, and this is rather unexpected because the prophecy is so short. Although in English it is traditional to speak of the "books" of the prophets, the translators of TEV felt here in verse 1 that the term "**account**" was more in keeping with the length of the document. Translators should bear this example in mind when choosing a term in their own languages. Some languages may have to use a verbal phrase for **book** or "account." One may say "Nahum wrote down the things he saw" or " . . . the things God showed him in a vision."

Nahum had a **vision** in which he saw the scenes described in the book. This may mean that he received his message while in a trance or some similar state. This word is quite common in the prophetic writings (compare Obadiah 1). The Hebrew term does not put any special emphasis on the means by which the prophet received his message, and there is no need for the translator to do so. It is not clear in the Old Testament how **visions** differ from "dreams." In some instances such as Job 20.8; 33.15, they are synonymous. In languages which do not distinguish between dreams and visions, the translator may have to use the word for "dream" in every instance where the word **vision** occurs.

The name **Nahum** means "full of comfort." It does not occur elsewhere in the Old Testament, though names with related meaning like Nehemiah and Menahem do. We know nothing about **Nahum** except for the fact stated here, that he was from **Elkosh**. This village has not been satisfactorily identified. Commentaries suggest at least four possible places, of which the most likely is in southwestern Judea. For the translator this is not an important question, and it will not be discussed further. Since **Elkosh** is an unfamiliar name, translators may wish to identify it with a generic term and say "from the village of Elkosh." Other possible translation models for this first verse are the following:

> This is a message from God concerning the city of Nineveh. God caused Nahum from the village of Elkosh to see these things in a vision (or, dream), and he wrote them down in this book.

Or:

> This book is a message from God concerning the city of Nineveh. Nahum from the village of Elkosh received this message in a vision (or, dream).

1.2-8

	RSV		TEV
2	The LORD is a jealous God and avenging, the LORD is avenging and wrathful; the LORD takes vengeance on his adversaries and keeps wrath for his enemies.	2	The LORD God tolerates no rivals; he punishes those who oppose him. In his anger he pays them back.
3	The LORD is slow to anger and of great might, and the LORD will by no means clear the guilty.	3	The LORD does not easily become angry, but he is powerful and never lets the guilty go unpunished.
			Where the LORD walks, storms arise;

THE LORD'S VENGEANCE AGAINST NINEVEH   Nahum 1.2-8

	His way is in whirlwind and storm,		the clouds are the dust raised by his feet!
4	He rebukes the sea and makes it dry, he dries up all the rivers; Bashan and Carmel wither, the bloom of Lebanon fades.	4	He commands the sea, and it dries up! He makes the rivers go dry. The fields of Bashan wither, Mount Carmel turns brown, and the flowers of Lebanon fade.
5	The mountains quake before him, the hills melt; the earth is laid waste before him, the world and all that dwell therein.	5	Mountains quake in the presence of the LORD; hills melt before him. The earth shakes when the LORD appears; the world and all its people tremble.
6	Who can stand before his indignation? Who can endure the heat of his anger? His wrath is poured out like fire, and the rocks are broken asunder by him.	6	When he is angry, who can survive? Who can survive his terrible fury? He pours out his flaming anger; rocks crumble to dust before him.
7	The LORD is good, a stronghold in the day of trouble; he knows those who take refuge in him.	7	The LORD is good; he protects his people in times of trouble; he takes care of those who turn to him.
8	But with an overflowing flood he will make a full end of his adversaries, and will pursue his enemies into darkness.	8	Like a great rushing flood he completely destroys his enemies; he sends to their death those who oppose him.

The difficulties of breaking this section into paragraphs have already been mentioned. Verses 2-8 have the form of an alphabetic poem, usually called an acrostic. Some scholars say that the poem extends to verse 10, others, to verse 14, but there is no general agreement. An acrostic poem is a poem in which the first word of each new line in Hebrew begins with a different letter of the Hebrew alphabet. The letters occur in alphabetical order. This type of poem is found in several places in the Old Testament; for instance, Psalm 25; 34; 37; 111; 112; 119; 145; Proverbs 31.10-31; Lamentations 1—4. In this case the poem goes only halfway through the alphabet, up to the eleventh of the twenty-two letters. In this respect its nearest parallel is found in Psalm 9, which uses ten of the first eleven letters. However, most of the remaining letters not used in Psalm 9 are used in Psalm 10, so that the cases are not exactly parallel.

Two things need to be said about this type of poem. The first is that it depends on the Hebrew alphabetical order and therefore can hardly ever be carried over into another language. Unless the other language also happened to have twenty-two letters, it would not even be possible to try. In any case the effort would be pointless unless readers were already accustomed to poems of this kind and appreciated them. Knox produced alphabetic patterns in his translation into English of the passages listed above, but probably he succeeded only in mystifying his readers.

The second thing to be said about acrostic poems is that the form required in the Hebrew can take precedence over the flow of thought. In a translation the alphabetic form is lost, and as a result the flow of thought may seem erratic or even illogical. There is not much that the translator can do about this, but he can help his readers if he includes a footnote to explain what has happened, as do *Bible de Jérusalem* (BJ), NEB, and TOB. Some translations even give the names of the Hebrew letters at the side of the page (BJ, JB, TOB). Few translators will find this useful, but if it is done it should certainly be explained in a footnote.

Verses 2-8 speak of the Lord's righteous anger and greatness. They describe the effect of the Lord's presence upon nature in a way which recalls such passages as Exodus 19.18; Psalms 18.7-12; 29; 97.1-5; 106.9; Amos 1.2; Micah

1.3-4. These verses have sometimes been referred to as Nahum's psalm. They do not say anything about the fall of Nineveh, but in speaking about the God who planned that fall, they form a fitting introduction to the following description of it.

SECTION HEADING: "**The LORD's Anger against Nineveh.**" The TEV heading for this section may need to be expanded slightly to say "The LORD is angry with the people of Nineveh." Other possibilities include "The LORD can be trusted to do right" (compare FrCL) or "The LORD's power to save" (compare GeCL).

1.2

RSV

The LORD is a jealous God and avenging,
the LORD is avenging and wrathful;
the LORD takes vengeance on his adversaries
and keeps wrath for his enemies.

TEV

The LORD God tolerates no rivals;
he punishes those who oppose him.
In his anger he pays them back.

Hebrew poetry is often repetitive, but this verse in Hebrew consists of four lines which are even more repetitive than usual. The identical phrase in Hebrew, "the LORD avenges," occurs in the first three of the four lines, though no major English version uses the same expression three times. Before attempting to translate the details of this verse, the translator will have to decide which of the following approaches will sound best in the receptor language:
(1) to use the same expression three times, as the Hebrew does;
(2) to use three related but slightly different expressions, as RSV does;
(3) to avoid the repetition and make the statements in different terms, as TEV does.

For the translation of **LORD**, see *A Translator's Handbook on the Book of Ruth*, page 10; *A Translator's Handbook on the Book of Jonah*, pages 6, 19; and *A Translator's Handbook on the Book of Amos*, page 66.

The LORD is a jealous God and avenging: this phrase recalls such passages as Exodus 20.5; 34.14; Deuteronomy 32.21. In English versions the traditional translation here is <u>jealous</u> (RSV and most other versions). Since the word <u>jealous</u> in modern English speech almost always carries bad overtones and means "resentful about and envious of that which belongs to someone else," it is not appropriate to apply it to God. The meaning when applied to God is rather "desirous to preserve that which is rightly his." TEV has therefore avoided the word <u>jealous</u>, and instead it has stated the real meaning in this context by saying "The LORD God tolerates no rivals." In some languages the idea of "rivals" may need to be made more explicit. It is possible to translate this as "The LORD God will not tolerate people worshiping other gods."

As mentioned above, the word <u>avenging</u> occurs three times in the Hebrew but only twice in RSV; TEV expresses it with the words "**punishes**" and "**pays . . . back.**" The word rendered as "**punishes**" in this context refers to a very strong action by God. So the translator should, if possible, use a word which conveys the idea of drastic punishment. The phrase "**pays . . . back**" is of course an English metaphor originally related to the use of money, but it is now in common use and has practically lost its figurative sense. This idiom carries the overtones of threat and goes well with the earlier word "**punishes**." Here the prophet means that God's enemies have done evil things against him in the past, and now God is going to punish them (pay them back) in a similar way.

The words <u>**adversaries**</u> and <u>**enemies**</u> are expressed in a single clause in TEV as "**those who oppose him**." But many languages will have two or more synonyms, as does the Hebrew. If a translator plans to use a structure similar to that in RSV, synonyms should certainly be employed. The two Hebrew terms <u>**wrathful**</u> and <u>**keeps wrath**</u> are expressed in TEV by the single phrase "**in his anger**." In certain languages it will be helpful to expand this sentence and say "He pays them back because they have made him angry" or "He is angry with his enemies, and so he pays them back." In some languages <u>**his adversaries**</u> (TEV "enemies") can be translated "those who hate him." <u>**Wrath**</u> (TEV "anger") in many languages is often stated in physiological terms as, for example, "hot heart" or "hot liver."

An alternative model for this verse is:

The LORD God will not tolerate (put up with) people worshiping other gods. He punishes those who hate him, and because they have made him angry, he pays them back.

1.3	RSV	TEV

**The LORD is slow to anger and of great might,
and the LORD will by no means clear the guilty.**

**His way is in whirlwind and storm,
and the clouds are the dust of his feet.**

**The LORD does not easily become angry,
but he is powerful
and never lets the guilty go unpunished.**

**Where the LORD walks, storms arise;
the clouds are the dust raised by his feet!**

This verse echoes the thought of such passages as Exodus 34.6 and Numbers 14.18. It gives a picture of the Lord's character which is complementary to the picture of anger in verse 2. The opening words say literally that the Lord is "long of nostril." In Hebrew the nostrils are associated with anger, and to be "long of nostril" means to be <u>**slow to anger**</u>. TEV puts this into more natural English as "**The LORD does not easily become angry.**" If translators have some figurative expression in their language which carries the meaning of "slow to get angry," this is a good place to use it. In certain languages this idea may be expressed as "does not become angry quickly" or "does not burst into anger." In other languages one may say "his heart (or, liver) does not rise (or burn, or pain) quickly." It is also possible in some languages to use the expression "has a cool heart." However, any expression used here must not sound disrespectful when applied to God.

In other places where the Lord is spoken of as <u>**slow to anger**</u>, the description usually goes on to say that he is "of great mercy" (Neh 9.17; Psa 86.15; 103.8; Joel 2.13; Jonah 4.2). Accordingly some scholars have suggested that the same

Hebrew words "of great mercy" should be inserted here to correct the text (compare Moffatt's translation [Mft]). However, the Hebrew text (**of great might**) makes perfectly good sense as it stands, and there is no need to emend it. In fact a similar expression occurs in Numbers 14.17 in a somewhat similar context. There the Lord's power seems to refer to his ability to keep his anger in check, and some commentators think it has the same meaning here. However, TEV links its equivalent phrase **"he is powerful"** with the next part of the verse (compare NAB), and this may be a useful example for translators to follow. **Great might** (TEV "powerful") here does not refer primarily to physical strength but rather to God's ruling power and authority as judge over the earth. Therefore translators should choose a term in the receptor language which is normally used to refer to the "greatness," "majesty," or "sovereignty" of a god, or of a political ruler such as a king or chief.

The LORD will by no means clear the guilty is translated in TEV as "he never lets the guilty go unpunished." This expression also occurs in earlier parts of the Old Testament (Exo 34.7; Num 14.18). In many languages it may be better to drop the double negative and say something like "he always punishes guilty people for their sins" or "he always punishes people who have done evil things."

The first half of verse 3, which has already been discussed, is linked in thought with verse 2 as a description of the character of the Lord. The latter half of verse 3 goes more closely in thought with verses 4-6, as it is part of a description of the effect of the Lord's presence on the world of nature. This is the reason why RSV and TEV start a new paragraph in the middle of verse 3.

The first part of the new paragraph says literally **His way is in whirlwind and storm**. TEV translates the two terms **whirlwind** and **storm** by the single word "storms" and turns the noun phrase **his way** into a verbal expression, "Where the LORD walks." The picture in the prophet's mind is of the Lord treading on the mountain tops (compare Micah 1.3) and thus causing storms ("storms arise" in TEV). In many languages storms do not **"arise"** but they "begin to blow." The Hebrew use of the word **whirlwind** provides the picture of a strong whirling wind. So a translator may render this sentence as "Where the LORD walks, great storms begin to blow" or "Where the LORD walks, a great whirling wind blows."

This picture is maintained in the last line of the verse, which says **the clouds are the dust of his feet**. Just as the approach of a traveler on the dry roads of Palestine could be seen by the dust clouds his feet raised, so the progress of the Lord along the mountain tops is said to be seen by observing **the clouds** which clustered around them. The prophet is of course using figurative language here to create a poetic effect. He did not really think of the Lord as a huge giant walking on the mountain tops. Since this type of picture language is quite common in the Old Testament, the translator should keep it if at all possible. TEV makes clear that **dust of his feet** means "dust raised by his feet." One may also render this phrase as "dust which his feet stir up."

1.4

RSV	TEV
He rebukes the sea and makes it dry, he dries up all the rivers; Bashan and Carmel wither, the bloom of Lebanon fades.	He commands the sea, and it dries up! He makes the rivers go dry. The fields of Bashan wither, Mount Carmel turns brown,

THE LORD'S VENGEANCE AGAINST NINEVEH   Nahum 1.4

           and the flowers of Lebanon
           fade.

 The description continues by emphasizing the terrifying and destructive effects of the Lord's presence, especially upon the waters and the vegetation that they support.

 The first line, **He rebukes the sea and makes it dry**, is probably an allusion to the time when the people of Israel crossed the Red Sea (Exo 14; compare Psa 106.9). **Rebukes** (TEV "**commands**") has the sense of "giving an order to" rather than "scolding." Some translators may wish to render this sentence as "He commands the sea to dry up, and it does so." In a similar manner the second line, **he dries up all the rivers**, alludes to the crossing of the River Jordan at the entrance to the promised land (Josh 3.16-17; 4.23). However, these two miraculous events, which were of special importance in the history of the Lord's people, are here taken as standing for the Lord's complete power over the whole of nature. So translators should not use language which indicates a particular sea or river.

 The second half of the verse deals with the results of the drying up of water supplies: even the most fertile parts of the land will suffer drought and lose their vegetation. **Bashan** was a well-watered area to the east of the Jordan and was famous for its flocks of sheep and herds of cattle (Amos 4.1; Micah 7.14). If it were to **wither**, there would be no grass left for the animals to eat, and so they would die. In many languages a country or territory cannot be referred to as "withering"; rather it is the fields or grass that "wither." In such a case translators will do well to translate in a similar way to TEV, which makes explicit the fact that **Bashan** has rich "**fields**," in order to help readers who do not know the area. In some languages it will be necessary to indicate that these are fields with abundant grass, rather than plowed fields where crops are grown.

 Carmel is the highest point along the Mediterranean coast of Palestine, near the modern town of Haifa. TEV makes it explicit that **Carmel** is a "**Mount**" to help readers who are not familiar with the name. The name **Carmel** means "orchard," and the slopes of the mountain, especially on the southern side, were famous for their fertility. If even **Carmel** dries up, then the rest of the land will be in a desperate condition. Some translators may wish to say "The trees on Mount Carmel die" (compare GeCL).

 The bloom of Lebanon fades: **bloom** here refers to "flowers," as TEV makes clear. **Lebanon** refers not to the whole of the modern country of Lebanon, but to the mountain range which runs north and south, more or less parallel to the coast. This range is much higher than Mount Carmel and is often snow-covered (the name **Lebanon** means "white"). As the snows melted, the slopes of the mountains received plenty of water and so had plentiful vegetation. When the prophet speaks of the Lord causing the well-watered Lebanon range to suffer from a drought, he is emphasizing the great power of the Lord.

 Taken together, the three places, **Bashan**, **Carmel**, and **Lebanon**, represent the most fertile parts of the land, as in Isaiah 33.9; 35.2. In some translations it may help to make this explicit and say "Even the most fertile parts of the land dry up, the fields of grass in Bashan, the orchards of Mount Carmel, and the flowers on the Lebanon mountains." These three places are shown on the map entitled "Division of Canaan" in the American edition of TEV, and on the map entitled "Divided Israelite Kingdoms" in the British edition.

1.5	RSV	TEV
	The mountains quake before him, the hills melt; the earth is laid waste before him, the world and all that dwell therein.	Mountains quake in the presence of the LORD; hills melt before him. The earth shakes when the LORD appears; the world and all its people tremble.

The mountains quake before him: first of all, Nahum uses earthquakes as symbols of the Lord's presence ("**Mountains quake in the presence of the LORD**" in TEV). Then, with the words **the hills melt**, he seems to picture torrents of water running down the sides of the hills, perhaps as a result of the storm of verse 3. However, translators should remember that the writer is here trying to create a dramatic impression of the awesome majesty and power of the Lord, rather than to give a logical description of an earthquake or of a thunderstorm. The words **the hills melt** may be simply a poetic parallel to **mountains quake** (compare Judges 5.4-5; Micah 1.4; Hab 3.6). In some translations the words **before him** may need to be rendered as "**when the LORD appears**," as TEV has done in the second half of the verse. The first half of the verse can then be rendered as "When the LORD appears, the mountains quake and the hills melt." In areas of the world which do not have mountains, it is possible to say "When the LORD appears, the high land (ground) quakes and melts." Another way of restructuring **before him** is "When the LORD shows his power . . . ."

In the second half of the verse, there is some uncertainty as to what **the earth** does when the Lord appears. The Hebrew text contains a verb which means "is upheaved" (Revised Version [RV]). However, two ancient translations, the Syriac and the Latin, appear to have read the Hebrew as a very similar word which means "crash in ruins, become desolate." RSV **is laid waste** follows these ancient versions but does not acknowledge this in a footnote (compare also JB, NAB, TOB). In fact in this context it hardly makes any difference to the overall meaning which alternative is followed. This third line of the verse, in parallel with the first, pictures the earth as being in violent motion because of the Lord's presence. Whether the motion is upwards (as in RV) or downwards (as especially in JB "collapses") really is of little importance. TEV's "**shakes**" can include both, and indeed can be derived from either of the possible Hebrew verbs, so that it is not entirely clear which one TEV has followed (compare NIV "trembles" and NEB "are in tumult").

In the final line the effect produced by the Lord's presence is extended to include both **the world** and **all that dwell therein**. The Hebrew word used here for **world** is different from the previous word for **earth** and refers particularly to those areas which are inhabited. In Hebrew the verb used to describe the action of **the earth** in the third line also applies to the action of the people in the fourth (compare RSV, JB, NAB, NIV, New Jewish Version [NJV], FrCL, GeCL). TEV gives the two lines a better balance by including the verb "**tremble**" in the fourth line. It is simply a synonym for shake and does not imply any significant difference in meaning. Translators may also use synonyms here, if these are available in their language and represent good style. In certain languages, though, translators may not be able to use the same word for upheaval both about people and about inanimate things such as the earth or world. In such a case one may translate the final line of the verse as "the world shakes and its people tremble" or "its people are in turmoil."

1.6

RSV	TEV
Who can stand before his indignation? Who can endure the heat of his anger? His wrath is poured out like fire, and the rocks are broken asunder by him.	When he is angry, who can survive? Who can survive his terrible fury? He pours out his flaming anger; rocks crumble to dust before him.

This verse shows some of the implications of the Lord's greatness and power. In **Who can stand before his indignation?** the literal **stand** means "stand firm" (as NAB; compare Psa 24.3; Amos 7.2,5; Mal 3.2). TEV expresses this as "Who can survive?" TEV thus keeps the form of a question but turns the noun phrase **his indignation** into a clause and says "When he is angry."

The implied answer to the two questions is that nobody can survive, and in languages which do not use questions in this way, the meaning can be expressed as a statement: "When he is angry no one can survive." **Endure** (TEV "survive") can also be rendered as "stay alive" or "keep on living."

The second line says practically the same thing again in different words: **Who can endure the heat of his anger?** The comparison of **anger** with **heat** is a figure of speech which is used in many languages, and often translators will be able to keep it here. TEV, however, expresses the meaning in nonfigurative language with "Who can survive his terrible fury?" In some languages it may be necessary to change the structure of this sentence and say "When his anger is very hot, no one will be able to live." In some languages the idea of **anger** (TEV "fury") can be expressed idiomatically; for example, "his burning heart." One can then say "When his heart burns fiercely, who will be able to live?" Note that where RSV has used two different English words, **stand** and **endure**, TEV has used the same term "**survive**" both times. Translators should use one word or two according to the vocabulary and style of their language.

The second half of the verse is in the form of statements again and picks up the theme of verse 5. The third line continues the picture of anger as being like heat and says **His wrath is poured out like fire**. This is a common figure of speech (compare Jer 7.20; 42.18; 44.6) and is perhaps based on the idea of molten lava pouring down the side of a mountain during a volcanic eruption. In languages where it may sound strange to talk about "pouring anger," it may be possible to use some other figurative expression and say "his fierce anger bursts forth" or "his fierce anger erupts." In some languages it will be helpful to say "His anger, like a flaming fire, bursts forth (erupts)."

The fourth line probably expresses the result of the third one: because of the **heat** of the Lord's **anger, the rocks are broken asunder by him**. Many translators will wish to avoid the passive and can follow TEV's rendering or say "and makes (causes) the rocks (to) break into pieces" or " . . . (to) split apart." Alternative translation models for the final part of this verse are "because he is very angry he makes the rocks break into pieces" or "because his heart is very hot he causes the rocks to break into pieces." The breaking of the rocks is a natural result of the Lord's power. Translators should avoid suggesting that the Lord goes around smashing rocks in a display of bad temper.

1.7   RSV   TEV

The LORD is good,   The LORD is good;
  a stronghold in the day of   he protects his people in times
  trouble;   of trouble;
he knows those who take ref-   he takes care of those who
  uge in him.   turn to him.

Verses 7 and 8 contrast with verses 2-6 and apply the Lord's greatness and power to his dealings with people, both to protect those who trust him (verse 7) and to punish his enemies (verse 8).

The LORD is good is a general statement which, in the second and third lines, is applied to the way he cares for his people. **Good** here probably emphasizes the Lord's kindness to those who trust him, and contrasts with his anger shown to those who oppose him (verses 2-3, 8-11).

The Hebrew says that he is **a stronghold in the day of trouble**. **A stronghold** is a fortified place that people can flee to when their enemies attack them. To speak of the Lord as a **stronghold** is a metaphor which means that "**he protects his people in times of trouble**," as TEV expresses it in nonfigurative language. (Compare Psa 37.39; Isa 25.4; Jer 16.19.) Some translators may wish to keep this metaphor and say something like the following: "He is like a stronghold which protects his people in time of trouble" or "He is like a fortified place which protects his people when they are in trouble." **Stronghold** may also be rendered as "a place with high strong walls." "In times of trouble" in certain languages can be rendered as "in times when his people receive troubles" or " . . . undergo troubles."

The third line says much the same thing over again, literally **he knows those who take refuge in him**. The Hebrew expression which is translated literally in RSV as **he knows** means "he takes care of" (TEV; compare NAB, NEB, NIV, FrCL, GeCL), and **take refuge in him** means "trust in him" (JB, NIV) or "**turn to him**" (TEV). Most translators will wish to follow the example of TEV and other modern English versions and express the meaning in plain language. Translators who keep the metaphor of **stronghold** in the first line may wish to render the second line as "he takes care of those who take refuge in him" or "he protects those who take refuge in him." For similar themes compare Psalms 1.6; 2.12; 5.11; 37.18; 144.2; Amos 3.2; Zephaniah 3.12.

1.8   RSV   TEV

But with an overflowing flood   Like a great rushing flood he
  he will make a full end of his   completely destroys his ene-
  adversaries,[a]   mies;[a]
and will pursue his enemies   he sends to their death those
  into darkness.   who oppose him.

THE LORD'S VENGEANCE AGAINST NINEVEH   Nahum 1.9-15

ᵃ Gk: Heb *her place*   ᵃ *Some ancient translations* his enemies; *Hebrew* its place.

But with an overflowing flood represents the first two words of the Hebrew of verse 8. Some modern versions take these words with verse 7 and translate "he calls to mind those who trust in him when the flood overtakes them" (JB) or "he takes care of those who have recourse to him, when the flood rages" (NAB, compare Mft, BJ, TOB, FrCL, GeCL). This makes good sense, but so does the text as punctuated in the Hebrew manuscripts, and there is no strong reason to depart from it. Indeed if the first two words are taken with the rest of verse 8, as in RSV, they can be seen more clearly as applying the Lord's power over nature (verses 3b-6) to his dealings with people. TEV also takes them this way and translates "**Like a great rushing flood.**" The word **flood** may be a reference to the account of the destruction of the wicked at the time of Noah (Gen 6—9). Another way of rendering this sentence is "He is like a great rushing flood which will completely destroy (or, will kill) his enemies" or "He is like a huge wave which crashes down on his enemies and kills all of them."

He will make a full end of his adversaries: RSV follows the ancient Greek translation, the Septuagint, in translating **adversaries** (compare BJ, JB, NAB, NEB, TEV, FrCL). The Hebrew at this point has "her place." Those modern versions which retain the Hebrew take the "her" to refer to Nineveh (TOB footnote, NIV; compare HOTTP). As Nineveh has not been mentioned since verse 1, this seems rather unlikely, and translators are advised to do as RSV and TEV have done and follow the Greek. TEV translates in more natural English as "**he completely destroys his enemies.**"

The second half of the verse repeats the thought of the first part in different words. The Hebrew uses a figure of speech which most English versions translate literally. RSV says that the Lord **will pursue his enemies into darkness**. The sentence can also mean "darkness will pursue his enemies," but this is less likely, since it involves a change of subject. **Darkness** stands for the darkness of the underworld, that is, death (compare Job 18.18), and some languages may be able to retain the figure. TEV expresses this in nonfigurative language as "**He sends to their death those who oppose him.**" One may also say "He sends to their death all those who hate him." In some languages "**he sends to their death**" may be a difficult expression. In such a case one can say "He causes those who oppose him (his enemies) to die."

1.9-15

RSV	TEV
9 What do you plot against the LORD? He will make a full end; he will not take vengeance twice on his foes.	9 What are you plotting against the LORD? He will destroy you. No one opposes him more than once.
10 Like entangled thorns they are consumed, like dry stubble.	10 Like tangled thorns and dry straw you drunkards will be burned up!
11 Did one not come out from you, who plotted evil against the LORD, and counseled villainy?	11 From you, Nineveh, there came a man full of wicked schemes, who plotted against the LORD.
12 Thus says the LORD, "Though they be strong and many, they will be cut off and pass away. Though I have afflicted you, I will afflict you no more.	12 This is what the LORD says to his people Israel: "Even though the Assyrians are strong and numerous, they will be destroyed and disappear. My people, I made you suffer, but I will not do it again. 13 I will now end Assyria's

Nahum 1.9-15 THE LORD'S VENGEANCE AGAINST NINEVEH

13 And now I will break his yoke from off you
    and will burst your bonds asunder."
14 The LORD has given commandment about you:
    "No more shall your name be perpetuated;
    from the house of your gods I will cut off the graven image and the molten image.
    I will make your grave, for you are vile."
15 Behold, on the mountains the feet of him who brings good tidings,
    who proclaims peace!
    Keep your feasts, O Judah,
    fulfil your vows,
    for never again shall the wicked come against you,
    he is utterly cut off.

power over you and break the chains that bind you."
14 This is what the LORD has decreed about the Assyrians: "They will have no descendants to carry on their name. I will destroy the idols that are in the temples of their gods. I am preparing a grave for the Assyrians—they don't deserve to live!"
15 Look, a messenger is coming over the mountains with good news! He is on his way to announce the victory! People of Judah, celebrate your festivals and give God what you solemnly promised him. The wicked will never invade your land again. They have been totally destroyed!

Some modern translations treat the rest of chapter 1 as a piece of consecutive text. Three versions, however, split it up (BJ, JB, TOB) and label the resulting parts as separate oracles addressed to Judah (verses 9-10), to Assyria (verse 11), to Judah (verses 12-13), to the king of Nineveh (verse 14), and to Judah (verse 15). This is indicated either in the margin as in JB, or in subheadings as in BJ, TOB. (After verse 15 these versions differ. For details see the introductory comments on chapter 2.)

Even versions which do not actually list the persons addressed in these verses may still agree with those which do. TEV and NIV make it clear in their texts that they regard verses 11 and 14 as addressed to Nineveh, and verses 12-13 and 15 as addressed to Judah. They differ only in not stating explicitly to whom they think verses 9-10 are addressed. (See detailed comments on verse 9.)

The variations between the versions, then, are more in their presentation than in their interpretation. Translators should consider which form of presentation will be easiest for their readers to follow. It is quite possible both to use subheadings and to include the names of the people addressed in the text itself, if that is felt to be best.

FrCL has a new section heading covering 1.9—2.3, which can be expressed in English as "Messages for Judah and Nineveh."

1.9 RSV

What do you plot against the LORD?
He will make a full end;
he will not take vengeance[b]
twice on his foes.[c]

[b] Gk: Heb *rise up*
[c] Cn: Heb *distress*

TEV

What are you plotting against the LORD?
He will destroy you.
No one opposes him more than once.

As mentioned above, some versions take verses 9 and 10 as addressed to the people of Judah (BJ, JB, TOB). JB translates the opening words of verse 9 as "How do you imagine Yahweh?" and some such meaning as this would make sense if addressed to Judah. However, the majority of versions and commentators

THE LORD'S VENGEANCE AGAINST NINEVEH   Nahum 1.10

think that these opening words have a different meaning: **What do you plot against the LORD?** (RSV; compare TEV, NEB, NIV, Mft, FrCL). This was the meaning understood by the ancient Greek and Latin translations, and the one which occurs again in a similar phrase in verse 11 (compare Dan 11.24; Hos 7.15), and it is therefore to be preferred here. If this meaning is accepted, the verse will continue the theme of punishment in verse 8, and the pronoun **you** will refer implicitly to the people of Nineveh. This fits the context better.

The word **plot** in English carries bad overtones; it implies "making evil plans" or "planning to do evil things," as does the Hebrew word it translates. Translators should try to find some expression with similar overtones in their own language if possible.

He will make a full end: **He** refers to the Lord, and the implied object is the **you** of the first line; thus, " . . . make a full end of you." TEV makes this explicit and translates in simple language as **"He will destroy you."** Some translators may say "He will cause you all to be destroyed" or "He will cause you all to die."

He will not take vengeance twice on his foes: the final line describes the result of the Lord's action in the second line. It says literally "oppression will not arise a second time" (compare JB, NIV, HOTTP). The meaning is that when the Lord destroys something, his destruction is complete, and no further trouble can ever come from the same source (compare 1 Sam 26.8; 2 Sam 20.10). Several translations understand the Hebrew word meaning "oppression" to be a figure of speech called a metonym and to stand for the people who cause the oppression. Thus TEV translates **"No one opposes him more than once"** (compare NAB, NEB, NJV). RSV obtains much the same result but does so by changing the Hebrew text to say **his foes** instead of "oppression." RSV also changes the Hebrew word for "arise" to say **take vengeance**, but this is unnecessary, since the Hebrew makes good sense as it stands. Translators are recommended to follow TEV here.

An alternative translation model for this verse is:

What evil things are you people of Nineveh planning to do against the LORD? He will cause you all to die. In fact no one is able to oppose him more than once.

1.10   RSV   TEV

Like entangled thorns they are   Like tangled thorns and dry
    consumed,^d   straw
like dry stubble.   you drunkards will be burned
                                                up!

^d Heb *are consumed, drunken as with their drink*

"This verse is rightly regarded as one of the most difficult in the Bible" (Delcor, page 372). "As it stands in the Massoretic Text, this verse is wholly unintelligible. Modern interpreters have for the most part abandoned it as hopeless and many declare the recovery of the original text impossible" (J.M.P. Smith, page 294). For a full discussion of the textual difficulties, translators are referred to the standard commentaries such as those cited in this paragraph.

A literal translation of the Hebrew text as it stands is given in RV: "For though they be like tangled thorns, and be drenched as it were in their drink, they shall be devoured utterly as dry stubble" (or "as stubble fully dry").

The basic problem in this verse is that the two words translated "and be drenched as it were in their drink" have no apparent connection with the rest of the verse. In Hebrew these two words are quite similar in sound to the previous two words, translated "tangled thorns" in RV. The majority of commentators and translators conclude that the two problem words are most likely a muddled repetition of the earlier words and should therefore be dropped from the text. This opinion is followed by RSV, BJ, JB, NAB, Mft, and earlier editions of TEV which omit the word **drunkards** in the text as quoted above. The problem words are retained by TOB, NIV, NJV, FrCL, GeCL, and later editions of TEV (compare HOTTP). RSV, BJ, NIV, NJV, and FrCL all have footnotes acknowledging the difficulty.

Those versions which retain the two problem words have to decide how to make sense of them. TOB places a dash before and after them to separate them from the rest of the verse. NIV renders "They will be entangled among thorns and drunk from their wine; they will be consumed like dry stubble." Thus it apparently ignores the lack of meaningful connection between the three clauses (compare NJV). FrCL says "They are like tangled thorns, those who drink till they are drunk." GeCL says "They can drink to gain courage as much as they like." These renderings make sense in themselves but do not establish any real connection between drinking and the rest of the paragraph.

Translators are recommended to follow the example of RSV and others and omit the problem words. This advice cannot be offered as a solution to the problems. Rather it is offered in this case as the course of action which will do most to make the verse intelligible.

Once the two problem words are omitted, the rest of the verse makes reasonable sense, and its parts have parallels elsewhere in the Old Testament. RSV translates **Like entangled thorns they are consumed, like dry stubble**. The picture is of fire spreading over fields in dry weather. Just as fire destroys dry thorn bushes or the stubble that is left when a field of grain has been harvested, so the Lord will destroy his enemies. TEV changes the third person verb to second person to make it clear that it regards this verse as referring to the people of Nineveh, called "you" in verse 9. TEV then expresses the meaning in simple English as "Like tangled thorns and dry straw you drunkards will be burned up!" The Lord's enemies are compared to thorns in 2 Samuel 23.6; Isaiah 10.17; 33.12; Micah 7.4; and to stubble in Isaiah 5.24; 33.11; 47.14; Obadiah 18. In languages which do not use the passive, the expression **they are consumed** ("you . . . will be burned up") can be rendered as "the fire will burn you up." But in some languages it will be necessary to restructure this verse and say "The fire will burn you up just as it burns tangled thorns and dry straw."

1.11

RSV	TEV
Did one not[e] come out from you, who plotted evil against the LORD, and counseled villainy?	From you, Nineveh, there came a man full of wicked schemes, who plotted against the LORD.

THE LORD'S VENGEANCE AGAINST NINEVEH   Nahum 1.12

^e Cn: Heb *fully*

GeCL has a section heading at this point covering verses 11-14. It can be expressed in English as "The LORD will finally end the power of Assyria."

RSV translates this verse as a question, whereas in other major versions it is a statement. What RSV has done here is to carry over into verse 11 the word which in Hebrew is the last word of verse 10, the word translated "utterly" in RV, JB. RSV has also changed one letter of the Hebrew word and assumed different vowels. Instead of "utterly" RSV's conjecture has the marker of a negative question, which accounts for the question form in RSV. Since verse 11 makes sense without this change, translators are not recommended to follow it.

In Hebrew the opening words of the verse are **from you**, and TEV adds the name "Nineveh" to make it explicit that the prophet is here addressing the capital city of Assyria (compare FrCL). The rest of the sentence is an accusation expressed in TEV as "**From you . . . came a man full of wicked schemes, who plotted against the LORD.**"

Who plotted evil against the LORD: the word for **plotted** is the same Hebrew word as that used in verse 9. The Hebrew says **plotted evil**, but because the word **plotted** already carries bad overtones, TEV has left the word **evil** implicit. However, in languages which do not have a single word for "plotted," it will be necessary to say something like "made evil plans" or "planned to do evil things against." This description is generally understood to be a reference to Sennacherib, who was king of Assyria from 705 to 681 B.C. and who besieged Jerusalem in 701 in the days when Hezekiah was king of Judah (see 2 Kgs 18.13—19.37). The prophet considers action against the city of Jerusalem to be the same as action **against the LORD**.

Counseled villainy: the word translated **villainy** is the word which appears in other passages in the King James Version (KJV) and in RV as the name "Belial" (compare for instance Judges 19.22; 1 Sam 2.12; 1 Kgs 21.10; 2 Cor 6.15). JB retains the word here as a name and translates "a man with the mind of Belial." The word "Belial" means "worthlessness," and in most languages it will be better to translate this meaning, since "Belial" as a name will not be very familiar to most readers. The words **counseled villainy** are expressed in more modern language in TEV as "**full of wicked schemes.**" This phrase may be rendered in some languages as "who gave wicked (worthless) advice."

1.12	RSV	TEV
	Thus says the LORD, "Though they be strong and many,^f they will be cut off and pass away. Though I have afflicted you, I will afflict you no more.	This is what the LORD says to his people Israel: "Even though the Assyrians are strong and numerous, they will be destroyed and disappear. My people, I made you suffer, but I will not do it again.

^f Heb uncertain

As can be seen from RSV, the Hebrew text does not state to whom this verse is addressed. The majority of modern translations indicate by means of section headings, footnotes, or a term of address in the text itself, that they regard this verse as spoken to the people of Israel (BJ, JB, NAB, NEB, TOB, TEV, NIV, FrCL).

The opening words of the verse are the familiar expression **Thus says the LORD**. TEV puts this into modern language and makes the addressees explicit by saying "**This is what the LORD says to his people Israel.**" Many translators will wish to do the same. However, the name "Israel" in TEV is misleading, since it normally refers to the northern kingdom of Israel, which no longer existed in Nahum's day. It would be clearer to say "to his people Judah."

The rest of the verse is in two parts, of which the first is to be understood as a statement about the Assyrians, and the second is about the Lord's people, to whom the prophet is speaking. TEV makes the two groups explicit. The first part describes the Assyrians as **strong and many**. There is some variation in the understanding of the word rendered **strong** in RSV and TEV. NAB has "vigorous," JB "equipped," and NIV "unscathed." Although these words are different in detail, the differences do not really affect the overall impact of the verse, which is to emphasize the power of the Assyrian army. Translators should choose a term in their own languages which will fit such a setting.

The full statement is that even **though they** (the Assyrians) **be strong and many, they will be cut off and pass away**. The Hebrew word translated **cut off** is actually a term used of shearing sheep, and NAB has kept a figure of speech by saying "they shall be mown down." Most translators will probably need to use nonfigurative language here, such as TEV's "**destroyed.**" For other ways to render "**destroyed**," see comments on "make a full end" in verse 9. The verb translated **pass away** is singular in Hebrew, in contrast to the plural verb translated **be cut off** (compare KJV, RV "cut down"). Some scholars see it as a further reference to the man "who plotted evil against the LORD" in verse 11, but most prefer to supply a singular collective noun such as "their people" as the subject of this verb. In this way it has in effect a plural subject like the previous verb, and thus an awkward change of person in English is avoided. **Pass away** or "disappear" probably means "vanish from the political scene," though it may perhaps mean "die." **They will be cut off and pass away** can be translated as "people will kill (destroy) them and they will disappear."

The second part of the verse is generally understood as addressed to the people of Judah, and TEV makes this explicit by saying "**My people.**" The message is one of encouragement: **Though I have afflicted you, I will afflict you no more**. The meaning is that in the past the Lord used the Assyrians to "discipline" (JB) his people for their sins (compare Isa 10.5), but he will not use them in this way again. TEV translates in simple language as "**I made you suffer, but I will not do it again.**"

It is also possible to understand this second part as addressed to the Assyrians. In that case it would mean "I will make you suffer in such a way that I will not make you suffer again." In other words, the Lord will punish the Assyrians so severely that no second punishment will ever be necessary. (Compare verse 9.) If this interpretation is followed, it will be better style to use the pronoun "them" instead of **you** in this sentence, and say "I will make them suffer in such a way that I will not need to make them suffer again."

There is no need to transpose this verse to follow verse 14, as NEB does.

THE LORD'S VENGEANCE AGAINST NINEVEH   Nahum 1.14

1.13   RSV   TEV

> And now I will break his yoke   I will now end Assyria's power over
> from off you   you and break the chains that bind
> and will burst your bonds   you."
> asunder."

This verse continues to give encouragement to the Lord's people with a promise of freedom from oppression by the Assyrians. The promise is given in Hebrew through a metaphor drawn from the way oxen were used for plowing. RSV gives a literal translation: **And now I will break his yoke from off you, and will burst your bonds asunder**. The **yoke** was the wooden bar that was put over the neck of the ox, and the **bonds** were the leather straps used to fasten the yoke to the animal's neck. If the **yoke** was broken and the **bonds** snapped, the animal would be free to go its own way and would not be forced to pull the plow or cart any more. This kind of language is often used in the Scriptures to speak about freedom from oppression. (See Lev 26.13; Psa 2.3; Isa 10.27; Jer 28.2,14; 30.8; Ezek 34.27; and compare Matt 11.29; Acts 15.10; Gal 5.1; 1 Tim 6.1.)

In areas where plowing is still done with animals under a yoke, the translator may be able to use similar picture language. However, in areas where this is not done, the translator can express the meaning in nonfigurative language. This is what TEV has done in the first part of the verse: "**I will now end Assyria's power over you.**" Another way to say this is "I will now cause Assyria to lose its power over you." If translators decided that the final line of verse 12 refers to the Assyrians, they should now clearly identify the referent of **you** here as "my people." One may say "And now my people, I will end Assyria's power over you" or "I will cause Assyria to stop ruling over you."

In the second part of the verse, TEV uses figurative language when it says "**I will . . . break the chains that bind you.**" This picture is quite a general one and is not closely linked to animals and plowing. Even translators who cannot keep the metaphor in the first part of the verse may be able to do something similar to TEV in this second part. However, if the translator cannot use figurative language, it is possible to say "and set you free." So an alternative translation model for this verse is: "I will now cause Assyria to lose its power over you and will set you free."

1.14   RSV   TEV

> The LORD has given command-   This is what the LORD has de-
>   ment about you: creed about the Assyrians: "They will
> "No more shall your name be   have no descendants to carry on their
>   perpetuated;   name. I will destroy the idols that are
> from the house of your gods I   in the temples of their gods. I am
>   will cut off   preparing a grave for the Assyrians—
>   the graven image and the mol-   they don't deserve to live!"
>   ten image.
> I will make your grave, for you
>   are vile."

The LORD has given commandment about you: the singular **you** is generally understood to be the king of Assyria (BJ, JB, NAB, TOB, GeCL) or the Assyrian nation as a whole (TEV, NIV, FrCL). TEV makes the addressees explicit by saying "**This is what the LORD has decreed about the Assyrians.**" In English the colon (:) shows that the following text states the content of the **commandment**, or what is "**decreed.**" In languages which do not use the colon, it will be helpful to render this sentence as "The LORD has decreed about the Assyrians, saying . . . ."

Most versions retain the second-person forms throughout the verse in English, but TEV has changed them all to third person, perhaps to emphasize the change of addressee from the previous two verses.

The **commandment** or "decree" itself is in three parts. The first one says literally "it shall not be sown from your name any more" (Driver). The word "sow" in this sense refers to having children, who serve as "seed" to carry on the family name. Thus RSV has **No more shall your name be perpetuated**. TEV expresses this meaning in plain language as "**They will have no descendants to carry on their name.**" The lack of descendants and loss of the family name was regarded as a serious matter in the ancient world (see Deut 7.24; 29.20; 1 Sam 24.21). In some cultures a single term for descendants may be difficult to find. Some languages say this by long, involved expressions such as "children, grandchildren, and great-grandchildren" or "the children of their children," meaning "descendants." Others have technical expressions similar to "species" or "lineage." Translators should pick the word or phrase which most naturally refers to those who come from a particular ancestor or group of ancestors.

The second part of the decree speaks of the fall of the gods of Assyria: **from the house of your gods I will cut off the graven image and the molten image**. The word translated **cut off** is a common way in Hebrew of referring to destruction (see also verse 12 for a discussion on **cut off**). Graven images were carved from stone or, more commonly, from wood. Molten images were made by melting metal and pouring it into a mold. Few languages nowadays have separate words for these two different kinds of image. NEB uses two words in English, "image and idol," but there is no particular need to do this. The use of the two words together in Hebrew is a way of referring to all kinds of images (compare Deut 27.15; Isa 48.5; Jer 10.14; Hab 2.18), and a general expression of this type is quite adequate. TEV uses just one English word and says "**I will destroy the idols that are in the temples of their gods.**"

It was the normal practice of the Assyrians, when they captured a city, to remove the images of the gods (metal or wooden statues) from its temples. This was to show that these gods were less powerful than the gods of Assyria. Nahum here says that the Lord will remove the Assyrian images from their temples to show that he is more powerful than they are. In English the supreme God is differentiated from lesser gods or deities by the use of a capital letter. In many other languages this device is not suitable, or the term for God is only used for the Christian God, so it will seem strange to refer to other gods. There are two possible solutions. Translators may use a term or terms which refer to supernatural beings which non-Christians in the culture worship, or they may use the term for the Christian God with an adjective; for example, "false gods" or "small gods." This will show that these are beings which are thought to be like God but are not really God. In such languages one can express the second part of the decree as follows: "I will destroy the idols that are in the temples of those false gods of theirs."

THE LORD'S VENGEANCE AGAINST NINEVEH   Nahum 1.15

The third part of the decree speaks of the deaths of the Assyrian people. The Lord says to the Assyrians, **I will make your grave**, that is, for them to be buried in when they are dead. In some languages it will be helpful to supply the words "and bury you" at the end of this sentence and say "I am making a grave for you Assyrians and will bury you . . . ." The picture seems to be of the whole people being killed at once. The reason for this is given as **for you are vile**. The Hebrew word translated **vile** means "of no account, worthy of contempt" (compare 1 Sam 2.30). TEV renders this as "They don't deserve to live!"

Some translators change the Hebrew words underlying **make** and **vile** (RSV) and translate "I intend to make your tomb an object of shame" (JB, compare NAB). However, the Hebrew makes good sense as it stands, and there is no need to make any change.

1.15^g
[2.1]

RSV	TEV
Behold, on the mountains the feet of him who brings good tidings, who proclaims peace! Keep your feasts, O Judah, fulfil your vows, for never again shall the wicked come against you, he is utterly cut off.	Look, a messenger is coming over the mountains with good news! He is on his way to announce the victory! People of Judah, celebrate your festivals and give God what you solemnly promised him. The wicked will never invade your land again. They have been totally destroyed!

^g Ch 2.1 in Heb

This is the first verse of chapter 2 in Hebrew, but in theme it goes more closely with the preceding verses and is better numbered 1.15. It is explicitly addressed to **Judah**, which, as TEV makes clear, means the "People of Judah." The opening invitation is to **Behold**, or as TEV puts it, to "Look." In languages which need to add a vocative with **Behold** or "Look," translators may transfer "People of Judah" to the beginning of the verse. In certain languages it is more natural for commands such as this to use a first person inclusive plural pronoun; for example, "Let us look, a messenger . . . ." The words **on the mountains the feet of him who brings good tidings** are the same in Hebrew as those found in Isaiah 52.7. The **feet** stand for the messenger as he travels, and TEV makes this explicit with "a messenger is coming over the mountains." In certain languages the phrase "over the mountains" may give the impression that the messenger is flying. In such a case it will be helpful to translate in a way similar to RSV and say "across the mountains" or "on top of the mountains." If translators wish to retain something of the figurative language, they may say "Look, a messenger's feet are bringing him across the mountains to tell us good news!" Or, "Look, the feet of the messenger are already treading the mountains as he comes to bring us good news!"

This messenger **brings good tidings** and **proclaims peace**. TEV uses a modern term "news" instead of **tidings** and makes the second clause a separate sentence. TEV's phrase "**with good news**" is a little difficult to reproduce in some languages. One other possibility is to render this phrase in a similar way to RSV and say "bringing good news." This sentence can then be rendered "Look, a messenger is coming over the mountains bringing good news." Presumably the messenger is coming toward the speaker and his intended hearers, the people of Judah. This direction will need to be indicated clearly in many languages. In this context TEV interprets **peace** to refer to the fall of Nineveh, and so translates as "**He is on his way to announce the victory!**" One may also translate "He is coming to announce the defeat of Assyria."

The rest of the verse states some results that the fall of Nineveh will bring for Judah. First of all the **people of Judah** will be able to **keep** ("celebrate" in TEV) their **feasts** in honor of the Lord with no fear of interruption, and the prophet calls upon them to do so. Secondly, he calls on them to **fulfil your vows**. This means to carry out the promises made to the Lord when the people were in fear of their enemy and were asking the Lord to help them. Compare Psalms 22.25; 66.13. TEV expresses this in nontechnical language as "**give God what you solemnly promised him.**" "**Promised**" may be expressed in certain languages as "things you said you would do." "Solemnly" means that the people had made a promise using something such as their name or head to show that it was a very strong promise. The name or head of an individual in many ancient cultures, including that of the Hebrews, was thought of as representing that person's power or "mana." God himself sometimes makes a solemn promise using his name (see Gen 22.16-17; compare Heb 6.13-18). If he fails to keep his promise, he is no longer God. The word "**what**" in TEV's rendering means "the things." It will be helpful in many languages to begin this final section with the equivalent of the English word "so"; for example, "So, people of Judah . . . ."

The last part of the verse emphasizes that the defeat of Assyria is complete and final: **never again shall the wicked come against you**. TEV expresses the meaning more fully as "the wicked will never invade your land again." The word translated **wicked** is in Hebrew *Belial*, as in verse 11, and refers either to the king of Nineveh or to the Assyrian nation as a whole. See the comments on verse 11. If translators understand the adjective **wicked** as referring to the Assyrian nation, it will be helpful to identify the subject by saying "the wicked people" or "the wicked nation." The **wicked** may also be rendered as "the bad people," "people who are evil," or "people who do evil things." The reason that the Assyrians will not trouble the Lord's people again is that they have been **utterly cut off**. As often elsewhere, **cut off** stands for "destroyed," and TEV translates in plain language as "They have been totally destroyed." (See verse 12 for a discussion of **cut off**.)

An alternative translation model for this verse is:

> Look, a messenger is coming across the mountains to tell us good things. He comes to announce that the Assyrians have been defeated. So, people of Judah, celebrate your festivals and give God the things you solemnly promised to give to him. Those wicked Assyrians will never attack your land again. They have all been killed.

SECTION 2: A DESCRIPTION OF THE FALL OF THE CITY
(Chapter 2.1—3.19)

Chapter 2

SECTION HEADING: the rest of the Book of Nahum is covered by a single section heading in TEV, "**The Fall of Nineveh.**" Some translators may need to expand it a little and say "The attackers capture the city of Nineveh." Many translators may wish to break this long section into several short ones. Suitable paragraph breaks may be found at 2.13 (RSV, NEB) or 3.1 (BJ, JB, NAB, TOB, NIV, NJV, FrCL, GeCL), and at 3.8 (RSV, BJ, JB, NAB, NEB, TOB, NIV, FrCL, GeCL), where TEV also implies a break by changing from poetic format to prose. Some translations add other breaks and section headings, but these are the most common.

For translators who wish to use more section headings than TEV, the following can be suggested: 2.1 "The enemy attacks the city of Nineveh"; 2.13 or 3.1 "The enemy takes the city"; 3.8 "Nineveh cannot defend itself" or "The inhabitants cannot defend Nineveh."

The topic of the whole section is indeed the fall of Nineveh. The description is abrupt, vivid, and disjointed, and the tone is one of triumph and rejoicing. Translators should try to give an atmosphere of exultation and mockery over the defeated enemy.

2.1-13

	RSV		TEV

1	The shatterer has come up against you.
	    Man the ramparts;
	        watch the road;
	    gird your loins;
	        collect all your strength.
		1	Nineveh, you are under attack!
			    The power that will shatter you has come.
			    Man the defenses!
			    Guard the road!
			    Prepare for battle!

2	(For the LORD is restoring the majesty of Jacob
	    as the majesty of Israel,
	for plunderers have stripped them
	    and ruined their branches.)
			(2 The LORD is about to restore the glory of Israel, as it was before her enemies plundered her.)

3	The shield of his mighty men is red,
	    his soldiers are clothed in scarlet.
	The chariots flash like flame
	    when mustered in array;
	    the chargers prance.
		3	The enemy soldiers carry red shields
			    and wear uniforms of red.
			They are preparing to attack!
			    Their chariots flash like fire!
			    Their horses prance!

4	The chariots rage in the streets,
	    they rush to and fro through the squares;
	they gleam like torches,
	    they dart like lightning.
		4	Chariots dash wildly through the streets,
			    rushing back and forth in the city squares.
			They flash like torches
			    and dart about like lightning.

5	The officers are summoned,
	    they stumble as they go,
	    they hasten to the wall,
		5	The officers are summoned;
			    they stumble as they press forward.

Nahum 2.1-13   THE FALL OF NINEVEH

	the mantelet is set up.		The attackers rush to the wall
6	The river gates are opened,		and set up the shield for the battering ram.
	the palace is in dismay;		
7	its mistress is stripped, she is carried off,	6	The gates by the river burst open;
	her maidens lamenting,		the palace is filled with terror.
	moaning like doves,	7	The queen is taken captive;
	and beating their breasts.		her servants moan like doves
8	Nineveh is like a pool		and beat their breasts in sorrow.
	whose waters run away.	8	Like water from a broken dam
	"Halt! Halt!" they cry;		the people rush from Nineveh!
	but none turns back.		"Stop! Stop!" the cry rings out—
9	Plunder the silver,		but no one turns back.
	plunder the gold!		
	There is no end of treasure,	9	Plunder the silver!
	or wealth of every precious thing.		Plunder the gold!
			The city is full of treasure!
10	Desolate! Desolation and ruin!		
	Hearts faint and knees tremble,	10	Nineveh is destroyed, deserted, desolate!
	anguish is on all loins,		Hearts melt with fear;
	all faces grow pale!		knees tremble, strength is gone;
11	Where is the lions' den,		faces grow pale.
	the cave of the young lions,		
	where the lion brought his prey,	11	Where now is the city
	where his cubs were, with none to disturb?		that was like a den of lions,
			the place where young lions were fed,
12	The lion tore enough for his whelps		where the lion and the lioness would go
	and strangled prey for his lionesses;		and their cubs would be safe?
	he filled his caves with prey	12	The lion killed his prey
	and his dens with torn flesh.		and tore it to pieces for his mate and her cubs;
			he filled his den with torn flesh.

13 Behold, I am against you, says the LORD of hosts, and I will burn your chariots in smoke, and the sword shall devour your young lions; I will cut off your prey from the earth, and the voice of your messengers shall no more be heard.

13 "I am your enemy!" says the LORD Almighty. "I will burn up your chariots. Your soldiers will be killed in war, and I will take away everything that you took from others. The demands of your envoys will no longer be heard."

In the comments on 1.9-15, it was pointed out that three modern translations split this section up into separate oracles addressed in turn to Judah and Assyria. A similar possibility exists in the opening verses of chapter 2, but the three versions concerned (BJ, JB, and TOB) differ in their handling of the text.

All three versions follow the Hebrew verse numbering, by which 1.15 in RSV and TEV is numbered 2.1 in the Hebrew text, 2.1 in RSV/TEV is 2.2, and 2.2 in RSV/TEV is 2.3. BJ treats the whole of chapter 2 as straightforward consecutive text. JB transposes 2.3 and 2.2 (RSV/TEV 2.2 and 2.1) and links 2.3 with 2.1 (RSV/TEV 1.15) as part of the last oracle addressed to Judah. Then it takes 2.2 (RSV/TEV 2.1) as beginning the consecutive text which runs through the rest of chapter 2. TOB keeps the verses in the traditional order but treats 2.2 (RSV/TEV 2.1) as a further oracle addressed to Nineveh, and 2.3 (RSV/TEV 2.2) as a further oracle to Judah. After that, the rest of the chapter is treated as consecutive text.

Other versions are also aware of a problem in following the theme of these verses. NAB and NEB transpose the same verses as JB and place a new section heading after the transposition, while RSV and TEV put 2.2 in round brackets. This shows that they consider it to be something apart from the surrounding verses. Only NIV translates the text in the traditional order, with no indication of any difficulty. Translators should consider what arrangement of the text will be most helpful to their own readers, bearing in mind the average level of biblical understanding. Probably in most cases it will be best to follow RSV and TEV in

THE FALL OF NINEVEH   Nahum 2.1

using round brackets for 2.2. This at least gives some indication that the verse is separate from its context, but does not change the numerical order, which may confuse some readers.

Because of the abruptness of the Hebrew, any further paragraph breaks are bound to be rather arbitrary, and there is much diversity among modern versions. The most common places for paragraph breaks are after 2.8 (TEV, NEB, TOB, Mft), 2.10 (TEV, BJ, JB, TOB, NIV, NJV, Mft, FrCL, GeCL), and 2.12 (RSV, TEV, NEB, NIV, Mft, GeCL). As always in making decisions of this kind, translators should consider the needs of their readers and the normal practice in their own languages.

2.1   RSV   TEV
[2.2]

    The shatterer has come up   **Nineveh, you are under attack!**
        against you.   **The power that will shatter you**
    Man the ramparts;   **has come.**
        watch the road;   **Man the defenses!**
    gird your loins;   **Guard the road!**
        collect all your strength.   **Prepare for battle!**

The prophet is speaking to a feminine <u>you</u> which TEV identifies as "Nineveh" (compare TOB, NIV). The word for "city" in Hebrew is feminine. The verse consists of a statement followed by four commands which are really consequences of the information given in the statement.

The shatterer has come up against you: the Hebrew word rendered **shatterer** is a form which does not occur elsewhere, and it is uncertain whether it is derived from a root meaning "to shatter" or from another one meaning "to scatter." If the latter is correct, then the reference is to the population of Nineveh fleeing from the city. This idea is found again in 2.8; 3.16-18. However, most versions prefer the former, in which the reference is to the enemy besieging Nineveh and breaking down the gates or walls with a battering ram (compare NEB "the battering-ram is mounted against your bastions"). This idea also occurs in verse 5 (see comments on verse 5).

Some scholars understand **the shatterer** to refer to some particular leader in the attack upon Nineveh, but there is no agreement as to who this could be. The most likely person is Cyaxares, the Median leader. This interpretation is perhaps shown in the NAB rendering, "The hammer comes up against you," as various historical figures who have been successful military leaders have been referred to as "the hammer." (For instance, this is the probable meaning of the second name of Judas Maccabaeus, a Jewish military leader in the second century B.C.) However, the majority of translations interpret the statement in a more general way. NIV, for example, has "An attacker advances against you."

TEV accepts this interpretation but translates with two separate sentences. The words **against you** are the basis of the opening sentence, "**Nineveh, you are under attack!**" This opening creates a vivid atmosphere for the whole chapter. The remaining words are translated by TEV as "**The power that will shatter you has come.**" "Shatter" means to "break into fragments or pieces." Other possible translation models are "The one who has the power to destroy you completely has come and is attacking you" or "People of Nineveh, the one who has the power . . . ."

THE FALL OF NINEVEH

The attack made by her enemies requires some response from the people of Nineveh, and in the rest of the verse, Nahum invites them to take defensive actions. The commands he gives are ironic, as he knows that the city will be captured anyway. The first command is **Man the ramparts**. The **ramparts** (RSV, JB, NAB) are the top part of the wall surrounding the city. Since few modern cities have defensive walls, most translators will find it necessary to use a more general term like **"defenses,"** as TEV does. However, a translator can capture the picture of walls with defensive positions on top of them by rendering this sentence as follows: "Place your soldiers along the top of the city walls."

The second command is **watch the road** in order to see the approaching enemy and to be informed of their movements. In some languages it will be necessary to identify the implicit direction of the road and say "guard the road leading to the city."

The third command is **gird your loins** (RSV, NAB). The people of those days normally wore long, flowing clothes, and when they were preparing for active work, they would tuck them up to give their legs more freedom of movement. JB translates here "tuck up your cloaks." However, this is really a figure of speech meaning "get ready for action" and occurs quite often in scripture (Exo 12.11; 1 Kgs 18.46; 2 Kgs 4.29; 9.1; Jer 1.17; Luke 12.35; 1 Peter 1.13). In the present context it may also be translated as "get ready to fight." In areas where people wear long clothes, it may be possible to use a figure of speech similar to that in the Hebrew.

The fourth command is **collect all your strength**, which means "gather your troops together" (compare JB "muster all your forces"; NIV "marshal all your strength"). TEV puts these third and fourth commands together into one and says simply **"Prepare for battle!"** Other translators may wish to put the two commands together without being quite as brief as TEV. A possible translation model is "gather your soldiers together and prepare to fight!"

2.2
[2.3]

RSV

(For the LORD is restoring the
majesty of Jacob
as the majesty of Israel,
for plunderers have stripped
them
and ruined their branches.)

TEV

(The LORD is about to restore the
glory of Israel, as it was before her
enemies plundered her.)

RSV and TEV enclose this verse in round brackets, and TEV prints it in prose format, to show that it is different in theme from the surrounding verses. As pointed out above, several versions move this verse to join it to the end of chapter 1, with which it has more in common in theme.

For the LORD is restoring the majesty of Jacob as the majesty of Israel: the verb translated **is restoring** is in the perfect tense in Hebrew (compare NJV "has restored"). This is generally taken to be a "prophetic perfect," in which the prophet speaks of something still future as though it had already happened. Thus TEV says "The LORD is about to restore" (compare NAB, NEB, NIV "will restore"). This sentence may also be rendered as "The LORD is about to cause Israel to regain its glory" or "The LORD is about to cause the people of Israel to regain their glory."

The Hebrew word translated **majesty** is very similar to the Hebrew word for "vine," and since the second half of the verse speaks about **branches**, some scholars think that the word for "vine" should be read in the first half of the verse. This view is followed by BJ, JB, NAB, and Mft. The vine is often used as a picture of the nation of Israel (Gen 49.22; Psa 80.8-16; Isa 5.1- 7; Jer 2.21; 12.10; compare John 15.1-6), and the overall theme of this verse is not really changed, whichever wording is followed. The difference is basically between a literal expression (**majesty**) and a figurative one ("vine").

The expression **restoring the majesty of Jacob as the majesty of Israel** can be puzzling. **Jacob** and **Israel** stand for the northern and southern kingdoms, though there is some disagreement as to which is which. There are three opinions. (1) Some scholars take **Jacob** to refer to the northern kingdom (destroyed by the Assyrians in 722 B.C.) and **Israel** to refer to the southern kingdom. They mention such passages as Amos 6.8; 8.7; and Micah 1.13-15 to support their view (NJV). (2) Others take **Jacob** to refer to the southern kingdom and **Israel** to the northern, and mention passages like Isaiah 43.1; 44.1; 46.3; Obadiah 18; Micah 3.1,8 for support (J.M.P. Smith, Lehrman). (3) Still others take the two terms together to refer to the entire nation, without distinguishing which is which (Gailey, Watts, GeCL). The second opinion above seems the most probable. The prophet is saying that, through the fall of Assyria, the Lord will restore the former glory of Judah just as he had promised to restore that of Israel (for instance in Hos 14.5-7). The prophetic hope was that all the twelve tribes would be restored, not just the tribes of the south, and this idea remains even in the New Testament (Rev 7.4-8).

TEV seems to follow the third of the three possibilities mentioned above. It drops the comparison of south with north and simply says "**The LORD is about to restore the glory of Israel**." This does, however, seem to lose something of the original meaning. A fuller translation model can be "The Lord is about to restore the glory of the people of Judah, just as he promised to restore the glory of the people of Israel." The words **majesty** or "glory" are difficult terms to translate in many languages, for the meaning changes according to the particular linguistic context. Here "glory" seems to refer to "honor and power." One can translate

Nahum 2.2

"The LORD is about to cause the people of Judah to regain their honor and power, just as he promised to do for the people of Israel."

The second half of the verse speaks of conditions as they existed at the time: **for plunderers have stripped them and ruined their branches**. This refers to the long period during which Assyria had dominated Israel and Judah, and which is now about to end. The picture of the nation as a vine is explicit here in the use of the word **branches**. TEV drops the figure of speech and runs the two parallel clauses into one, simply saying **"as it was before her enemies plundered her."** If a translator wishes to keep the figure of the "vine," he may say "as it was before her enemies had taken her possessions away by force, as people strip and ruin the branches of a vine." Other possible translation models for this verse are "The LORD is about to cause his people Israel to regain the honor and power which they had before their enemies took away all their possessions by force" or "Enemies took away by force all the possessions of the people of Israel, but now the LORD is going to give back to his people the honor and power they had before that happened."

2.3
[2.4]

RSV	TEV
The shield of his mighty men is red, his soldiers are clothed in scarlet. The chariots flash like flame[h] when mustered in array; the chargers[i] prance.	The enemy soldiers carry red shields and wear uniforms of red. They are preparing to attack! Their chariots flash like fire! Their horses[b] prance!

[h] Cn: The meaning of the Hebrew word is uncertain
[i] Cn Compare Gk Syr: Heb *cypresses*

[b] *Some ancient translations* horses; *Hebrew* cypresses.

In this verse Nahum describes the appearance of the enemy soldiers as they begin their attack on Nineveh. The description takes up the theme of verse 1. In the phrase **his mighty men, his** refers back to "the shatterer" or "The power that will shatter" (TEV) in verse 1. TEV makes the meaning more explicit by saying **"The enemy soldiers."**

Two facts are stated about these soldiers: they **"carry red shields and wear uniforms of red"** (TEV). It is not certain whether the shields looked red because they were covered with dyed leather (compare FrCL, GeCL) or because they were made of copper which reflected the sun (compare 1 Maccabees 6.39). The clause **"wear uniforms of red"** may be rendered as "wear red uniforms" or "wear clothing made of red cloth."

The Hebrew word used to describe the color of the uniforms is a different word from that used to describe the color of the shields, and perhaps implies a different shade of **red** (compare **scarlet** in RSV and most other modern English versions). However, in many languages there is only one word for **red**, and it is quite adequate to translate both terms by the same word, as TEV does. Red uniforms were in fact characteristic of the Medes and Babylonians (Ezek 23.14), who captured Nineveh.

The chariots flash like flame: the word translated **flash** is a word which does not occur anywhere else in the Hebrew Bible and whose meaning is unknown. Some scholars think it means "steel" (RV, JB, NAB; compare NIV) and speaks of the material from which the **chariots** were made. Others relate it to a word of similar spelling which means "torches" (NJV). Others see instead a word which means **flash**. RSV and TEV are in this last group, and TEV translates "**Their chariots flash like fire!**" This may again be a reference to the sun reflecting off the polished metal of the chariots. **Chariots** were light two-wheeled carts pulled by two horses and used in battle. Usually two or three people would ride in them, one to drive and the others to fight. **Chariots** in some languages will need to be translated by a phrase; for example, "horse-drawn war carts" or "war carts pulled by horses."

The last two words of the clause are clear in their meaning, but it is not certain exactly what aspect of the battle they refer to. They say literally "in the day of his preparation" (KJV, RV). Most translations link them with the description of the chariots. Thus RSV has **when mustered in array**, and NEB has "when the line is formed." TEV treats these two words as a more general description of the enemy preparations and says "**They are preparing to attack!**" TEV places these words before the mention of the chariots in order to give the general statement before the more specific ones. In many languages it will be helpful to designate the object of the verb "**attack**" and say "they are preparing to attack Nineveh."

The chargers prance: in this last line the Hebrew contains a word that refers to a kind of tree ("fir" in KJV, "cypress" in NJV, "pine" in NIV). If this wording is correct, the name of the tree stands for the weapons made from its wood ("arrows" in NJV, "spears" in NIV, compare TOB, FrCL, GeCL). This interpretation is not paralleled anywhere else in the Old Testament but makes good sense here, provided one uses a verb that can apply to weapons, such as "the spears of pine are brandished" (NIV). However, the ancient Greek translation, the Septuagint, understands here a similar word which occurs in 3.3 and means "horsemen" (JB) or "**horses**" (NAB, TEV). RSV accepts this possibility but uses the word **chargers**, which means horses specially trained for use in battle.

Prance describes the impatient movements of the horses as they wait for the battle to begin. In areas where horses are not well known, the languages may not have a single word for this kind of movement. In such cases translators may say something like "the horses wait impatiently for action" (compare JB). Another way to express the prancing action is to say "the horses move their feet impatiently as they wait for battle." It may also be possible to use here a term that ordinarily describes the foot movements of some animals other than horses.

2.4 [2.5]	RSV	TEV
	The chariots rage in the streets, they rush to and fro through the squares; they gleam like torches, they dart like lightning.	Chariots dash wildly through the streets, rushing back and forth in the city squares. They flash like torches and dart about like lightning.

Nahum 2.4

The majority of commentators take this verse as continuing to describe the attackers, though TEV seems to treat it as referring to the defenders by linking it with the first part of verse 5. The majority view seems more probable. Since the assault on the city walls is not mentioned until verse 5, the **streets** and **squares** here must refer to areas in the suburbs of Nineveh that were outside the main fortifications. The **squares** were more open areas where the **chariots** would have more room to turn (compare NAB "wheel in the squares").

The terms used for the movements of the **chariots** are very vivid. (See comments on verse 3 for other ways to translate **chariots**.) For **rage** TEV uses the expression "dash wildly." The actual type of movement involved is not so important as the picture the words create of a situation which is frantic and disorderly. Translators should try to create a similar impression by the terms they choose; for example, "run in a confused way," "race madly," or "run in an uncontrolled way."

They gleam like torches, they dart like lightning: these words probably refer again to the way the sun was reflected from the polished metal of the chariots. A torch was a long pole with rags that were soaked in olive oil and then attached to one end of the pole. When the rags were set on fire, the torch gave out light. The comparison with **torches** stresses brightness, and the comparison with **lightning** stresses both brightness and speed. These two sentences can be rendered "They gleam like the light from flaming torches, and dart about like flashes of lightning." The word **dart** refers to very fast movement, first in one direction and then in another. In languages which do not have a single term for the idea of **dart**, translators may have to use a phrase; for example, "they rush in one direction and then in another."

2.5
[2.6]

RSV	TEV
The officers are summoned, they stumble as they go, they hasten to the wall, the mantelet is set up.	The officers are summoned; they stumble as they press forward. The attackers rush to the wall and set up the shield for the battering ram.

The difficulty with the first half of this verse lies in deciding whether it speaks of the attackers or the defenders. There are two main problems. The first is that the verse opens with a singular verb in Hebrew ("He summons" in NIV; "He commands" in NJV). The nearest singular subject for the "he" to refer to is "the shatterer" of verse 1. If this is indeed the subject, then the description must be of the attackers.

However, the second problem is the occurrence of the word **stumble**, which seems out of place if applied to well-organized attackers. One of the marks of such an army is that its men do not stumble (Isa 5.27). The word **stumble** is more appropriate if used about unready defenders hurrying to man the walls. But if this is the case, there is no real subject for the singular verb "summons."

Those who take this verse to refer to the attackers (HOTTP) may explain the stumbling as caused by their eagerness and haste (Watts). Or else they may change

THE FALL OF NINEVEH   Nahum 2.6

the Hebrew by one letter to form a similar word and translate "they take command of their companies" (J.M.P. Smith).

Those who take the verse to refer to the defenders have to assume that it is the king of Assyria who summons **the officers** (TOB, FrCL, GeCL; Lehrman). This would be rather odd, since he has not previously been mentioned, but it is not impossible in such an abrupt passage as this.

Another possibility is to read a different form of the verb for "summon," as RSV does, and to translate **The officers are summoned**. This wording seems to have the support of the ancient Greek translation but does not in itself resolve the question of whether the attackers or the defenders are in view. RSV applies the words to the attackers (compare JB, NAB). TEV uses the same words "**The officers are summoned**" but applies them to the defenders.

This is one of those cases where it is virtually impossible to be certain what the original writer intended. It seems more likely that the whole of verses 3-5 describes the attackers. However, translators will do well to consider which interpretation sounds best in their own languages. For languages which do not use the passive, a translator can restructure and say "The officers receive a summons," or else introduce a nonspecific subject and say "they summon (call) the officers." If the second choice is taken, the next sentence will then need to be rendered as "who stumble as they go," so that the subject refers to **officers**.

They hasten to the wall: in the second half of the verse the description is definitely of the attackers. TEV makes this explicit: "**The attackers rush to the wall**," that is, the wall which protects the inner city.

The mantelet is set up: in ancient warfare the attackers would attempt to break down the gates of a city with a battering ram. This was usually a large tree trunk with an iron tip in the shape of an ax head. It was either carried by soldiers or mounted on a frame which allowed it to be swung at the gates. In either case the attacking soldiers would be exposed to missiles hurled by the defenders. In order to protect their men, the attackers would place over the battering ram a kind of movable shelter called a **mantelet** (RSV, JB, NAB, NEB). This is what TEV refers to with the words "**set up the shield for the battering ram**." It will be useful in some languages to say "set up a protective shield (protective device) over the battering ram." It may be helpful to include an explanatory footnote here, as FrCL does. "Battering ram" may need to be rephrased as "the tree trunk for battering the walls or gates."

Another translation model for this verse is:

They call the officers, who stumble as they press forward.
The attackers [enemy soldiers] run quickly up to the wall
   and set up the shelter for the tree trunk to batter the wall.

2.6   RSV   TEV
[2.7]
      The river gates are opened,   **The gates by the river burst open;**
         the palace is in dismay;   **the palace is filled with terror.**

Nineveh was located on the east bank of the Tigris River and was protected both by the river itself and by a series of walls and moats. It is not certain exactly what **the river gates** (RSV, NAB, NIV) refer to. They may be the "sluices" (NEB), or gates which controlled the flow of water through the moats. If the sluices were captured by the attackers, it could either mean that the water was diverted away from the moats and the enemy could therefore approach closer to the walls (Lehrman), or else that the water was somehow released into the city, causing damage by flooding (NEB, NIV, NJV). It is not necessary to state which effect is in mind. TEV simply gives the bare fact as **"The gates by the river burst open."** However, if the translator decides that the subject of the passive construction **opened** is "the attackers," this sentence may be rendered "They open the sluices on the river" or "The enemy opens the gates that control the waters of the river."

The palace is in dismay: the Hebrew says literally "the palace is dissolved" (RV). This may refer to the result of a supposed flood which caused the palace to collapse physically (NEB, NIV, FrCL), or it may refer to the psychological effect on the people who lived in the palace (RSV, JB, GeCL). TEV follows this second interpretation and says **"the palace is filled with terror."** It will be helpful in many languages to provide a subject for **"filled with terror"** and translate as "the people in the palace are filled with terror" or "the people in the palace are shaking with fear." **Dismay** (TEV "terror") in some languages is described with idiomatic expressions; for example, "The people in the palace, their souls flee and bile stirs up so that they shake all over."

2.7   RSV   TEV
[2.8]

    its mistress[j] is stripped, she is   The queen is taken captive;
        carried off,   her servants moan like doves
    her maidens lamenting,   and beat their breasts in sor-
        moaning like doves,   row.
        and beating their breasts.

[j] The meaning of the Hebrew is uncertain

The Hebrew word translated **its mistress** in RSV and "The queen" in TEV is a word which does not occur anywhere else in the Old Testament. It may be taken as a verb form (compare NIV "It is decreed"), but this is unlikely. Most commentators take the word as a proper name ("Huzzab" in KJV, RV, NJV) and understand it as referring either to the queen of Assyria (HOTTP, RSV, NAB, TEV, Mft, GeCL) or to the statue of the goddess Ishtar (BJ, JB, TOB, FrCL), who was worshiped at Nineveh.

The Hebrew text states that this Huzzab **is stripped, she is carried off**. If the queen is meant, stripping her or forcing her to remove her clothes would have been a way of humiliating and dishonoring her (compare 3.5). If the statue is meant, the stripping refers to the removal of its valuable decorations. This action would both supply booty for the conquerors and dishonor the goddess (compare 1.14). Many translators will need to supply an agent or person doing the action in this passive construction. Clearly, the attacking soldiers are implied. If the translators understand the word to mean "removing clothes," they can say "They strip the queen of her clothes," or "They remove the clothes from the queen by force," or "They compel the queen to remove all her clothes."

Many translations use different Hebrew vowels when reading the word translated in RSV as **is stripped**, and this produces a word that means "is exiled"

(NJV; compare BJ, JB, NAB, NEB). TEV follows this interpretation and combines this word with the next one (<u>she is carried off</u> in RSV) in the single statement that "**The queen is taken captive.**" In some languages this sentence will need to be expressed in the active voice: "They capture the queen" or "They make the queen a prisoner."

The second half of the verse describes the reactions of **her maidens**. If the queen was the subject of the first part of the verse, the **maidens** are "her servants" (TEV) or attendants. TEV leaves it implicit that these servants were females, but some translators may wish to say explicitly "female servants." If the goddess was the subject of the first part of the verse, then the **maidens** are the sacred prostitutes who served in her temple. Compare the comments on 3.4.

These women are doing three things: **lamenting, moaning like doves, and beating their breasts**. The second and third of these actions are ways of demonstrating the first action. With the words "**her servants moan like doves and beat their breasts in sorrow**," TEV translates the actions of **moaning** and **beating** as verbs, but renders the **lamenting** with the words "**in sorrow**," to explain the meaning of the actions.

The sound made by **doves** or pigeons was often taken as a picture of the moaning of people expressing their sorrow (compare Isa 38.14; 59.11; Ezek 7.16). This sentence may be translated "Her female servants weep, making a sound like the moaning of doves." Beating the breast or chest was a common way of showing sorrow (Isa 32.12; compare Luke 18.13; 23.48). "**In sorrow**" can also be rendered "to show their sorrow" or "to show that their hearts are filled with sorrow." In some languages it will be necessary to say "they use their hands to beat their breasts to show their sorrow."

2.8
[2.9]

RSV	TEV
Nineveh is like a pool whose waters[k] **run away.** **"Halt! Halt!" they cry; but none turns back.**	**Like water from a broken dam the people rush from Nineveh!**[c] **"Stop! Stop!" the cry rings out— but no one turns back.**

[k] Cn Compare Gk: Heb *from the days that she has become, and they*

[c] *Probable text* Like water ... Nineveh; *Hebrew unclear.*

If the Hebrew text is correct as it stands, the meaning is "Nineveh has been like a [placid] pool of water from earliest times. Now they flee" (NJV). The words here translated "from earliest times" are probably the result of a copying error. The majority of modern translations change them in accordance with the ancient Greek translation, the Septuagint. RSV, for instance, translates **Nineveh is like a pool whose waters run away** (compare JB, NAB, NIV, FrCL, GeCL). Since this is the first mention of **Nineveh** in the Hebrew text since 1.1, it will be helpful in many languages to say "The city of Nineveh."

TEV follows this wording but makes the point of the comparison explicit: "**Like water from a broken dam the people rush from Nineveh!**" This refers of course to the people trying to escape when the city is captured. In some languages the second line needs to be placed first: "The people rush from the city of Nineveh just as water pours out of a broken dam."

The second half of the verse gives a vivid picture of the officers trying in vain to stop the defending troops from fleeing with everyone else. They call out **"Halt! Halt!" . . . but none turns back**. The words **they cry** are not in the Hebrew but are inserted in several modern versions (RSV, NEB, NIV; compare FrCL, GeCL) to make clear that the previous words **"Halt! Halt!"** are direct speech. TEV uses the idiomatic English expression **"the cry rings out"** to make the effect more vivid and dramatic. In many languages it will be necessary to state explicitly who is crying out; for example, "The officers shout, 'Stop! Stop!' But no one turns around and comes back."

2.9   RSV   TEV
[2.10]

    Plunder the silver,   Plunder the silver!
      plunder the gold!   Plunder the gold!
    There is no end of treasure,   The city is full of treasure!
      or wealth of every precious
      thing.

Nahum here turns to address the attackers, who can take what they want from Nineveh, now that the defending soldiers have fled. **Plunder the silver, plunder the gold!**: **silver** and **gold** would be the most obvious and most valuable items to attract the attacking soldiers. The word **plunder** refers to violent action like "taking by force" or "seizing" (see also verse 2, where "plunderers" occurs).

But there were many other things beside **silver** and **gold**. Nineveh contained the goods captured by the Assyrian armies in many previous campaigns, as well as the annual tribute which subject nations were forced to give. These other things are described in general terms as **There is no end of treasure, or wealth of every precious thing**. TEV combines these two clauses into one and says simply "The city is full of treasure!" Some translators may wish to use a broader expression more like the Hebrew and say "treasure of every kind" or "precious things of every kind."

2.10   RSV   TEV
[2.11]

    Desolate! Desolation and ruin!   Nineveh is destroyed, deserted,
      Hearts faint and knees trem-   desolate!
        ble,   Hearts melt with fear;
    anguish is on all loins,   knees tremble, strength is
      all faces grow pale!   gone;
                                                  faces grow pale.

Desolate! Desolation and ruin!: the first three words in Hebrew are similar to each other in both sound and meaning (*buqah umebuqah umebullaqah*). A number of English versions try to reproduce the same effect: "Raid and ravage and ruin" (JB); "Desolation, devastation and destruction" (NJV); "desolate, dreary, drained" (Mft). TEV has the same approach but makes the subject explicit and says **"Nineveh is destroyed, deserted, desolate!"** If translators can find three terms in their own languages that are similar in sound, that would be good though it is not essential. As in some earlier verses the overall impression created by the verse is more important than the exact meaning of the individual terms. In languages which do not use the passive, this sentence poses problems. However, most languages without a passive form of the verb can describe these conditions by using alternative forms such as "suffer" or "receive"; for example, "Nineveh has suffered destruction, desertion, and desolation" or "Nineveh has received destruction . . . ."

The rest of the verse describes the effect of the capture of Nineveh on its inhabitants. The language is pictorial, and translators should try to use appropriate pictures in their own languages rather than necessarily to translate literally the pictures of the Hebrew. In languages which have ideophones this may be a good place to use them.

Hearts faint and knees tremble: these are two aspects of the physical reactions of the people of Nineveh. The **hearts** are regarded as the source of courage. If their **hearts faint** (TEV "melt"), the people will not be able to fight. If their **knees tremble**, they will not be able to run away either. Most languages have similar idioms which translators should try to use. Examples are "The heart flees and turns over" or "The heart falls." Compare the description of Belshazzar's reactions to the writing on the wall in Daniel 5.6.

Anguish is on all loins: it is not certain whether this is a description of a woman having labor pains (compare Isa 21.3), or whether the **loins** are regarded as the source of physical strength (compare Job 40.16). TEV adopts the latter interpretation and drops the figure of speech, saying just "**strength is gone**." If some part of the body other than the **loins** is regarded as the source of physical strength, translators may be able to refer to it here.

The last word of the verse in Hebrew is of uncertain meaning. It refers to some color, but it is not clear what color. Some translators render it as "black" (Mft) or "crimson" (TOB), but the majority think that paleness fits better with a description of fear (compare Joel 2.6). Thus RSV says **all faces grow pale** (compare JB, TEV, NIV, FrCL). Other modern versions have expressions of similar meaning: "blanched" (NAB), "drained of colour" (NEB), and "ashen" (NJV, compare GeCL). Translators should use word pictures or idioms which are natural in their languages for expressing reactions to fear; for example, "soul (guardian spirit) disappears and bile is stirred up" (Thai) or "teeth chatter uncontrollably."

2.11-12 RSV	TEV
[2.12-13]	
11 Where is the lions' den, the cave[1] of the young lions, where the lion brought his prey, where his cubs were, with none to disturb?	11 Where now is the city that was like a den of lions, the place where young lions were fed, where the lion and the lioness would go and their cubs would be safe?
12 The lion tore enough for his whelps and strangled prey for his lionesses; he filled his caves with prey and his dens with torn flesh.	12 The lion killed his prey and tore it to pieces for his mate and her cubs; he filled his den with torn flesh.

[1] Cn: Heb *pasture*

Nahum 2.11-12

These two verses together compare the city of Nineveh to a **lions' den**, and its people to **lions**. The lion was a favorite figure in Assyrian sculpture, and in their inscriptions the Assyrians often boasted of the cruel way they had treated people whom they had conquered. Thus it is particularly apt that Nahum should use the habits of the lion as the basis for his comparison. He starts in verse 11 with a mocking question which in effect rejoices over the fall of Nineveh; then he goes on in verse 12 with a description of the way **the lion** of Nineveh used to behave in the days of his power. In some languages it will be easier to run the two verses together and first give the description of what Nineveh used to be like, before making the statement of what it is like now that it has fallen. See comments below on verse 12.

The figure of speech in verse 11 is in Hebrew a metaphor, **Where is the lions' den . . . ?** The **lions' den** refers of course to the city of Nineveh, and TEV makes this explicit by turning the metaphor into a simile, saying "**Where now is the city that was like a den of lions . . . ?**" **Lions' den** may also be expressed as "cave of lions," or "cave where lions live," or "place where lions live." In cultures where the **lion** is unknown and there is no word for this animal, it will be helpful to say "wild animal named 'lion,' " or use a generic term in the language meaning "wild animal" or "predator (flesh eater)" and append the name "lion" to it.

The clause **Where is . . .** can be rendered "What has happened to . . . " in many languages. This question, which includes the whole of verse 11, is a rhetorical question, and is really a way of making a strong statement meaning "Nineveh is now nowhere, it is destroyed." Compare the use of the questions "Where is . . . God?" in Psalms 42.3,10; 115.2; Micah 7.10, and "Where are the gods of . . . ?" in Isaiah 36.19. Some translators may find it more appropriate to use a statement here and say "The city that was like a den of lions . . . has now been destroyed."

The cave of the young lions: TEV has "**the place where young lions were fed**," and this translates the Hebrew text as it stands (compare HOTTP, NIV, NJV, TOB, FrCL, GeCL). However, because the Hebrew word for feeding place normally refers to a place where cattle or sheep graze (compare NJV "pasture"), a number of scholars think that it does not fit well in a passage that is speaking about lions. By changing the order of two of the letters in the Hebrew, a word meaning **cave** is obtained instead, and this wording is followed by RSV, BJ, JB, NAB, and NEB. This gives a better parallelism between the first two lines. If translators follow the **cave** interpretation, these two lines can be translated as:

What has happened to the city
  that was like a den of lions,
  the cave where young lions live?

Where the lion brought his prey: TEV again follows the Hebrew text as it stands, with "**where the lion and the lioness would go**" (compare NIV). The Hebrew word for "lioness" was understood by the ancient Greek translators as a slightly different word meaning "to enter." Some modern translators follow this interpretation and understand the word "to enter" as referring to the lion's return to his den after being out hunting. Thus Mft has "whither the Lion withdrew." This interpretation also seems to be followed by RSV, with its **where the lion brought his prey**. Many languages have no single word for **prey**. Some translators may have to use a phrase such as "the animals he killed."

Even translators who follow the Hebrew as its stands are not all agreed as to its meaning. An alternative to the TEV understanding can be seen in the JB rendering, "When the lion made his foray the lioness stayed behind."

The last line is literally **where his cubs were, with none to disturb**. In some languages this sentence may be expressed "Where nothing can hurt his cubs." TEV gives the same meaning but with simpler wording, **"and their cubs would be safe."** **Cubs** is a word for the young of wild animals such as lions.

Verse 12 continues the comparison of Nineveh with a group of lions, and describes the conduct of the Assyrian soldiers in the past in terms of a lion hunting to feed his family.

The first two lines are parallel with each other: **The lion tore enough for his whelps and strangled prey for his lionesses**. **Whelps** is another word for the young of the lion, especially when they are very small. The picture is of the lion killing some other animal and taking some of its meat back for the lionesses and their offspring to eat. The word **strangled** is probably best understood as a forceful way of expressing the general meaning "kill." Lions do in fact strangle their prey by biting the throat to cut off the air supply, especially when they attack larger animals. NEB translates "broke the neck"; this is another way lions kill their victims, but it is not the intended meaning of this text. The Hebrew word used here occurs elsewhere only at 2 Samuel 17.23. TEV drops the parallel structure and expresses the meaning in logical order as **"The lion killed his prey and tore it to pieces for his mate and her cubs."** **Prey** here may be rendered as "the animal he hunted." **For his lionesses . . .** may be expressed as "so that his mates . . . may eat it." A male lion often has more than one mate.

The second two lines are again parallel with each other: **he filled his caves with prey, and his dens with torn flesh**. Since these two lines say the same thing twice, they are put together into one line in TEV as **"he filled his den with torn flesh."**

If translators wish to run the two verses together and avoid a rhetorical question, the following may be a suitable translation model (compare GeCL):

> 11-12 In the past Nineveh was like a den of lions, where the lion and lioness would go, where young lions were fed, and the cubs were safe. The lion used to kill his prey and tear it to pieces for his mates and cubs. He would fill his den with torn flesh. But now Nineveh has lost all its power! (Or, But now Nineveh has itself been destroyed!)

2.13 [2.14]

RSV	TEV
Behold, I am against you, says the LORD of hosts, and I will burn your^m chariots in smoke, and the sword shall devour your young lions; I will cut off your prey from the earth, and the voice of your messengers shall no more be heard.	"I am your enemy!" says the LORD Almighty. "I will burn up your chariots. Your soldiers will be killed in war, and I will take away everything that you took from others. The demands of your envoys will no longer be heard."

^{m} Heb *her*

There is some doubt whether this verse is to be linked more closely with those that precede or those that follow. In some respects it seems to continue the picture of Nineveh as a den of lions, which would link it with verses 11 and 12. On the other hand, the opening words, **Behold, I am against you, says the LORD of hosts**, are repeated in 3.5, which may suggest that in both places a new paragraph is beginning. This analysis would link verse 13 with 3.1-4.

The uncertainty is reflected in the paragraph divisions of the various versions. RSV begins a new paragraph with verse 13 and continues it into chapter 3, and NEB includes 2.13-3.6 under one section heading. The majority of versions (BJ, JB, NAB, TOB, NIV, NJV, FrCL, GeCL) join verse 13 to the preceding verses. TEV makes it a separate paragraph from the surrounding verses by printing it as prose instead of poetry. In view of the uncertainties, perhaps this is the most practical solution.

The word translated **Behold** is a way of attracting the attention of the hearer or reader (compare 1.15; 3.5; Hab 2.13,19; Zeph 3.19). It is hardly used in modern English, and a number of modern versions (NAB, NEB, NIV, NJV) simply omit it here. TEV tries to give the effect of the Hebrew word by translating the rest of the phrase as a separate sentence with an exclamation mark: "I am your enemy!" However, many languages have words or phrases similar to the Hebrew that are used to attract the attention of the hearer or reader. Such terms should certainly be used here and elsewhere. Examples are "Look!" "Think carefully!" or "Hear this!"

The words "I am your enemy!" are simply a modern way of saying **I am against you**. For other ways to translate **enemy**, see 1.8 and comments. The speaker here is **the LORD of hosts**. This title for the Lord emphasizes his military help in the history of his people and is very appropriate here in a passage dealing with the downfall of Judah's greatest enemy. The exact meaning of **hosts** is not certain but definitely includes a reference to the Lord's power. Thus TEV translates "the LORD Almighty" (compare Hab 2.13; Zeph 2.9-10). "Almighty" may also be rendered "all powerful," "the one who has the greatest power," and so on. In some languages translators may need to place the phrase **says the LORD of hosts** at the beginning of this sentence for stylistic reasons: "The LORD, the all-powerful one, says, 'I am your enemy.' "

I will burn your chariots in smoke: for the translation of **chariots** see comments on verse 3. To speak of burning something **in smoke** sounds odd in English, so TEV simply says "I will burn up your chariots." The ancient Greek Septuagint translators understood a different word instead of **chariots**, and some scholars today prefer to change the Hebrew. Thus NEB has here "I will smoke out your pride." "Pride" is intended in its normal sense, not as a technical term meaning a family of lions. The picture of the lions in the previous verses is found again in the next line, **and the sword shall devour your young lions**. But as this picture is not carried through to the end of the verse, TEV drops the figurative language and expresses the meaning in nonfigurative speech, "**Your soldiers will be killed in war.**" In some languages it may be possible to retain the picture language of **sword** referring to "killing" or "war." In such cases one may say "The sword shall eat up your soldiers." In languages which do not use the passive, and where translators wish to drop the picture language, this clause may be rendered as "Your enemies will kill your soldiers in war."

The picture of the lions occurs again in the next clause, **I will cut off your prey from the earth**. The **prey** here refers to the plunder which the Assyrians had taken from the nations they had defeated. TEV again expresses this in nonfigurative language as "**I will take away everything that you took from others.**"

The last line, **the voice of your messengers shall no more be heard**, refers to the envoys sent by the Assyrians to other nations, to threaten them or to demand from them submission or tribute. An example of this is found in Isaiah 36.1-22; compare 2 Kings 18.13-37. Nineveh would never again send out such messengers. TEV translates this with modern diplomatic terms as "**The demands of your envoys will no longer be heard.**" One may also restructure this sentence and say "You will no longer send envoys to make demands on other nations" or "Your envoys (messengers) will no longer go to other nations to make demands." When an envoy makes demands, he is using the authority of the person who sent him to ask for or require others to do certain things.

The term translated **your messengers** is changed by some scholars to "your feeding" (NEB). If this change is accepted, this is a further reference to the lions in their den. However, the majority of modern versions do not accept the change, and since the Hebrew makes perfectly good sense as it is, translators are recommended to follow the traditional text.

Chapter 3

3.1-7

	RSV		TEV

1	Woe to the bloody city,
	    all full of lies and booty—
	        no end to the plunder!
		1	Doomed is the lying, murderous city,
			    full of wealth to be looted and plundered!

2	The crack of whip, and rumble of wheel,
	    galloping horse and bounding chariot!
		2	Listen! The crack of the whip,
			    the rattle of wheels,
			    the gallop of horses,
			    the jolting of chariots!

3	Horsemen charging,
	    flashing sword and glittering spear,
	hosts of slain,
	    heaps of corpses,
	dead bodies without end—
	    they stumble over the bodies!
		3	Horsemen charge,
			    swords flash, spears gleam!
			Corpses are piled high,
			    dead bodies without number—
			    men stumble over them!

4	And all for the countless harlotries of the harlot,
	    graceful and of deadly charms,
	who betrays nations with her harlotries,
	    and peoples with her charms.
		4	Nineveh the whore is being punished.
			Attractive and full of deadly charms,
			    she enchanted nations and enslaved them.

5	Behold, I am against you,
	    says the LORD of hosts,
	    and will lift up your skirts over your face;
	and I will let nations look on your nakedness
	    and kingdoms on your shame.
		5	The LORD Almighty says,
			"I will punish you, Nineveh!
			I will strip you naked
			and let the nations see you,
			    see you in all your shame.

6	I will throw filth at you
	    and treat you with contempt,
	    and make you a gazingstock.
		6	I will treat you with contempt
			    and cover you with filth.
			People will stare at you in horror.

7	And all who look on you will shrink from you and say, Wasted is Nineveh; who will bemoan her? whence shall I seek comforters for her?	7	All who see you will shrink back. They will say, 'Nineveh lies in ruins! Who has any sympathy for her? Who will want to comfort her?'"

The text continues to be rather abrupt, with a series of short statements rather than a continuous discourse, and again there are many differences in paragraph breaks between the various modern versions. The most favored places for beginning new paragraphs are 3.8 (RSV, BJ, JB, NAB, TOB, TEV, NIV, FrCL, GeCL), 3.15b (RSV, BJ, JB, NAB, TOB, TEV, FrCL), and 3.18 (BJ, JB, NAB, TOB, TEV, NIV, NJV, FrCL, GeCL). Translators should include at least this many new paragraphs, but may also include others at points which seem suitable in their language.

For possible additional section headings, see the introductory notes to chapter 2.

THE FALL OF NINEVEH

3.1   RSV   TEV

**Woe to the bloody city,
all full of lies and booty—
no end to the plunder!**

**Doomed is the lying, murderous city,
full of wealth to be looted and plundered!**

The first three verses of chapter 3 continue to picture the fall of Nineveh begun in chapter 2. They are very vivid and very abrupt, and in fact do not form full sentences in Hebrew. They are mainly phrases strung together without formal connection. Their effect is to reinforce the impression of confusion and panic, and translators should try to create a similar effect in their own language. Some may be able to use a string of phrases like the Hebrew, while for others, this may result in nonsense. Some languages have special grammatical constructions to express a series of dramatic descriptive phrases such as those in verse 2. Each translator has to make the decision how best to achieve an effect equivalent to that of the Hebrew in the receptor language.

TEV varies in its approach, using short but complete sentences in verses 1 and 3, and a string of separate phrases in verse 2.

The Hebrew in verse 1 consists of two parts, the first describing the characteristics of the city at the height of its power, and the second the riches for its conqueror to plunder.

Woe to the bloody city: **Woe to** here is a statement rather than a wish, as it sometimes is elsewhere. "**Doomed is the . . . city**" (TEV) may also be rendered as "The . . . city will certainly be destroyed" or "There is no escape for the . . . city." In some cultures there are no human settlements which are the equivalent of cities, but people live in villages or small groups of houses, sometimes without any walls for protection. In such cases it will be necessary to refer to a city as "a large group of houses surrounded by a strong wall," or perhaps as "the large (or, chief) village."

The word **bloody** is used here in its original meaning, "causing bloodshed," and is not to be misunderstood as the common swear word used in many dialects of English.

The city is called **bloody** and **full of lies**, referring to the cruelty of its armies toward the people they had conquered, and to the deceitfulness of the rulers in making false promises. TEV reverses the order of these statements and says "**Doomed is the lying, murderous city**." Since murder is generally reckoned to be more serious than telling lies, this sequence forms a better climax in English. "**Murderous city**" can also be phrased as "city full of murderers." Another translation model for these first two clauses is "The city full of liars and murderers will certainly be destroyed."

The second half of the verse says the city is **full of . . . booty—no end to the plunder**. The Hebrew word translated **plunder** is the same word as that used for **prey** in 2.12,13 and thus gives a hint that the comparison of Nineveh with a den of lions is still in the prophet's mind. TEV expresses the Hebrew nouns as verbs and says "**full of wealth to be looted and plundered**." Nineveh was full of rich and luxurious goods of all kinds, many of which the Assyrians had previously taken from other cities which they had captured. Languages which do not use the passive will need to restructure this sentence. One possible translation model is "full of wealth that your enemies will loot and plunder." See also

2.2 and 2.9 on translation choices for **plunder**. The word "looted" in TEV is used as a synonym for "**plundered**."

It is also possible to understand the second half of the verse as parallel to the first half and continuing the description of the Assyrians in the days of their power. Thus JB has "stuffed with booty, whose plunderings know no end!" and NIV has "full of plunder, never without victims!" It does not really matter much which interpretation the translator follows, because, as has already been pointed out, the most important feature of this passage is its overall effect rather than its details.

3.2   RSV   TEV

The crack of whip, and rumble of wheel, galloping horse and bounding chariot!	Listen! The crack of the whip, the rattle of wheels, the gallop of horses, the jolting of chariots!

Here Nahum imagines he is watching the final assault of the enemy chariots as the city falls. In four phrases he picks out four outstanding features of the scene. TEV introduces the verse with "**Listen!**" an exclamation which is intended to make the reader feel as if he too were present at the scene.

The crack of whip: **crack** is a term in English to describe the noise made by the whips. Whips were used to encourage horses to go faster. Another way of rendering this clause is "the cracking sound of whips." In certain languages in Africa and elsewhere, this verse may be a good place to use ideophones.

Rumble of wheel is the noise made by the wheels of the attacking chariots as they rush forward. TEV "**rattle**" is probably more appropriate. Here again an ideophone can be used to good effect in certain languages.

Galloping horse: the word translated **galloping** does not occur anywhere else and its meaning is not certain. Some form of the word "gallop" is used by most English translations. This gives an impression both of swift movement and of the noise of the horses' hoofs beating on the ground. One can also say "the thud of horses' hoofs."

Bounding chariot: for notes on **chariot** see comments on 2.3. The chariots bounce as they speed over the uneven ground. There is a similarity of sound between the two Hebrew words in this phrase. One can obtain something of the same effect in English by saying "the charging of chariots," but it is not possible to do this in many languages, and it is not of any great importance to do so. A possible rendering is "the rattling sound of racing chariots."

In RSV the nouns of this verse, **whip**, **wheel**, **horse**, and **chariot**, are all singular. The prophet mentions one sample of each item as representing many. In other languages it may be more appropriate to translate as plural, as TEV does (compare Mft, NAB, NEB, NIV, TOB, FrCL).

3.3   RSV   TEV

Horsemen charging, flashing sword and glittering spear,	Horsemen charge, swords flash, spears gleam! Corpses are piled high,

hosts of slain,
  heaps of corpses,
dead bodies without end—
  they stumble over the bodies!
	dead bodies without number—
	men stumble over them!

The graphic picture of the final attack on Nineveh continues. **Horsemen charging**: the term translated **charging** here may be understood as "rearing" (NEB). In that case the description is of the horses rather than the riders, and it speaks of them raising themselves up on their hind legs. However, if this is understood as a charging action, another possible rendering is "Horsemen urge their horses forward" or "Horsemen urge their horses to race forward to fight." In other languages one must be even more explicit and say "The soldiers riding horses urge their horses . . . ."

Flashing sword and glittering spear: these words speak of the reflection of the sun on the metal weapons of the attackers (compare 2.3-4).

Hosts of slain, heaps of corpses: the attackers kill so many of the people of Nineveh that the bodies lie in **heaps**. Assyrian inscriptions record that this is exactly how the Assyrians had treated peoples whom they had conquered, so the prophet is here speaking of a just punishment upon them. TEV reduces these two phrases to one clause, "**corpses are piled high**." Some translations will need to say "dead bodies lie in huge mounds" or "the dead bodies are piled up in high mounds."

Dead bodies without end: these words emphasize the greatness of the slaughter. They are largely parallel in meaning with the previous words, and some translators may prefer to give all the information in a single clause. They can say something like "Dead bodies too many to count are piled high," or "countless dead bodies are piled high," or "dead bodies without number are piled high."

They stumble over the bodies: there are so many dead people lying around that the attacking soldiers can hardly step over them, and so they **stumble**. **They** (RSV) or "**men**" (TEV) may need to be rendered "the enemy soldiers."

3.4	RSV	TEV

	And all for the countless harlotries of the harlot,
	  graceful and of deadly charms,
	who betrays nations with her harlotries,
	  and peoples with her charms.
		Nineveh the whore is being punished.
		Attractive and full of deadly charms,
		  she enchanted nations and enslaved[d] them.

[d] enslaved; *or* seduced.

Here a new metaphor begins in which the city of Nineveh is compared to a prostitute, or woman who receives payment for allowing men to have sexual relations with her. This metaphor extends over verses 4-7. In the Old Testament, prostitution is often used as a picture of unfaithfulness to the Lord. In this meaning it is of course applied to the Lord's own people, who are linked to him in a covenant relationship as a wife is to her husband (compare for instance Ezek 16; Hos 2). Assyria was a pagan nation and could not really be accused of unfaithfulness to the Lord in the same way. The comparison of Nineveh with a prostitute is not therefore to be understood as speaking primarily of her idolatrous religion. Rather it speaks of the way in which her power attracted other nations, who became subject to her and who later regretted their association with her. In the same way, a prostitute presents an attractive outward appearance in order to lure men to their ruin. In some languages one may need to change the metaphor to a simile and say "Nineveh is like . . . ."

One of the nations which had fallen under the power of Assyria's false charms was Judah. King Ahaz, despite the warnings given by the prophet Isaiah (Isa 7.1—8.8) had asked for the help of the Assyrians against his enemies (2 Kgs 16.7-9). The help was given, but Judah became subject to Assyria and even followed the pattern of Assyrian idolatry (2 Kgs 16.10-16).

There is also another sense in which the comparison of Nineveh with a prostitute is very apt. The chief deity of Nineveh was the goddess Ishtar, in whose worship sacred prostitution played a large part. Some of her own worshipers even referred to her as a prostitute. Insofar as the city reflected the characteristics of its goddess, it is appropriate that Nahum should liken it to a prostitute.

The picture of the enemies of God's people as a prostitute is also found elsewhere in scripture, especially in Revelation 17—18 (compare Isa 47).

And all for the countless harlotries of the harlot: the words **And all for** refer back to the destruction of the city and the death of its inhabitants as described in verses 1-3. The expression means that all that punishment is coming upon Nineveh because of its past conduct. TEV makes this more explicit by saying "**Nineveh the whore is being punished**." This clause can also be translated "Because Nineveh is a prostitute, she is being punished" or "Because Nineveh is a prostitute, God is punishing her."

There are numerous terms in English to speak of a prostitute. The word "prostitute" itself is probably the most general, and its emotional effect is rather neutral and colorless. The term **harlot** used in RSV (compare NAB, NIV, NJV) is a somewhat stronger term but sounds rather old fashioned. The word "**whore**" used by TEV and JB is also a stronger word and is still in use today. It carries overtones of scorn and disgust, but it is not out of place in a formal setting such as a scripture translation. Many languages will have a lot of terms covering this area of meaning, and if possible, translators should choose here some term which carries a strong emotive force, but which is not offensive in polite conversation. If no such term can be found, then it will be best to use a neutral term equivalent to the English "prostitute," rather than a stronger word which may cause offense during the public reading of scripture.

Graceful and of deadly charms: this is literally "fair and charming, a mistress of witchcraft" (NAB). In this case "witchcraft" refers to spells, potions, and even secret objects which were thought to arouse the sexual instinct in the men who went to a prostitute. TEV translates in plain language as "**Attractive and full of deadly charms**." "Deadly charms" may also be rendered "charms which lead to death," or even more explicitly, "magic charms which lead to death."

The third and fourth lines in Hebrew repeat key words from the first and second lines. This pattern can be seen in the literal translation of RSV, **who betrays nations with her harlotries, and peoples with her charms**. TEV runs these two lines into one and says "She enchanted nations and enslaved them." The term translated **betrays** or "enslaved" is literally "sold" (compare KJV, RV). Several modern English versions take this to imply "sold into slavery" and translate in a way similar to TEV (JB, NAB, NIV). Others, like RSV, interpret the word in the sense of "deceived," and this possibility is shown in the footnote of TEV, "seduced" (compare NEB, NJV, Mft). Both meanings fit the context very well.

Another translation model for this verse is:

> Because Nineveh is a prostitute, God is punishing her.
>   She is attractive and full of magic charms which lead (people) to death.
>   So she used her charms to attract nations to her and made them her slaves.

3.5

RSV

Behold, I am against you,
  says the LORD of hosts,
  and will lift up your skirts over
    your face;
  and I will let nations look on
    your nakedness
  and kingdoms on your shame.

TEV

The LORD Almighty says,
  "I will punish you, Nineveh!
  I will strip you naked
  and let the nations see you,
  see you in all your shame.

The opening words of this verse, **Behold, I am against you**, are identical with those of 2.13. It is possible that in both cases they mark the beginning of a new paragraph, as the format of RSV suggests (see comments on 2.13). Against this view is the fact that in both cases a metaphor begun in the previous verse is continued as if no break were intended. TEV, like RSV and GeCL, begins a new paragraph at verse 5, but other versions (BJ, JB, NAB, NEB, TOB, NJV, FrCL) treat verses 4-7 as all one paragraph. On the whole, this second format seems preferable.

For comments on the opening words, see 2.13. Note that here in verse 5, the wording of TEV is not exactly the same as in 2.13. The TEV translators evidently thought that the words "**I will punish you**" fitted the present context better than the words they had used in 2.13. In cases like this translators should be aware of places where Hebrew wording is repeated, but they have to make their own decisions whether or not to use identical wording in their translation. The decision must be made according to the content of the passage and the stylistic needs of their own language. In general, where the Hebrew repeats itself, especially in longer passages (for example, 2 Kgs 18.13—20.19; and Isa 36—39), a translation should do the same unless there is good reason not to. Where the repeated section is shorter (as here), there is more room for variety in the translation, as the context may require.

I . . . will lift up your skirts over your face: the punishment which was to be given to the prostitute Nineveh was that given customarily to women who had been found guilty of adultery. (Compare Jer 13.26; Ezek 16.36-38; Hos 2.10.) Her clothing (**skirts**) would be lifted up **over** her **face** so that her **nakedness** was exposed to view. TEV drops the details about the way in which the clothing was raised, and expresses the meaning in a more general statement, "**I will strip you naked.**" This changes the meaning somewhat, as the skirt was probably not completely removed. If nakedness is mentioned, it will be necessary in some languages to use a euphemism in order not to give offense to readers.

Nahum 3.5

I will let nations look on your nakedness and kingdoms on your shame: **nakedness** is here a euphemism for sexual organs. Just as the Assyrians had humiliated other nations, so now they in turn would be publicly humiliated.

The last line in Hebrew is parallel with the previous line, and one verb covers both lines: "I will show the nations your nakedness and the kingdoms your shame" (NIV). Since there is no real difference in meaning between "nations" and "kingdoms," TEV drops the repetition but adds emphasis in a way which is more natural in English, by repeating the words "see you" in "see you in all your shame." These three lines can be rendered as "I will pull your skirts up over your face, and make you ashamed by letting the nations see your private parts (sexual organs)."

3.6   RSV   TEV

I will throw filth at you
  and treat you with contempt,
  and make you a gazingstock.
	I will treat you with contempt
	  and cover you with filth.
	People will stare at you in horror.

I will throw filth at you and treat you with contempt: TEV reverses the order of the first two lines as found in the Hebrew and in RSV. The reason for this is probably to explain the general meaning of the action stated, before describing what the specific action was. Thus in TEV "**I will treat you with contempt**" comes before "**and cover you with filth**." Here filth probably refers to all sorts of household rubbish. It may be that the treatment spoken of here is that given at the time to women who were known to have committed adultery. Not only were they stripped in public (verse 5), but they were also mocked by having rubbish thrown at them. **I will throw filth at you and treat you with contempt** may be expressed in some languages as "I will show you how much I despise you by throwing rubbish (filth) at you." Some translators may wish to follow RSV's ordering of these clauses and say "I will throw rubbish at you to show how much I despise you."

The last line, **I will . . . make you a gazingstock**, means that Nineveh will be made an object of public ridicule and scorn. JB has "I am going to . . . make you a public show." TEV "**in horror**" is not quite the right meaning; "in scorn" would be more accurate.

Some scholars think that the word translated **gazingstock** has a different meaning, namely excrement or feces. If so, then this line is parallel in sense with the first one. NEB, the only major English version to follow this interpretation, translates "I will treat you like excrement."

3.7   RSV   TEV

And all who look on you will shrink from you and say, Wasted is Nineveh; who will bemoan her?	All who see you will shrink back. They will say, 'Nineveh lies in ruins! Who has any sympathy for her?

whence shall I seek comforters for her?ⁿ	Who will want to comfort her?' "

ⁿ Gk: Heb *you*

    This verse continues to describe the reaction of those who see the terrible things that happen to Nineveh. The sight of her destruction is so dreadful that **All who look on you will shrink from you** or "turn their backs on you" (JB). **Shrink from** in this context has the sense of "avoidance," or even "revulsion and horror." Therefore this sentence may be translated in many languages as "And every person who sees you will turn their backs on you because of their disgust (revulsion) and say . . . " or "And all who see you will turn their eyes away because they feel so disgusted. Then they will say . . . ." Translators need to find expressions that describe the actions of people who feel great disgust or revulsion. In some languages this is described by physical actions such as "turn away," "shrink back," or similar expressions. **All** may be rendered "Every person."

    These onlookers then speak **and say, Wasted is Nineveh**. This is of course a result of being destroyed by the armies which captured the city. These words also give the meaning of the picture language about the treatment of the prostitute in verses 5 and 6. TEV puts this meaning in plain language as "**Nineveh lies in ruins**." In some languages it will be necessary to designate Nineveh again as "The city of Nineveh." **Wasted** refers to the pile of rubble, wood, and bricks which remains after the city has been torn down by the enemy soldiers. So the phrase **Wasted is Nineveh** may be rendered as "All the buildings in Nineveh have been destroyed" or "All the buildings in Nineveh lie in ruins."

    The main problem in this verse is to decide where the quotation ends. Some translators end the quotation after this first sentence (BJ, JB, NJV). Others include the next sentence, **Who will bemoan her?** (NEB, TOB, NIV, GeCL). Yet others include the third sentence, **Whence shall I seek comforters for her?** (NAB, TEV, Mft, FrCL). When the opinions of scholars are so evenly divided, it is very hard to give firm advice to translators. There is, however, one slight argument against the third of these possibilities. This is the fact that the Hebrew text actually says "Where shall I look for anyone to comfort you?" (NEB, NJV). If these words are included within the quotation, the pronoun "I" has no real antecedent, and it is also necessary to follow the ancient Greek translation, the Septuagint, and say "her" instead of "you" (see RSV footnote). The fact that there is a variation between the Hebrew text and the Greek translation shows that the problem is a very old one. The Hebrew words for "you" and "her" differ by only one letter, and the argument against following the Greek text is not a very strong one. However, the punctuation of the Hebrew text places the main break in the verse after **Who will bemoan her?** and this also tends to support the view that the quotation may not extend to the end of the verse. On the whole, therefore, it seems best to suggest following NEB, TOB, NIV, and GeCL, and ending the quotation after **Who will bemoan her?** If this is done, then in the third sentence the pronoun **I** refers to the Lord, as in verses 5 and 6. In languages which use special pronouns for God and royalty, such a pronoun will then be required. In other languages which do not have special pronouns for God, if the translator decides that God is speaking in the third line, it will be helpful to identify the speaker clearly by saying "From where shall I, the LORD, find . . . ," or by changing to a statement, "I, the LORD, cannot find anyone to comfort her

(Nineveh)." The word **bemoan** means "to mourn for" or "to weep" as though a person had died.

The meaning of the last two clauses is given in clear modern language in TEV as "**Who has any sympathy for her?**" and "**Who will want to comfort her?**" Whether the last sentence is included within the quotation or not, translators should note that the two questions are both rhetorical questions, and both imply the answer "Nobody." In some languages the meaning may be clearer if these questions are restructured as negative statements, such as "No one has any sympathy for her. I shall find no one to comfort you (or, her)" or "No one will mourn (shed tears) for her. . . . "

3.8-15a

	RSV	TEV

8	Are you better than Thebes
	  that sat by the Nile,
	with water around her,
	  her rampart a sea,
	  and water her wall?
		8 Nineveh, are you any better than Thebes, the capital of Egypt? She too had a river to protect her like a wall—the Nile was her defense. 9 She ruled Sudan and Egypt, there was no limit to her power; Libya was her ally. 10 Yet the people of Thebes were carried off into exile. At every street corner their children were beaten to death. Their leading men were carried off in chains and divided among their captors.
		11 Nineveh, you too will fall into a drunken stupor! You too will try to escape from your enemies. 12 All your fortresses will be like fig trees with ripe figs: shake the trees, and the fruit falls right into your mouth! 13 Your soldiers are like women, and your country stands defenseless before your enemies. Fire will destroy the bars across your gates. 14 Draw water to prepare for a siege, and strengthen your fortresses! Trample the clay to make bricks, and get the brick molds ready! 15 No matter what you do, you will still be burned to death or killed in battle. You will be wiped out like crops eaten up by locusts.

9	Ethiopia was her strength,
	  Egypt too, and that without limit;
	  Put and the Libyans were her helpers.	

10	Yet she was carried away,
	  she went into captivity;
	her little ones were dashed in pieces
	  at the head of every street;
	for her honored men lots were cast,
	  and all her great men were bound in chains.	

11	You also will be drunken,
	  you will be dazed;
	you will seek
	  a refuge from the enemy.	

12	All your fortresses are like fig trees
	  with first-ripe figs—
	if shaken they fall
	  into the mouth of the eater.	

13	Behold, your troops
	  are women in your midst.
	The gates of your land
	  are wide open to your foes;
	fire has devoured your bars.	

14	Draw water for the siege,
	  strengthen your forts;
	go into the clay,
	  tread the mortar,
	  take hold of the brick mold!	

15a	There will the fire devour you, the sword will cut you off. It will devour you like the locust.	

At this point TEV changes from poetic format back to prose, which continues to the end of the book. Some translators may wish to add a section heading here such as "Nineveh cannot defend itself" or "The inhabitants cannot defend Nineveh," as suggested in the introductory remarks to chapter 2. Verses 8-10 challenge Nineveh to compare herself with the city of Thebes in Egypt, which the Assyrians themselves had captured in 663 B.C.

| 3.8 | RSV | TEV |

RSV:
Are you better than Thebes°
that sat by the Nile,
with water around her,
her rampart a sea,
and water her wall?

TEV:
Nineveh, are you any better than Thebes, the capital of Egypt? She too had a river to protect her like a wall—the Nile was her defense.

° Heb *No-amon*

Are you better than Thebes: this is another rhetorical question, and again the implied answer is "No." TEV makes it explicit that the prophet is addressing Nineveh by including the name again here: "**Nineveh, are you any better than Thebes, the capital of Egypt?**" Or the sentence may be rendered as a statement by saying "Nineveh, you are no better than Thebes, the capital city of Egypt." The words "**the capital of Egypt**" do not appear in the Hebrew but are included in TEV to make explicit the location and importance of Thebes, which would otherwise be an unfamiliar name to most readers. In some languages "**capital**" will be rendered as "the most important city," "the city where the king (chief) lives," "the most important group of houses," or even "the largest group of houses." **Thebes** is in fact the Greek name for the city, which was situated on the River Nile about 650 kilometers (400 miles) south of Cairo, the present capital. In Hebrew the name is *No-amon,* as noted in the RSV footnote (compare BJ, JB, NAB, NEB, NJV). This means "the city under the care of the god Amon." It was indeed a great city, perhaps the greatest of the ancient world. Its massive temple ruins can still be seen at the places today called Karnak and Luxor.

The city was on the east bank of the River Nile, hence the description **that sat by the Nile**. It will be helpful in some languages to translate "that is situated beside the River Nile." The words **with water around her** are somewhat vague. So far as is known Thebes was not surrounded by the river or by canals. It is unlikely that Nahum had visited Thebes, and the description is probably based on hearsay and designed to emphasize a general similarity with Nineveh rather than to give precise details.

The last part of the verse speaks in two parallel phrases of the way in which the River Nile protected Thebes, just as the Tigris protected Nineveh. It says literally "whose rampart was the sea and her wall was of the sea" (RV). The word translated **rampart** means an outer defense, while the word translated **wall** refers to the main fortification around a city. In saying that Thebes' "rampart was the sea" (RV), Nahum is referring to the River Nile, which was about a kilometer (half a mile) wide at that point. The Nile is referred to as "the sea" elsewhere also (see the Hebrew of Isa 18.2; 19.5). TEV drops the distinction between outer and inner defenses and translates by a single, general term, "**wall**."

And water her wall: in this line the Hebrew word for "sea" occurs in the traditional Hebrew text (RV "of the sea"), but scholars usually assume different vowels, so that they read it as "waters" instead of "of the sea." This does not change the meaning of the verse but gives better parallelism between the last two phrases of the verse, as seen in RSV **her rampart a sea, and water her walls** (compare BJ, JB, NAB, NEB, NIV).

TEV drops the parallelism and restructures the sentence to give, first, a general statement emphasizing the similarity between Thebes and Nineveh, "**She too had a river to protect her like a wall**," and second, a more detailed statement about Thebes, **"the Nile was her defense."** In cultures which do not have cities protected by rivers, it will be necessary to expand the final part of the verse and say something like "The Nile River was around the city protecting it just like a wall."

Nahum's point in all this is that, in spite of her greatness, Thebes had not been able to avoid capture by the Assyrians. In the same way Nineveh, despite its greatness, will not be able to avoid capture by its attackers.

3.9	RSV	TEV
	Ethiopia was her strength, Egypt too, and that without limit; Put and the Libyans were her^p helpers.	She ruled Sudan and Egypt, there was no limit to her power; Libya was her ally.

^p Gk: Heb *your*

Ethiopia was her strength, Egypt too, and that without limit: the description of Thebes at the height of her powers is continued. In the years before her capture in 663 B.C., Thebes was the center of an empire which included both **Egypt** itself and the area to the south of Egypt called Cush in Hebrew. This region was called **Ethiopia** in Greco-Roman times and is so named in Greek translations of the Old Testament (so RSV, KJV, JB, NAB). The area referred to included most of modern Sudan and some of present-day Ethiopia (Abyssinia). Thus TEV translates "**She ruled Sudan and Egypt, there was no limit to her power.**" In certain languages it will be necessary to translate as "The city of Thebes ruled the countries of Sudan and Egypt. There was no limit . . . ," or even "The kings in the city of Thebes ruled the countries of . . . ." The kings of the twenty-fifth Egyptian dynasty, which ruled from 715-663 B.C., were actually of Sudanese origin, and this is why the two countries were ruled as one at that time. (See also comments on Zeph 1.1; 2.12; 3.10.) **And that without limit** ("**There was no limit to her power**"): in certain languages this sentence will need to be restructured as "her power had no limit."

Put and the Libyans were her helpers: in addition to the people of their own territories, the kings who had ruled in Thebes could also call upon neighboring countries as allies, or friends who had a treaty or agreement with Thebes and would come to its aid in time of war. The two countries mentioned are "Put and Libya" (NIV). Libya is the country immediately west of Egypt, but there is some doubt where Put was. The majority of scholars think that it was along the African coast at the southern end of the Red Sea, in the country now called Somalia. Others think that it was close to or even part of Libya. TEV holds this latter view and thus translates the one name only: "**Libya was her ally.**"

Since **Put** is here distinguished from Libya, this solution seems a little improbable, and translators should probably retain both names, as do FrCL and GeCL. Since it has been several lines since the name "Thebes" has been mentioned, it will be helpful to repeat it here; for example, "Put and Libya were the allies of Thebes," or even "The people of Put and Libya were the allies of Thebes" (compare NIV). In some languages it may be necessary to expand this

THE FALL OF NINEVEH   Nahum 3.10

sentence slightly and say "The people of the countries of Put and Libya were the allies (friends) of the people of Thebes."

3.10	RSV	TEV

<blockquote>

Yet she was carried away,
  she went into captivity;
her little ones were dashed in pieces
  at the head of every street;
for her honored men lots were cast,
  and all her great men were bound in chains.

</blockquote>

<blockquote>

Yet the people of Thebes were carried off into exile. At every street corner their children were beaten to death. Their leading men were carried off in chains and divided among their captors.

</blockquote>

The events mentioned in this verse do not seem to follow a logical or chronological order. The first clause makes a general statement about the result of the capture of Thebes, and the other three clauses state other events associated with that capture. The clauses can be reordered if this is helpful in a receptor language.

Despite the great power Thebes had enjoyed, **yet she was carried away, she went into captivity**. This the Assyrians would know very well, because it was their own armies under King Asshurbanipal that had captured Thebes and exiled its people. TEV makes it explicit that **she** refers to the inhabitants rather than the city, by saying "**the people of Thebes**."

The Hebrew actually uses two verbs (**carried away** and **went into captivity** in RSV), but TEV runs these together into the one English phrase "**were carried off into exile**." "Exile" means being forced to live in another place, usually a distant country. Other ways of translating this sentence are "Yet their enemies carried away the people of Thebes into exile" or "Yet their enemies led off the people of Thebes as prisoners into a distant country."

The rest of the verse describes what the Assyrian soldiers had done when they captured Thebes, and carries the implied threat that the same sort of things will be done to the people of Nineveh.

Her little ones were dashed in pieces at the head of every street: **Little ones** (RSV, JB, NAB) refers to small children; compare "infants" (NEB, NIV), "babes" (NJV). Such cruel actions were not uncommon in the ancient world (compare 2 Kgs 8.12; Psa 137.9; Isa 13.16; Hos 13.16). TEV's "**beaten to death**" is not as vivid as RSV's **dashed in pieces** but states the meaning in very general terms. In some languages it will be necessary to expand this clause and say "the children were taken and smashed against the stones until they died," or in languages which do not use the passive, one may say "the enemy soldiers took the children and smashed them against the stones . . . ." If possible, translators should use strong words that will carry the deep emotional effect of the passage.

The words **at the head of every street** are not necessarily to be taken literally. They mean "in public view, and at many places all over the city" (compare Isa 51.20; Lam 2.19).

The last part of the verse speaks of what happened to the honored men of Thebes. **Lots were cast** for them and they **were bound in chains**. In both these clauses it will be necessary in many languages to state the agent doing the action and say "The enemy soldiers cast lots for the leading men of Thebes and bound them with chains." The purpose of casting lots was to decide who would get each man as a slave. It is not certain what type of **lots** were used here. However, in many cultures stones with people's names written on them would be shaken in some sort of container and then thrown on the ground. The first stone to reach the ground showed the person chosen. In the case in this verse, slaves were being picked. Certain cultures today have similar methods for choosing, and translators in such cultures will have no problem selecting vocabulary that will suit this context. However, if in a particular culture such a practice as casting **lots** does not exist, translators may follow TEV as a translation model. TEV reverses the order of these two actions and gives them in the sequence in which they probably happened: "**Their leading men were carried off in chains and divided among their captors.**" In cultures where chains are not used, one may say "Their leading men were made captives, and their hands and feet were tied with ropes made of metal." There is no significant difference in meaning between the two phrases **honored men** and **great men**. TEV therefore avoids repetition by using just the one phrase "**leading men.**" In other languages there may be pairs of synonymous expressions which can be used here.

Another translation model for the entire verse is the following:

> Yet the enemy soldiers captured the people of Thebes and led them off to a distant country. They dashed their children to pieces at many places all over the city. Their captors bound Thebes' leading men with chains and divided them up among themselves by casting lots.

3.11   RSV   TEV

You also will be drunken,   Nineveh, you too will fall into a
  you will be dazed;   drunken stupor! You too will try to
you will seek   escape from your enemies.
  a refuge from the enemy.

Verses 11-13 draw the conclusion that Nineveh will be captured just as Thebes had been, and they speak of the uselessness of her defenses.

You also will be drunken, you will be dazed: as in verse 8, TEV uses the name "Nineveh" here as a term of address, to remind the reader who is being spoken to. The word also emphasizes the similarity between the fate of Thebes and the fate of Nineveh. TEV translates two verbal phrases in Hebrew by the single expression "**fall into a drunken stupor.**" Drunkenness is quite often used in Hebrew as a picture of suffering the effects of God's anger (compare Psa 60.3; Isa 51.17; Jer 25.15-27; Lam 4.21; Ezek 23.31-34), which is sometimes compared to a cup of wine.

The word translated **be dazed** in RSV is of uncertain meaning. The form in the Hebrew text as it stands usually means "to hide" (compare NIV "you will go into hiding"), but that does not make very good sense here. Some scholars change one letter to make another word that means "to be faint" and which occurs in similar descriptions in Isaiah 51.20; Ezekiel 31.15. Other scholars think that the word as it stands in the text can also mean "to be faint." This sense fits the context well and is adopted by RSV (**be dazed**), NAB ("faint away"), and NJV ("be ... overcome"). TEV also follows this interpretation but expresses it by the noun "**stupor**." Another way of rendering these two clauses is "Nineveh, you will fall into a stupor from drinking too much intoxicating liquor," or in languages where one cannot speak about cities drinking, one may say "You Assyrians will fall ...." TEV's expression "**drunken stupor**" refers to the condition of a drunk person when he has no more control over himself. Most languages have idioms or picturesque phrases to describe such a condition; for example, "sway (stagger) with drunkenness" (see Isa 24.20), or "three sheets to the wind," an English idiom originally applied to a drunken sailor. Translators should look for a descriptive phrase or idiom in their own language that will fit not only the context of this verse but the level of style as well.

In many languages it may be better to translate the first half of this verse as a simile rather than a metaphor. One can say "Nineveh, you too will feel as though you are drunk and dazed."

<u>You will seek a refuge from the enemy</u>: just as the people of Thebes had tried in vain to escape from the Assyrians, so the Assyrians in their turn would try to escape. <u>Seek a refuge</u> (RSV, NAB, NJV) means to look for a place to flee to, where they would be safe. Other translation models for this clause are "you will look for a place to hide where you will be safe from your enemies" or "you will look for a place where your enemies cannot find you." In some languages it may be necessary to make it explicit that the search will be unsuccessful. One may, for instance, add "but you will not find such a place."

3.12	RSV	TEV
	All your fortresses are like fig trees with first-ripe figs— if shaken they fall into the mouth of the eater.	All your fortresses will be like fig trees with ripe figs: shake the trees, and the fruit falls right into your mouth!

<u>Fortresses</u>, in this context, were towns or cities with especially strong and high walls, and which guarded Assyria's borders from attack. They were often situated at mountain passes, where enemies would be most likely to try to invade the land. If no better term is available, <u>fortresses</u> may be translated "cities with strong walls," "cities protected by strong walls," or "large groups of houses surrounded by strong walls."

The Assyrians will not be able to escape anywhere (see previous verse) because all their fortresses will be captured by their enemies. This is stated in a vivid metaphor which compares the fortresses to trees full of ripe fruit. <u>All your fortresses are like fig trees with first-ripe figs</u>: <u>fig trees</u> were common in Palestine, and the <u>first-ripe figs</u> were considered a delicacy. The fig tree usually grows about three to five meters (ten to fifteen feet) tall. The fruit has a high sugar content and can be dried, made into pressed cakes, and then stored like raisins for later use. (See *Fauna and Flora of the Bible*, pages 118-119, for further information.) In areas where <u>fig trees</u> are not known, translators are urged to use a generic word for "tree" followed by the word "fig"; for example, "with first-ripe fruit from the tree called 'fig.'" It is also possible to use a general term like "fruit trees." It is better to translate in this way than to substitute the name of some other fruit tree like the mango or the papaw (pawpaw, papaya) which were not known in Palestine. It will also be helpful to have a descriptive footnote or an entry in the word list. If a translator has used the name Nineveh in the previous verse, it will be helpful in this verse to say "All the fortresses of you Assyrians" or something similar. Otherwise readers may understand the pronoun **your** as referring to the city of Nineveh, rather than to the Assyrian empire with Nineveh as its capital.

The second half of the verse is literally a conditional sentence, as in RSV **if shaken, they fall**. In English one way to express the condition is by using an imperative, and this is what TEV has done: "shake the trees, and the fruit falls." Most languages will not be able to express a condition in this way and may have to say something like the following: "When you shake the trees . . . ." Translators should use whatever construction is natural in their language.

The last part of the sentence, **they fall into the mouth of the eater**, is of course an exaggeration for a special effect. The Hebrews did not make a habit of shaking fig trees and catching the fruit in their mouths! The meaning is that the figs are so ripe that they are absolutely ready to eat as soon as they come off the tree. Some translators may need to state this meaning without the use of exaggeration. A translation base for this whole sentence can be "when you shake the tree, the fruit falls off, ready to eat at once."

In saying that the Assyrian **fortresses are like fig trees with first-ripe figs**, Nahum means that they will easily be captured by their attackers. In some languages it may be necessary to restructure the whole verse to make the basis of the comparison explicit. One can say, for instance, "Just as ripe figs are ready to eat, and fall as soon as someone shakes the tree, so your fortresses are ready to fall to your enemies as soon as they attack."

3.13

RSV	TEV
Behold, your troops are women in your midst. The gates of your land are wide open to your foes; fire has devoured your bars.	Your soldiers are like women, and your country stands defenseless before your enemies. Fire will destroy the bars across your gates.

Behold is omitted by several modern English translations (Mft, NEB, TEV). Compare comments on 2.13.

Your troops are women in your midst means that they have lost their military skill and courage and cannot fight the enemy (compare Isa 19.16; Jer 51.30). In certain languages it will be necessary to explain this implicit meaning and say "Your soldiers have lost their fighting skill and courage and have become like women." The Hebrew actually says "your people" (JB), but clearly the **troops** (TEV's "**soldiers**") are in mind, and RSV makes this explicit (compare NAB, NEB, NIV, NJV).

Because the defenders cannot fight, **the gates of your land are wide open to your foes**. It is not certain whether **the gates of your land** refers to the gates of the city of Nineveh itself (compare Jer 15.7) or to the mountain passes that gave entry to the country of Assyria as a whole. The use of **your land** rather than "your city" suggests the latter, and TEV seems to take it that way. TEV also drops the figurative use of **gates** and expresses the meaning in plain language as "**your country stands defenseless before your enemies.**" One may also translate this sentence as "And there is no one to defend you as your enemies attack." For the translation of **enemies**, see 1.2.

Fire has devoured your bars: these are the bars used to fasten shut the gates of cities (compare Amos 1.5), but it is not clear whether the sense here is literal or figurative. If figurative, then the **bars** probably stand for the fortresses that guarded the mountain passes which were called **gates** in the previous clause. If literal, then the bars would be the wooden beams which prevented the gates of Nineveh itself from being opened. TEV follows this interpretation and says "**Fire will destroy the bars across your gates.**" Probably it is better either to take the **gates** and **bars** as both literal, or as both figurative. If translators take both the **gates** and **bars** as figurative, a possible translation model is the following: "The borders of your land are wide open to your enemies, and fire will destroy your fortresses."

Has devoured: the perfect tense has been translated as future in TEV ("will destroy"), as this event is still part of things which will happen in the future.

3.14 RSV TEV

Draw water for the siege, Draw water to prepare for a siege, and
   strengthen your forts;   strengthen your fortresses! Trample
go into the clay,   the clay to make bricks, and get the
   tread the mortar,   brick molds ready!
   take hold of the brick mold!

Nahum now gives further commands to the people of Nineveh to prepare themselves for a siege (compare 2.1). Again these commands are ironic, for Nahum goes on to say in verse 15 that the city will be captured anyway.

The first command is **Draw water for the siege**. During a siege, a good water supply is essential for the defenders. However, since Nineveh was situated on the bank of a major river, water was not likely to be a serious problem for its inhabitants. Because of this some scholars think that this command refers to filling the moats which were part of the city's defenses. However, all available English translations use the word **draw**, which normally refers to a supply of drinking water, and translators are recommended to follow this interpretation. The word **draw** in English normally signifies the action of using some container such as a bucket to take water out of a well or some other place where there was a water supply. This first sentence may also be translated "You must draw water to prepare for the time when your enemies surround your city."

Strengthen your forts means make any necessary repairs so that the forts will be in good condition to resist attack. **Forts** here probably refers to the strongest places in the wall of the city itself. The main building material that was used in Assyria was brick, and many bricks would be needed to repair the fortifications of the city.

The rest of the verse speaks about various parts of the process of making bricks. The first two are **go into the clay, tread the mortar**. They refer to the trampling of **the clay** underfoot to make it soft enough to be shaped. TEV drops the repetition and expresses this aspect of the brick making in a single clause, "Trample the clay to make bricks." When the clay was soft enough, it was put into a **brick mold**, which was a wooden container that would form each brick into the same shape and size as the other bricks. The bricks were then removed from

Nahum 3.14

the mold to dry in the sun. Nahum tells the people of Nineveh to **take hold of the brick mold**, or as TEV puts it more clearly, "**get the brick molds ready!**" This sentence can also be translated as "Trample the clay which you use to make bricks, and prepare the brick molds" or "Use your feet to soften the clay which will be used to make bricks . . . ."

SLAVES MAKING BRICKS

3.15a

RSV	TEV
There will the fire devour you, the sword will cut you off. It will devour you like the locust.	No matter what you do, you will still be burned to death or killed in battle. You will be wiped out like crops eaten up by locusts.

This verse gives an implicit contrast with the previous one. Even if the people of Nineveh make careful preparations to defend themselves, they will still be defeated. TEV brings out this contrast with the words "**No matter what you do.**"

The defeat of the Ninevites is described in two figurative statements, **There will the fire devour you, the sword will cut you off**. **There** has no real antecedent in Hebrew, and it is not clear what place is referred to, though the place where the bricks were being made is most likely. Some versions take it in a temporal sense (NEB "even then"; compare BJ). Probably this is what TEV has done in translating "still." A captured city was often set on fire after it had been plundered (compare Josh 6.24; 8.19; 2 Kgs 25.9). **The sword** stands for any weapon of war with which people are killed. TEV drops the figures of speech and expresses the meaning in plain language as "**you will still be burned to death or killed in battle.**" If the figures of speech can be meaningfully retained, they should be.

The next line says literally **It will devour you like the locust**. There are three problems to be solved in connection with this line. The first is to decide what **It** refers to. The nearest noun is **sword**, but it is also possible that the **It** refers back to the previous noun **fire**. The second problem is to decide whether **like the locust** is related to the subject of the verb **devour** or to the object. These two problems give four possible meanings to the phrase as a whole. When the comparisons are filled out and made explicit, these four possibilities are:

(a) The sword will devour you as it devours the locust;
(b) The sword will devour you as the locust devours crops;
(c) The fire will devour you as it devours the locust;
(d) The fire will devour you as the locust devours crops.

Of these, (a) hardly makes sense, since swords were not used to kill locusts; (c) is possible in the context, since fire was one means of getting rid of locusts, but (c) and (d) are both rather doubtful because they do not take the nearest noun as the antecedent to the pronoun it; on the whole (b) seems to be the most likely meaning and is followed by TEV, "**You will be wiped out like crops eaten by locusts.**" (For the use of the English metaphor "wipe out" in place of a Hebrew metaphor, compare TEV Zeph 3.6.) **Wiped out** can also be rendered "destroyed."

TOB, NIV, NJV, and FrCL adopt the same interpretation as TEV, but BJ, JB, NAB, and NEB omit this line altogether, because they believe it to be a mistaken duplication of material which follows in the rest of verse 15 and verse 16. This solution is not to be recommended, since the line gives a reasonable meaning in its context.

The third problem in the line concerns the exact meaning of the Hebrew term *yeleq* translated **locust** in RSV and TEV, "grasshoppers" in NIV, and "grub" in NJV. In verses 15-17 no less than four different Hebrew words for locust occur. Their exact meanings have been fully and clearly discussed by John A. Thompson in *The Bible Translator*, Volume 25 (1974), pages 405-411. The paragraph in which he deals with Nahum 3.15-17 is worth quoting in full, as follows:

> In Nah 3.15, 16, 17 five [sic] words for locust are found, in verse 15 *yeleq* twice and *'arbeh*, in verse 16 *yeleq*, and in verse 17 *'arbeh*, *gobh*, and *gobhai*. The translation of *yeleq* here depends to some extent on the interpretation of the verb in the second part of verse 16. The Hebrew-English lexicon edited by Brown, Driver, and Briggs gives the meaning of the verb in this verse as "stripping off (sheaths of wings)," and that edited by Koehler and Baumgartner has "strip off the skin." So the meaning of *yeleq* in verse 16 must be "young locust," which sheds its skin and becomes the mature locust with usable wings. The two occurrences of *yeleq* in the immediately preceding verse 15 would presumably have the same meaning. Verse 15 compares the fire kindled by the attackers of Nineveh and their killing swords to young locusts who eat and destroy plants. The young locust is a more destructive eater than the mature locust. "Young locust" is suggested here as the meaning of *yeleq*, rather than "newly-hatched" as in Joel, because a newly-hatched locust must go through several stages before it is able to fly. It is not surprising that there should be a shift of meaning between the specific "newly hatched" and the general "young" according to the context. Several modern translations (RSV, Jerusalem Bible, New American Bible) have not followed the lexicons and give the verb of verse 16 the meaning "spread wings" or "spread out." This meaning of "spread" is not found elsewhere in the Bible for this verb, and "wings" must be supplied. Moreover if this translation of the verb were correct, then *yeleq* would refer to an adult locust with usable wings, which is not the meaning of *yeleq* elsewhere. For *'arbeh* in verse 15 I have suggested the meaning "mature locust" to distinguish it from *yeleq* in the same verse. *Gobh* and *gobhai* in verse 17 seem to mean "swarm of locusts," and the use of both nouns may emphasize the great number of Assyrian officials."

Nahum 3.15a   THE FALL OF NINEVEH

Thompson's comments will be very helpful to translators in areas where locusts are well known, but in other areas translators may do better to use a single general term like the English word **locust**. If locusts are completely unknown, it will probably be necessary in this passage to borrow a word from English or some other major language, and to explain its meaning in a footnote or in a word list. In some of the other passages where locusts are mentioned, it may be possible to substitute the name of some other creature, but here the habits of locusts are stated in some detail, and it is unlikely that any other creature can be spoken of instead.

3.15b-17

	RSV	TEV
15b	Multiply yourselves like the locust, multiply like the grasshopper!	You multiplied like locusts! 16 You produced more merchants than there are stars in the sky! But now they are gone, like locusts that spread their wings and fly away. 17 Your officials are like a swarm of locusts that stay in the walls on a cold day. But when the sun comes out, they fly away, and no one knows where they have gone!
16	You increased your merchants more than the stars of the heavens. The locust spreads its wings and flies away.	
17	Your princes are like grasshoppers, your scribes like clouds of locusts settling on the fences in a day of cold— when the sun rises, they fly away; no one knows where they are.	

In the last part of verse 15, a new figure of speech begins which continues through verses 16 and 17. In this passage the leading men of Nineveh are compared with locusts, but this time the comparison is based on the large numbers in which locusts swarm, rather than on their destructiveness as in the previous line. Because of this change of emphasis, a number of translations begin a new paragraph here in the middle of verse 15 (RSV, BJ, JB, TOB, TEV, FrCL).

3.15b	RSV	TEV
	Multiply yourselves like the locust, multiply like the grasshopper!	You multiplied like locusts!

The last part of verse 15 consists of two lines which are closely parallel in structure and meaning: **Multiply yourselves like the locust, multiply like the grasshopper!** The Hebrew verb form is imperative (as RSV **Multiply**). In this context the imperative is not really a command but rather an ironic statement, and this is why TEV has translated as a statement ("**You multiplied**"). This produces a smoother connection with the statements in the following verse.

The Hebrew words for **locust** (*yeleq*) and **grasshopper** (*'arbeh*) refer, according to Thompson, to different stages in the development of the insect, rather than to two different species. Since English does not have much vocabulary for speaking about locusts, TEV here drops the parallelism and expresses the meaning just once: "**You multiplied like locusts!**" In other languages with similar vocabulary problems, translators will need to do the same. **You multiplied** in certain languages may be expressed as "You increased in number . . . ."

58

THE FALL OF NINEVEH   Nahum 3.17

3.16   RSV   TEV

You increased your merchants   You produced more merchants than
    more than the stars of the   there are stars in the sky! But now
    heavens.   they are gone, like locusts that spread
The locust spreads its wings   their wings and fly away.
    and flies away.

You increased your merchants more than the stars of the heavens: TEV expresses the meaning in more natural English as "**You produced more merchants than there are stars in the sky!**" The use of **the stars of the heavens** as an example of great quantity is common in scripture (compare Gen 15.5; Exo 32.13; Deut 1.10; Heb 11.12). Nineveh was indeed a great commercial center where many **merchants** lived. Probably most communities in the world have the equivalent of **merchants**, those people who engage in buying and selling for profit. In some languages they are referred to as "shop (stall) owners (managers)," while in other languages they will be described idiomatically; for example, "father (mother) who buys sells." But in still other languages it will be necessary to render this first sentence in a more general way and say "You increased the number of people who buy and sell until they were more numerous than the stars in the sky."

The last part of the verse returns abruptly to the picture of the locusts: **The locust** (Hebrew *yeleq*) **spreads its wings and flies away**. Some scholars think that this sentence would be more appropriate near the end of verse 17, and some translations print it at that point (BJ, JB, NAB). Others, however, try to show how it can fit here, and there is no need to move it. TEV compares the merchants with locusts in the way they fly off: "**But now they are gone, like locusts that spread their wings and fly away.**" NIV is even more explicit about the point of the comparison: "like locusts, they strip the land and then fly away." It is often true that when danger threatens a city, the merchants are the first to leave and take themselves and their wealth off somewhere else.

3.17   RSV   TEV

Your princes are like grasshop-   Your officials are like a swarm of
    pers,   locusts that stay in the walls on a cold
    your scribes^q like clouds of   day. But when the sun comes out, they
        locusts   fly away, and no one knows where
settling on the fences   they have gone!
    in a day of cold—
when the sun rises, they fly
    away;
no one knows where they are.

^q Or *marshals*

The first two lines are closely parallel to each other in both structure and sense, and both contain words of uncertain meaning. RSV renders **Your princes are like grasshoppers** (Hebrew *'arbeh*), **your scribes are like clouds of locusts** (Hebrew *gobh gobhai*). The words translated **princes** and **scribes** are probably both

Assyrian words which Nahum has borrowed. The first one is perhaps related to a Hebrew word for "crown," which suggests the meaning **princes**. Scholars have proposed a number of other possible meanings, and several English translations prefer the word "guards" (JB, NIV, NJV). FrCL and GeCL have words meaning "inspectors" or "overseers." At any rate, a word should be used which denotes a class of people who are numerous, since that is the point of the comparison with locusts. On that basis "guards" or "overseers" are more likely than **princes**.

The second of the two words thought to be Assyrian is almost certainly the word for scribe. The equivalent word in Hebrew came to have a military meaning as well, and some scholars think that this was also the case with the Assyrian word. This gives rise to the term "marshals" in the RSV footnote (compare RV, NJV). However, **scribes** understood in the sense of "civil servants, officials" seems on the whole more probable here. In some languages **scribes** may be rendered as "servants of the king (chief)." Another translation model for the first two lines is "Your guards are as numerous as grasshoppers, and the servants of your king (chief) as a cloud (swarm) of locusts."

Since the exact meanings of these two key words are uncertain and the lines are closely parallel, TEV runs them together into one and includes the meanings of the two Assyrian words under one general term, "**officials**." For a discussion of the Hebrew words used here for **clouds of locusts**, see the comments of Thompson quoted under verse 15. **Clouds of locusts** or "a swarm of locusts" can also be rendered as "a huge crowd of locusts" or "great numbers of locusts which resemble a cloud." The emphasis here is on the tremendous number of the insects.

Settling on the fences in a day of cold: the second half of verse 17 speaks of the way locusts are affected by changes of temperature. As TEV puts it, they "stay in the walls on a cold day" and move about only a little if at all. "Walls" refers not to the walls of houses but to the stone walls around a field, which would have plenty of spaces for the locusts to shelter in. Probably the word **fences** is a better one (RSV, NAB, NJV). However, in many languages it will be better to say "fences made of stone," or perhaps "walls made of stone which surround your fields."

When the sun rises, they fly away: when the locusts are warm again, they are able to **fly away** once more. In the same way the officials of Nineveh, instead of fighting, will run away when the city is attacked. TEV marks the contrast with the previous line by using the introductory "**But**."

No one knows where they are: just as people cannot keep up with a swarm of locusts when they fly away, so no one will be able to find the officials of Nineveh and bring them back to defend the city.

3.18-19

RSV	TEV

18 Your shepherds are asleep,
    O king of Assyria;
    your nobles slumber.
    Your people are scattered on the mountains
    with none to gather them.
19 There is no assuaging your hurt,
    your wound is grievous.
    All who hear the news of you
    clap their hands over you.
	18 Emperor of Assyria, your governors are dead, and your noblemen are asleep forever! Your people are scattered on the mountains, and there is no one to bring them home again. 19 There is no remedy for your injuries, and your wounds cannot be healed. All those who hear the news of your destruction clap their hands for joy. Did anyone escape your endless cruelty?

THE FALL OF NINEVEH   Nahum 3.18

> For upon whom has not come
> your unceasing evil?

The last two verses do not continue the description of the fall of Nineveh, but rather rejoice over the defeat of the city and its king. The language is still figurative, but the figure changes from the locusts of verses 15-17 to one of shepherds and sheep.

3.18   RSV   TEV

Your shepherds are asleep,   Emperor of Assyria, your gover-
   O king of Assyria;   nors are dead, and your noblemen are
your nobles slumber.   asleep forever! Your people are scat-
Your people are scattered on the   tered on the mountains, and there is
   mountains   no one to bring them home again.
   with none to gather them.

Unlike the earlier parts of the prophecy, which are addressed to the city as a feminine figure, these verses are addressed directly to the **king of Assyria** himself. TEV makes this change clear by putting the words "Emperor of Assyria" first. Assyria was not only a country but also an empire. This is probably the reason TEV uses "**Emperor**" here rather than **king** as in RSV. A **king** normally rules over a city or one country. An "**Emperor**," on the other hand, rules over a large number of countries and has many kings under him. Some languages refer to this type of ruler as "supreme ruler (chief)," "chief ruler," or "ruler over many kings." Others have had to borrow the English word "emperor," with a footnote or explanatory note in the glossary.

Your shepherds are asleep: it is quite common in Hebrew to speak of kings and rulers as **shepherds** (compare Jer 3.15; Ezek 34; 37.24), but this picture will not be clear to many modern readers unless sheep are important in their culture, and it may even give a wrong meaning. TEV has therefore dropped it and stated its meaning in plain language as "**your governors.**" The use of the word **Your** here does not mean that the **shepherds** (TEV "**governors**") rule over the king; rather, they and the nobles hold authority under him. In some languages this first clause may be rendered as "Supreme ruler of Assyria, your chief servants are dead" or " . . . the people who help you rule are dead."

Asleep here is usually understood as a picture of death, and TEV has made this explicit by saying "**your governors are dead.**" (Compare Psa 76.5; Jer 51.39,57.) If the figure of speech can be retained with the right meaning, it should be.

Your nobles slumber is parallel in meaning, but in this line TEV keeps the figure of speech, saying "**your noblemen are asleep forever!**" The inclusion of the word "**forever**" makes it clear that here the sleep is the permanent sleep of death. **Nobles** (TEV "**noblemen**") refers to people of high rank in the society. So one may translate "Your people of great honor (status) . . . ."

In the second half of the verse, the same figure is continued: **Your people are scattered on the mountains with none to gather them**. Since the rulers are compared to shepherds, the **people** are by implication compared to sheep, who now have no one to look after them. Because of this they are easily **scattered on the mountains**. This is another picture which is common in scripture. (See Num

61

27.17; 1 Kgs 22.17; Ezek 34.6; Zech 13.7; and compare Matt 9.36; Mark 6.34.) In many languages it will be difficult to translate the stative expression **are scattered**. One possibility is to say "Your people have gone in all directions on the mountains, just like sheep." **To gather them** is expressed more fully in TEV as "to bring them home again."

In areas where sheep are known, it may be possible to keep the figure of speech in translation. But in such cases it may be better to fill in more of the details, to make the basis of the comparison clearer. A possible translation model for the whole verse is:

> King of Assyria, your governors and noblemen are like shepherds who are dead and sleep forever. Because of this, your people are like sheep which are scattered on the mountains and have no one to bring them home again.

3.19

RSV	TEV
There is no assuaging your hurt, your wound is grievous. All who hear the news of you clap their hands over you. For upon whom has not come your unceasing evil?	There is no remedy for your injuries, and your wounds cannot be healed. All those who hear the news of your destruction clap their hands for joy. Did anyone escape your endless cruelty?

There is no assuaging your hurt, your wound is grievous: the picture changes again, and this time the defeat of the king of Nineveh is compared to a fatal **wound** which cannot be assuaged, or healed. This metaphor, though quite common in the Old Testament (compare Isa 1.5-6; Jer 14.17; 30.12), does not depend on anything specific to Hebrew culture. It will therefore probably be widely understood, and TEV keeps it: "**There is no remedy for your injuries, and your wounds cannot be healed.**" Many translators will be able to use the same figure, though they may find it helpful to turn the metaphor into a simile and perhaps drop the parallelism. A possible translation model is "You are like a wounded man, whose injuries no medicine can heal."

The last part of the verse turns from mocking the king of Assyria to describing the joy that his defeat will bring to other nations: **All who hear the news of you clap their hands over you**. TEV makes it explicit that **the news of you** means "the news of your destruction." TEV also explains the significance of hand clapping: "**All those who hear ... clap their hands for joy.**" This use of clapping the hands to show appreciation or joy is fairly widely understood, but some translators may need to substitute some other actions which carry the same meaning in their culture; for example, "whistle," "stamp their feet," or "shout with glee."

The book ends with a rhetorical question, **For upon whom has not come your unceasing evil?** TEV keeps the question form but expresses the meaning in more natural English as "**Did anyone escape your endless cruelty?**" The answer is that none of the smaller states of Western Asia had escaped, and that is why they will all rejoice when they hear of Nineveh's destruction. In some languages it may be necessary to replace the question by a negative statement and say "No one escaped your endless cruelty." **Evil** (TEV "cruelty") refers to cruel or evil actions by the Assyrians. One may translate "No one escaped from your endless evil actions" or "You did cruel things to people continuously. No one escaped." In some languages it may be necessary to change the order of clauses in the second half of the verse so as to put the cause before the effect. One may then say "You did cruel things to people continuously. No one escaped. Because of that, those who hear the news that you have been destroyed will clap their hands for joy."

Translating the Book of Habakkuk

How can God, who is holy and just, use evil men to fulfil his purposes in the world? This question is the main topic of the prophecy of Habakkuk. The book is therefore unusual in that it deals with the prophet's challenge to God rather than God's challenge to his people.

Of Habakkuk himself we know for sure only what is stated in 1.1 and 3.1, that he was a prophet. Even the meaning of his name, which occurs nowhere else in the Hebrew Old Testament, is uncertain. Some scholars have linked it with the name of an Assyrian garden flower, and others with a Hebrew verb meaning "to embrace." Later Jewish tradition regarded Habakkuk as a Levite, but this cannot be proved or disproved. He is mentioned in the deuterocanonical story of Bel and the Dragon, verses 33-39.

The whole of the book of Habakkuk (except 1.1; 2.6a; and 3.1) is set out as poetry in RSV. In TEV only 3.2-19 is set out in this way. As with the Book of Nahum, translators should decide for themselves what parts of this book are suitable for poetry in their own languages. In most cases chapters 1 and 2 will need to be translated into prose. Since chapter 3 is a psalm, many translators will wish to handle it in the same way as they handle the Book of Psalms.

We may note that Habakkuk 2.4 is quoted three times in the New Testament (Rom 1.17; Gal 3.11; Heb 10.37-38). For more on this, see the comments on 2.4.

We may also note that the Dead Sea Scrolls include a commentary on the first two chapters of Habakkuk. This shows how the community at Qumran applied the words of Habakkuk to their own day. It contains some differences from the traditional Hebrew text, but these are not of major importance for translators. The differences are referred to where necessary in the comments.

Outline

The structure of the book is quite clear, especially in the first two chapters.

Introduction (1.1)

    1. Questions and answers (1.2-2.5)
      (a) Habakkuk's first question (1.2-4)
      (b) The Lord's first answer (1.5-11)
      (c) Habakkuk's second question (1.12-17)
      (d) The Lord's second answer (2.1-5)

    2. Taunts against the wicked (2.6-20)
      (a) The first taunt (2.6-8)
      (b) The second taunt (2.9-11)
      (c) The third taunt (2.12-14)

(d) The fourth taunt (2.15-17)
(e) The fifth taunt (2.18-20)

3. Habakkuk's prayer: a psalm expressing trust in the LORD (3.1-19)

Background and Date

In the case of Habakkuk, the interpretation particularly in the first chapter is closely connected with the date assumed for the book. It is therefore necessary in this case to say more about the date and background than is usual in translators' Handbooks.

The book itself does not state any dates. The first two chapters are usually said to come from the last few years before 600 B.C., but there has been much debate over their exact dating. The main events of the period were as follows: In 612 B.C. the Assyrian capital Nineveh was captured by the Babylonians and Medes, and the Assyrian empire came to an end. The Egyptians saw this as an opportunity for them to take control of the smaller states west of the river Euphrates. King Josiah of Judah attempted to resist them and was killed at the battle of Megiddo in 609 (2 Kgs 23.29-30). The Egyptians took the new King Jehoahaz, who was one of Josiah's sons, as a prisoner to Egypt. In his place they appointed another of Josiah's sons called Jehoiakim (2 Kgs 23.31-34). Jehoiakim proved to be a selfish and oppressive ruler (Jer 22.13-17), and during his reign (609-598) there was a breakdown in law and order, and an increase in idolatry.

In 605 B.C. the Egyptians were decisively defeated at the battle of Carchemish by the Babylonians under Nebuchadnezzar. From then on the Babylonians dominated the whole of Western Asia. King Jehoiakim submitted to the Babylonians for three years but then rebelled against them (2 Kgs 24.1). This rebellion eventually led to a Babylonian invasion of Judah, and the deportation of Jehoiakim's son and successor, King Jehoiachin, in 598.

The exact dating of the book of Habakkuk within this period depends on whether the wicked people described in 1.2-4 and 1.12-17 are understood to be Judean citizens or foreign enemies. The matter is discussed thoroughly in other commentaries, and the arguments will not be repeated here. The view taken in this handbook may be summed up as follows:

(1) There is no need to assume that the whole of chapters 1 and 2 were written at once. The opening question "How long?" (1.2) suggests that Habakkuk had meditated on the problems that troubled him for a considerable time, and it therefore seems quite reasonable to suggest that his written record of them may also have taken some time.

(2) The description in 1.2-4 seems to fit the evil days of King Jehoiakim very well, and we take it that these verses speak of evildoers within Judah.

(3) The answer to the question raised in 1.2-4 is given in 1.5-11. In 1.5-6 the rise of the Babylonians ("Chaldeans" in 1.6 RSV) is spoken of as something still future, and so it seems probable that this paragraph dates from before the battle of Carchemish in 605, though perhaps not long before.

(4) The description of the wicked in 1.12-17 seems to be speaking of the same people as those mentioned in 1.5-11, that is, the Babylonians. This suggests that it comes from a time somewhat later than 605, when Judah was already experiencing the practical effects of Babylonian rule.

(5) The answer to the question raised in 1.12-17 is to be dated at about the same time as the question. This answer is given in 2.2-5 in RSV (2.2-4 in TEV).

(6) The rest of chapter 2 and the whole of chapter 3 are not as closely linked with specific historical events. Their dating is therefore of less importance to translators.

We may note in passing that some scholars have tried to find a much later date for Habakkuk 1–2, in the Greek period. This view is closely related to suggestions for rearranging the order of the text and for changing "Chaldeans" in 1.6 to "Greeks." Since translators have to deal with the text as it is in the manuscripts rather than to rewrite it, this view is of little importance to them and is not discussed further in this Handbook.

Chapter 1

1.1   RSV   TEV

        The oracle of God which Habakkuk the prophet saw.   **This is the message that the LORD revealed to the prophet Habakkuk.**

    This verse serves as a title for the first two chapters. The first verse of chapter 3 gives a new title for the rest of the book.

    The word translated <u>oracle</u> is a common word in the prophetic books (compare Nahum 1.1) and is often used when the prophet speaks against pagan nations (for example Isa 13.1). In modern English it means "message" (TEV). The Hebrew word implies that the message is a religious one, and so RSV translates it as <u>The oracle of God</u>. The terms <u>God</u> and "the LORD" both occur in Habakkuk, but since "LORD" occurs in verse 2, it may be better to use it also in verse 1. This is what TEV has done ("**This is the message that the LORD revealed**"). For comments on the translation of "LORD," please see the sources referred to under Nahum 1.2.

    The term <u>oracle</u> or "message" is applied to the whole of chapters 1 and 2, even though they include Habakkuk's questions as well as the Lord's answers.

    For notes on the name of <u>Habakkuk</u>, see the introduction above, "Translating the Book of Habakkuk." **The prophet** translates a common Hebrew word and means "one who proclaims the Lord's message." It is unusual for this term to be used in the title of a prophetic book. It occurs in a similar position elsewhere only in Haggai 1.1 and Zechariah 1.1.

    The Hebrew word for <u>saw</u> is often used to describe prophetic activity (compare Micah 1.1). It usually implies that the prophet received his message in a trance or some similar condition. Thus JB and NEB render it as "received in a vision." For further discussion on "vision" see Nahum 1.1. TEV restructures as "**the message that the LORD revealed.**" The word "**revealed**" emphasizes the divine origin of the message but does not indicate the method by which it reached the prophet. An alternative translation model for this verse is:

        Here is the message that the LORD caused the prophet Habakkuk
        to see in a vision (dream).

1.2-4

RSV	TEV
	Habakkuk Complains of Injustice
2 O LORD, how long shall I cry for help, and thou wilt not hear? Or cry to thee "Violence!" and thou wilt not save? 3 Why dost thou make me see wrongs and look upon trouble? Destruction and violence are before me; strife and contention arise. 4 So the law is slacked and justice never goes forth. For the wicked surround the righteous, so justice goes forth perverted.	2 O LORD, how long must I call for help before you listen, before you save us from violence? 3 Why do you make me see such trouble? How can you stand to look on such wrongdoing? Destruction and violence are all around me, and there is fighting and quarreling everywhere. 4 The law is weak and useless, and justice is never done. Evil men get the better of the righteous, and so justice is perverted.

In this paragraph Habakkuk makes his first complaint to the Lord. He declares that there is wrongdoing all around him, but the Lord has taken no action to bring it to an end. He demands a reason for the Lord's apparent lack of interest.

SECTION HEADING: TEV places a section heading before verse 2, "**Habakkuk Complains of Injustice**." In some languages it is better to avoid the abstract term "**Injustice**" and say "Habakkuk complains that people act wickedly" or "Habakkuk complains that God does not punish the wicked people."

1.2

RSV	TEV
O LORD, how long shall I cry for help, and thou wilt not hear? Or cry to thee "Violence!" and thou wilt not save?	O LORD, how long must I call for help before you listen, before you save us from violence?

This verse has the grammatical form of a question but is really a way for Habakkuk to express his complaint. Translators should retain the form of a question, unless it will be misunderstood as a simple request for information. This is not just a rhetorical question, since the prophet does expect to get some response. This response is given in verses 5-11. Although the response deals with the question in a general way, it does not answer the question in the terms in which it is asked.

Verse 2 falls into two halves which are more or less parallel in meaning. In the first sentence the question **how long** echoes other parts of the Old Testament (compare Psa 13.1,2; Jer 12.4). It implies that the problem has been troubling the speaker for a long time already. The words **cry for help** translate a single Hebrew word. In some languages translators will need to supply a goal or object of **cry** and say "cry to you to help."

And thou wilt not hear implies that the Lord has given no response up to the present time, but does not imply that he never will respond. Indeed it is the hope that the Lord will eventually respond that makes the prophet keep on asking. This is brought out more clearly by TEV, "how long must I call for help before you listen." RSV's rendering **how long shall I cry for help and thou wilt not hear** will in some languages give the impression that the Lord has already been helping Habakkuk. On the contrary, the prophet now wants to know how much longer he must cry for help in order to stop the Lord from ignoring him. Therefore for many translators the use of the word "**before**" (TEV) instead of **and** will be helpful.

Or cry to thee "Violence!" and thou wilt not save? In the second sentence the word **cry** translates a different Hebrew verb from that used in the first sentence, and has a slight difference in emphasis. The previous verb means "to cry for help," whereas this one means "to cry out in distress or horror." Compare Mft "cry out . . . complain" and NIV "call . . . cry out." In some languages it is not easy to make this distinction, and many translators will need to do as RSV, NAB, NEB, and JB have done, and use the same word twice. The Hebrew word for "violence" is repeated in verses 3 and 9 and is one of the key words which links the question (verses 2-4) with the answer (verses 5-11). **Violence** may also be rendered as "cruel deeds" or "hurtful actions." The clause in TEV "**save us from violence**" can then be translated as "help us to escape from those who would treat us cruelly" or "prevent our enemies from doing cruel things to us." The exclusive pronoun "**us**" is not present in the Hebrew, but it is permissible to include it, because the prophet is speaking not only for himself but also for the minority of people in Judah, who are honest and who share his outlook. One can also say "before you save your people from violence." See the above comment on the problem of translating RSV's rendering of this verse literally. The word **save** is an important term in the Old Testament and is often used of the Lord's mighty acts on behalf of his people. Habakkuk feels that such acts are badly needed in his own situation. (The same Hebrew root occurs in 3.8,13,18.) In some languages **save** will be rendered by a phrase; for example, "help us to escape" (see above comment on **Violence**).

TEV has combined the two halves of the verse into one sentence. It has avoided repeating the verb phrase "**call for help**" and thus shortens the second half of the verse to "**before you save us from violence.**"

An alternative translation model for this verse is:

> O LORD, I have been crying out to you for a long time to help me. When will you listen to me? When will you help me (or us [exclusive], or your people) to escape those who want to do cruel things to me (or us, or them)?

1.3

RSV	TEV
Why dost thou make me see wrongs and look upon trouble? Destruction and violence are before me; strife and contention arise.	Why do you make me see such trouble? How can you stand to look on such wrongdoing? Destruction and violence are all around me, and there is fighting and quarreling everywhere.

The first half of the verse has the form of a double question in RSV. TEV turns it into two separate sentences. As in verse 2, the question form is an indirect way for Habakkuk to make his complaint against God. Again, it should be retained in translation if possible.

Habakkuk's first question — Hab 1.4

Why dost thou make me see wrongs and look upon trouble? First of all, it must be noted that the word translated **wrongs** in RSV is translated "trouble" in TEV, and the word translated **trouble** in RSV is translated "wrongdoing" in TEV. This may make it appear that TEV has reversed the order of the first two clauses, but in fact this is not the case. Several other modern English versions also prefer to use "wrong" or "wrongdoing" in the second clause rather than the first (NEB, NIV, NJV). The words **make me see** are causative in sense; the prophet is boldly blaming God for the problems in his situation. TEV expresses this more naturally as **"Why do you make me see such trouble?"** This means not just to look at the troubles of other people, but to experience trouble oneself. The sentence may also be phrased as "Why do you make me meet with such trouble?" or "Why do you make me receive trouble like this?" or even "Why do you bring such trouble upon me?" **Wrongs** is rendered as "ruin" (NAB), "misery" (NEB), "injustice" (JB, NIV), or "iniquity" (NJV).

The rest of the sentence, **and look upon trouble**, is ambiguous in RSV. The obvious interpretation in English is that **Why dost thou make** from the first clause is to be repeated in the second. This would give the meaning "Why do you make me look upon trouble?" However, this is wrong, and the Hebrew actually means "Why do you look upon trouble?" The prophet implies that the Lord is watching without taking any action to put things right. This meaning is expressed more clearly in TEV, **"How can you stand to look on such wrongdoing"** (American edition) or **"How can you endure to look on such wrongdoing"** (British edition). Compare NIV "Why do you tolerate wrong?" In many languages it will be necessary to show who is the subject of **"wrongdoing."** Therefore other ways of rendering this clause are "Why do you tolerate people doing such evil things?" or "When you see people doing such evil things, why do you not pay attention (or, take action)?"

The terms **Destruction and violence** often go together (compare Jer 6.7; 20.8; Ezek 45.9; Amos 3.10). Here the prophet says that they are **"all around me"** (TEV).

The last part of the verse has another pair of nouns, **strife and contention**, which balance **Destruction and violence**. TEV translates these in modern terms as **"there is fighting and quarreling everywhere."**

In some languages it will be necessary to use verbs to express the meaning of the second part of the verse. One may say "All around me people are attacking and oppressing others. Everywhere people are fighting and quarreling."

1.4

RSV	TEV
So the law is slacked 　and justice never goes forth. For the wicked surround the 　righteous, so justice goes forth perverted.	The law is weak and useless, and justice is never done. Evil men get the better of the righteous, and so justice is perverted.

This verse describes the results of the conditions stated in the second half of verse 3. The relationship between the verses is expressed by the word **So**, and in many languages it will be helpful to follow RSV here. **The law** here probably has a general sense rather than referring specifically to religious teaching. Because violence was so common, the social order was breaking down, and the courts were ineffectual. This is the sense of **slacked**, and TEV expresses it forcefully as "**The law is weak and useless.**" Compare "the law loses its hold" (JB) and "The law is paralysed" (NIV). In some languages it will be helpful to render this sentence as "The law has become weak and useless." **Justice never goes forth** is expressed in plain modern English in TEV as "**justice is never done.**" It means that judges are judging unfairly, and in many cases they are taking bribes. In languages which do not use the passive, this clause may be rendered as "judges never judge rightly," "judges never give justice," or "judges always judge in an unjust way."

In the second half of the verse, the Hebrew words for **the wicked** and **the righteous** are singular, but they stand for groups rather than individuals. It is therefore necessary to translate them as plural in many languages; for example, "wicked people" and "innocent people."

Surround is used with a hostile sense (compare Psa 22.12), and so TEV translates as "**Evil men get the better of the righteous.**" The implication is that the judges are corrupt, and the wicked bribe them in order to win their cases. Because of this, innocent people are deprived of their rights. Therefore one may translate "The wicked people always defeat innocent people in the law courts."

The sentence **So justice goes forth perverted** sums up the previous statements. **Goes forth perverted** means that justice is "bent," "distorted," "polluted," "turned upside down," and so on.

An alternative translation model for this verse is:

> The law has become weak and useless, and judges always judge in an unjust way. Wicked people always defeat innocent people in the law courts, so justice is turned upside down.

Both parts of the verse seem to say practically the same thing, and so in some languages it may be better to combine the two parts of the verse into one and avoid repetition by saying:

> Evil people always defeat innocent people in the law courts, and judges always judge unfairly. Because of this the law becomes weak and useless.

1.5-11

RSV

5 Look among the nations, and see;
    wonder and be astounded.
  For I am doing a work in your days
    that you would not believe if told.
6 For lo, I am rousing the Chaldeans,
    that bitter and hasty nation,
  who march through the breadth of the earth,
    to seize habitations not their own.
7 Dread and terrible are they;
    their justice and dignity proceed from themselves.
8 Their horses are swifter than leopards,
    more fierce than the evening wolves;
    their horsemen press proudly on.
  Yea, their horsemen come from afar;

TEV
The LORD's Reply

5 Then the LORD said to his people, "Keep watching the nations around you, and you will be astonished at what you see. I am going to do something that you will not believe when you hear about it. 6 I am bringing the Babylonians to power, those fierce, restless people. They are marching out across the world to conquer other lands. 7 They spread fear and terror, and in their pride they are a law to themselves.

8 "Their horses are faster than leopards, fiercer than hungry wolves. Their horsemen come riding from distant lands; their horses paw the ground. They come swooping down like eagles attacking their prey.

9 "Their armies advance in violent con-

The Lord's first answer Hab 1.5

<table>
<tr><td></td><td>they fly like an eagle swift to devour.</td><td>quest, and everyone is terrified as they approach. Their captives are as numerous as grains of sand. 10 They treat kings with contempt and laugh at high officials. No fortress can stop them—they pile up earth against it and capture it. 11 Then they sweep on like the wind and are gone, these men whose power is their god."</td></tr>
<tr><td>9</td><td>They all come for violence;
terror of them goes before them.
They gather captives like sand.</td><td></td></tr>
<tr><td>10</td><td>At kings they scoff,
and of rulers they make sport.
They laugh at every fortress,
for they heap up earth and take it.</td><td></td></tr>
<tr><td>11</td><td>Then they sweep by like the wind and go on,
guilty men, whose own might is their god!</td><td></td></tr>
</table>

In these verses the prophet receives the Lord's response to the questions of 1.2-4. The questions are not answered in the form in which they were asked, but nevertheless the Lord assures Habakkuk that he knows about the problems and is taking steps to deal with them.

SECTION HEADING: "**The Lord's Reply**"; this may be translated as "The LORD replies to the prophet" or "The LORD answers the prophet's questions."

1.5

RSV	TEV
Look among the nations, and see; wonder and be astounded. For I am doing a work in your days that you would not believe if told.	Then the LORD said to his people, "Keep watching the nations around you, and you will be astonished at what you see. I am going to do something that you will not believe when you hear about it.

In the text of RSV there is no indication that a new speech by a new speaker begins here. It is important in many languages to make this kind of information explicit. TEV has done so by adding the words "**Then the LORD said to his people**," and many translators will need to do something similar, as have FrCL ("says the Lord") and GeCL ("The Lord answers"). In Hebrew the second person verbs in verse 5 are all plural, making clear that the message is not for Habakkuk alone. The words of TEV "**to his people**" indicate that the message is for all those who shared Habakkuk's attitude toward the events of his day.

<u>Look among the nations, and see</u>: the words <u>Look</u> and <u>see</u> may need to be translated by a single word in some languages. Instead of the Hebrew word translated <u>among the nations</u>, the Septuagint, the ancient Greek translation of the Old Testament, understood the text to have a different Hebrew word, which occurs also in 1.13 and 2.5. This understanding is followed by NEB, which translates as "you treacherous people." Based on this interpretation, the whole paragraph, verses 5-11, is addressed to "the wicked" that Habakkuk complained about in verse 4. However, the Hebrew as it stands makes perfectly good sense, and translators are recommended to follow it rather than the Septuagint at this point (compare HOTTP).

<u>Wonder and be astounded</u> translate two forms of the same verb in Hebrew. Some translators may choose to follow RSV at this point and use two synonyms meaning "amazed" or "astounded." TEV, however, has translated only once, "**you will be astonished**." Other versions use only one verb but intensify it (NIV "utterly amazed"; NJV "utterly astounded"), and many translators will wish to follow this example. The idea of <u>astounded</u> in many languages will be expressed

in an idiomatic way, referring to the heart or some other bodily organ such as the liver; for example, "heart is uncomfortable," "heart feels strange," or "liver moves."

I am doing a work translates a Hebrew participle with no subject expressed (compare NAB "a work is being done"). In more natural English one can say "Something is going to happen" or "Events are about to take place" (compare FrCL, GeCL). However, in this context, as verse 6 makes clear, the subject can only be the Lord, and so several translations make the subject **I** explicit in verse 5 (RSV, JB, TEV, NIV). The Hebrew words used here have the overtones of referring back to the great deeds that the Lord performed at the time of the exodus from Egypt (compare Psa 44.1; 95.9). The use of the participle in Hebrew gives the impression that the events referred to will take place very soon. TEV tries to express this with "**I am going to do something.**" One can also say "I am about to do something."

In your days means "during your lifetime." The implication is that the events will take place soon, and the hearers will see them for themselves. TEV has omitted any equivalent to this phrase, but most translators will have no difficulty expressing it in their language; for example, the use of the expression "about to" (see comment above) will convey this idea. Or one may say "In the very near future (very soon) I am going to . . . ."

That you would not believe if told indicates that what follows will be a surprise to the hearers. It thus prepares the way for Habakkuk's second complaint in verses 12-17.

The passive expression **if told** may be difficult to translate in some languages. An alternative expression is "when someone tells you" or, as in TEV, "**when you hear about it.**"

In Acts 13.41 this verse is quoted in the Septuagint translation, which is somewhat longer than the Hebrew. Translators should not alter either verse to make them more alike than they really are.

1.6	RSV	TEV
	For lo, I am rousing the Chaldeans, that bitter and hasty nation, who march through the breadth of the earth, to seize habitations not their own.	I am bringing the Babylonians to power, those fierce, restless people. They are marching out across the world to conquer other lands.

This verse gives the content of the surprise promised in verse 5. This relationship is expressed by the first word of the RSV **For**. In many languages it will be necessary to show this relationship clearly with an introductory word of some kind.

The next word **lo** is an old-fashioned word which only draws attention to what follows. In modern English one may say "look" or "see" (NAB). However, TEV and several other modern versions (JB, NIV, FrCL, GeCL) simply omit it. Many languages will render **For lo** as "So look!" or "So pay attention."

Rousing or "raising up" (NAB, NEB, NIV) is expressed in political terms in TEV as "**bringing . . . to power.**" One may also say "I am causing the

The Lord's first answer   Hab 1.7

Babylonians . . . to become powerful (politically)" or "I am causing the Babylonians . . . to gain political power."

The Chaldeans were originally the inhabitants of southern Babylonia, but by the time of Habakkuk, this name carried a wider meaning. Thus it is translated by the more general word "**Babylonians**" in TEV and NIV. The Babylonians had lived in lower Mesopotamia for many centuries, but their recent conquest of Assyria had made them a major world power for the first time.

The words translated **bitter and hasty** have similar sounds in Hebrew. Some translators have tried to keep this similarity in English. Mft and JB use "fierce and fiery" for instance. If other languages have two words of similar sound that can be used together here, that will be good. However, if such a pair of words will not sound natural, it should not be forced. **Bitter** (TEV "**fierce**") emphasizes the cruelty of the Babylonians, and the Hebrew word translated **hasty** emphasizes the speed with which they conquered most of western Asia.

Another translation model for the first half of this verse is "So pay attention, because I am causing those cruel and restless Babylonians to gain political power."

The pronouns and possessives from verses 6b-11 are singular in Hebrew, agreeing with the singular noun **nation**. However, they are collective in meaning and are translated as plural in RSV and most other English versions. Some translators may be able to use a collective singular, but many will need to use the plural in these verses.

The second half of the verse strengthens the description and adds more detail. **March through the breadth of the earth** means "march everywhere in the world" (JB "march miles across country"). **To seize habitations not their own** means "to capture other people's homes." TEV makes this into a more general statement and says "**They are marching out across the world to conquer other lands.**" Some translators may find it helpful to follow this example. The word **march** in English always carries the overtones of soldiers on the move. So in some languages it will be helpful to render this sentence as "Their soldiers march everywhere in the world to conquer . . . ."

1.7   RSV   TEV

Dread and terrible are they; their justice and dignity proceed from themselves.

They spread fear and terror, and in their pride they are a law to themselves.

Verses 7-11 give a vivid description of the military power and arrogant attitude of the Babylonians.

The Babylonians are described as **Dread and terrible**. TEV expresses this in a more personal way as "**They spread fear and terror.**" One may also translate this clause as "They cause people everywhere to shake with fear." In some languages, however, "**terror**" is described idiomatically; for example, "They cause the hearts of people in countries everywhere to shrink so that their bodies tremble." In still other languages it may be necessary to state this from the opposite point of view and say "People in other nations fear them very much" or "People in other nations are so afraid of them that their bodies tremble."

The second half of the verse is not very clear in RSV. The meaning is that the Babylonians do not acknowledge any other power greater than themselves, and so they set their own rules for the treatment of other people. (Compare "whose own might is their god" in verse 11). **Dignity** in this context refers to "pride." TEV expresses this in rather idiomatic English as **"in their pride they are a law to themselves."** Another way to express this clause is "They are so proud that they feel (consider) that anything they do is right and lawful," or one can say "They are so proud that they feel (consider) that nothing they do is wrong or unlawful."

1.8   RSV   TEV

Their horses are swifter than leopards, more fierce than the evening wolves; their horsemen press proudly on. Yea, their horsemen come from afar; they fly like an eagle swift to devour.	"Their horses are faster than leopards, fiercer than hungry wolves. Their horsemen come riding from distant lands; their horses paw the ground. They come swooping down like eagles attacking their prey.

Verses 8-10 describe the military power of the Babylonians in rather traditional language (compare Isa 5.26-30; Jer 4.13; Hos 13.7). There is some poetic exaggeration in the figurative description. If this will be misunderstood in a literal translation, then the translator should try to make it clear that the figurative description ought not to be taken literally. One way to do this is to say "Their horses seem to run faster than leopards . . . ," and similarly with the other figures.

Leopards are large, wild, catlike animals, whose fur has spots which enable them to hide very easily in the shadow of trees. Here the comparison may be with a cheetah, an animal similar to a leopard, since cheetahs are well known for their speed and are sometimes captured and trained for hunting. See *Fauna and Flora of the Bible*, pages 48-49. If a cheetah is more familiar than a leopard, the word for cheetah may be used here. If neither animal is known, translators may make the comparison by referring to any large, swift predatory animal which is well known. In areas like the Pacific islands, where no such animals exist, it may be necessary to borrow a term from some other language and explain it in a footnote.

The expression **evening wolves** is a literal translation of the Hebrew. The thought behind the expression is that the wolves of Palestine normally hunted by night, and so in the evening, when they began their hunt, they were more hungry than at other times. TEV here translates the meaning into plain English and says **"fiercer than hungry wolves."** It is also possible that the word translated **evening** may mean "desert." Thus NEB translates "wolves of the plain," and NJV "wolves of the steppe." The Septuagint at this point understands the text to have a slightly different Hebrew word and translates it as "wolves of Arabia," but no modern English version does this. The word **evening** with the meaning "hungry" makes perfectly good sense, and translators are recommended to follow this interpretation. The same problem occurs in Zephaniah 3.3. In some cultures where **wolves** do not exist, other translation models are "hungry wild dogs which hunt at night," or even "hungry wild animals that . . . ." **Fierce** in this context means "cruel" or even "bloodthirsty."

The second part of the verse has several difficulties. The Hebrew word which RSV twice translates as **horsemen** may refer either to horses or to their riders. The Hebrew verb translated **press proudly on** in RSV is used elsewhere of cattle leaping about (Jer 50.11, "are wanton"; Mal 4.2, "leaping"), and seems to make better sense here if the subject is taken as "horses" rather than their riders. It is translated as "leap" in FrCL and "gallop" in NIV. In the second case the verb **come from afar** in RSV seems to refer to the riders more than the horses. English versions vary in the way they handle the problem. RSV and JB translate as **horsemen** both times (compare HOTTP). NJV does the opposite and translates as "steeds" (that is, horses) both times. Some versions avoid the difficulty by using the English word "cavalry" (Mft, NEB, NIV), which includes both the horses and their riders. This is a good solution in languages which have such a term (compare GeCL). NAB and TEV translate as "**horses**" in one instance and "**horsemen**" in the other. The "**horses paw the ground**" (NAB "prance"), while the "**horsemen come riding from distant lands.**" This is perhaps the best solution for languages that have no term equivalent to "cavalry" in English. The phrase "**horses paw the ground**" refers to the action of horses stamping their front hooves (feet) on the ground to show excitement. As noted above, this word may also be translated "gallop." **Horsemen** in some languages will be rendered as "horse soldiers," or even "soldiers who ride horses."

TEV changes the order of these two clauses and mentions the "horsemen" first. This is probably because the translators thought that the focus was more on the men than on the horses. Translators in other languages should follow the TEV order only if it would have the same effect on the focus of the sentence as it does in English.

The last part of the verse contains another simile or comparison. The cavalry **fly like an eagle swift to devour**. The word translated **eagle** in RSV probably means a vulture, and TEV translates it as "vulture" in other contexts such as Micah 1.16. (See *Fauna and Flora of the Bible*, pages 82-84.) However, in English the eagle is used as a symbol of power and strength, and so here TEV translates as "eagles," since it fits the context better. Translators should consider whether any of the large birds in their area are regarded as symbols of power. In this context it is more important to create the right impression on the reader than to give the correct zoological name of the bird. Compare Zephaniah 2.14.

The last sentence of the verse is expanded a little in TEV to give a more vivid effect: "**They come swooping down like eagles attacking their prey.**" The word "**swooping**" is used especially of a bird diving downward in flight. "**Prey**" is a term applied to any creature which another creature wishes to catch as food. It is not clear in TEV who "**they**" refers to in the final sentence, since "horses" were mentioned in the previous clause. If translators think that "they" refers to "horsemen" (compare RSV), it will be helpful to make that meaning explicit and say "Their horsemen come swooping . . . ." If it is impossible in certain languages to talk about "horsemen" swooping down on something, one may say "Their horsemen (soldiers on horses) suddenly attack their enemies like eagles (large birds of prey) swooping down on their victims."

Another translation model for this verse is:

> The horses of the Babylonians run swifter than leopards (cheetahs) and are fiercer than hungry wolves (wild dogs). The Babylonian

Hab 1.8

horse soldiers ride their horses (coming) from distant lands; the horses paw the ground (or, gallop). The horse soldiers suddenly attack like eagles (large birds of prey) swooping down on their victims.

1.9 RSV	TEV
They all come for violence; terror[a] of them goes before them. They gather captives like sand.	"Their armies advance in violent conquest, and everyone is terrified as they approach.[a] Their captives are as numerous as grains of sand.

[a] Cn: Heb uncertain

[a] *Probable text* and everyone ... approach; *Hebrew unclear.*

They all refers to the Babylonian soldiers, and TEV makes this clearer by translating "**Their armies.**"

Come for violence means "come with the intention of conquering by force." TEV translates as "**advance in violent conquest.**"

Another way of rendering this clause is "Their armies advance conquering everyone violently"; or else one may restructure as follows: "As the Babylonian armies advance, they conquer everyone with great force and cruelty" or " . . . they use great force and cruelty to conquer everyone."

In the second line of the verse, the Hebrew is practically unintelligible. The first of three Hebrew words that make up the line occurs nowhere else, and its meaning can only be guessed. Some scholars link it with a word meaning "to eat" (compare KJV "their faces shall sup up"). Others link it with a different word meaning "to desire" (compare RV "their faces are set eagerly"). A third group connect it with an Arabic root that means "to be abundant" and translate as "hordes" (NIV). Perhaps NEB's "a sea of faces" follows this interpretation. Another group of scholars thinks that the traditional Hebrew text contains a mistake and needs to be corrected. RSV and TEV both belong to this group, and both correct the problem word to one which means **terror**.

The third word of the Hebrew line means "east wind" (KJV, RV, JB), "desert wind" (NIV), or "stormwind" (NAB). Some scholars think that this word also contains a spelling mistake, and they correct it to give a word meaning "in front of." RSV and TEV both make this change. RSV says **terror of them goes before them**, and TEV expresses this more clearly as "**everyone is terrified as they approach.**" For help on the translation of **terror**, see the comments on Nahum 2.6.

Another possibility is given in the Dead Sea Scroll commentary on Habakkuk: "the set of their faces is like the east wind." This means that the Babylonians are as fierce as the hot east winds that blow toward Palestine from the desert.

There is no really satisfactory solution to these problems. The meaning given by RSV and TEV is clear and fits the context adequately, so translators may as well follow it rather than any of the other possibilities.

They gather captives like sand: the last line speaks of the effect of the Babylonian advance: they defeat their enemies and take many prisoners. TEV makes the meaning of the comparison explicit with "**Their captives are as**

The Lord's first answer Hab 1.10

numerous as grains of sand." One can also render this clause as "take captives in great numbers like grains of sand." The mention of (grains of) sand as a picture of vast quantity is common in the Old Testament (compare Gen 22.17; 41.49; Judges 7.12; 2 Sam 17.11). In certain languages where sand is not normally used as a figure for huge numbers, one may say "take so many people captive that it is impossible to count them."

An alternative translation model for this verse is:

> As all the Babylonian soldiers go forward (advance), they use great force and cruelty to conquer everyone. As they approach, the hearts of people everywhere are filled with fear. They take so many people captive that it is impossible to count them.

1.10

RSV	TEV
At kings they scoff, and of rulers they make sport. They laugh at every fortress, for they heap up earth and take it.	They treat kings with contempt and laugh at high officials. No fortress can stop them—they pile up earth against it and capture it.

RSV, TEV, and most English versions appear to ignore the fact that in this verse the Hebrew pronouns in **they scoff** and **they laugh** are emphatic. JB comes closest to representing this, with "They are a people that scoff at kings." Another way in English to show the emphasis is "These Babylonians are a people who . . . ." This can be repeated at the beginning of the second half of the verse.

The first half of the verse says essentially the same thing twice, as is clear from RSV, **At kings they scoff, and of rulers they make sport**. **Scoff** means to mock or scorn, and **make sport** means make fun of. It has nothing to do with athletic sports. The idea of **scoff** (TEV "**treat . . . with contempt**") can be translated in a variety of ways; for example, "They treat kings as if they were nothing," "They look down their noses at kings," "They sneer at . . . ," or "They shake their fingers at . . . ." **Make sport of** (TEV "laugh at") is similar in meaning but is a more active form of contempt. Here the conquerors are trying to show the defeated rulers how weak and foolish they are. In some languages **make sport** can be translated as "cause to lose face." For **rulers**, see the translation note on "princes" in Nahum 3.17.

The second half of the verse is also in two parts, but in this case the second is not parallel in meaning to the first, so they cannot be combined. The first part is similar to the statements in the first half of the verse (**They laugh at every fortress** in RSV). However, it sounds a little odd in English to laugh at something which is not personal, so TEV turns this statement around and expresses its meaning in plain language as "**No fortress can stop them.**" **Fortress** may be translated as "city with strong walls," or in certain languages as "large group of houses with a strong high wall around it" (see comment on Nahum 3.12). "**Stop them**" may also be translated as "prevent them from entering," or "defend itself against them," or "is an obstacle to them."

The words **they heap up earth and take it** refer to one ancient method of besieging a town or fortress. This involved heaping a ramp of earth against its wall until the top of the ramp was level with the top of the wall. Then the

Hab 1.10

attackers could climb the ramp, cross the wall, and capture the town or fortress. See the illustration at the discussion of Nahum 2.1.

Another translation model for this verse is:

> The Babylonian soldiers make fun of kings and laugh at their high officials (the chief servants of the kings). No city with strong walls can keep them from entering. They pile up earth against the walls and capture the city.

1.11   RSV   TEV

Then they sweep by like the wind and go on, guilty men, whose own might is their god!

Then they sweep on like the wind and are gone, these men whose power is their god."

There are several difficulties in this verse.

(1) The Hebrew word translated **wind** in RSV and TEV may also mean "mind" (KJV) or "spirit" (TOB). Which meaning is more appropriate here?

(2) Is this word the subject of the verbs translated **sweep by** and **go on** in RSV, or not?

(3) Does the Hebrew word translated **guilty men** in RSV go with the first part of the verse, as the Hebrew punctuation suggests, or does it go with the second part, as most modern scholars and translators believe?

(4) Is this Hebrew word to be read as in the traditional Hebrew text, or as in the Dead Sea Scroll of Habakkuk, which has one letter different?

In response to (1), if the meaning is taken to be "mind" or "spirit," then the sense of the verse is that the Babylonians go beyond the command God had given them and become proud of their own strength (TOB footnote). However, most scholars and translators (RV, RSV, BJ, JB, NAB, NEB, TEV, NIV, NJV, FrCL, GeCL) prefer to take the meaning as "wind."

In answer to (2), if "wind" is taken as the subject (JB "Then the wind changes and is gone"), then the first sentence is a metaphor. Its meaning is that the Babylonians, after conquering one place, **"sweep on"** to attack other places. **Sweep by** means to pass by, moving along at great speed. However, most translations take the Babylonians as the subject and translate as **"like the wind**
(or, storm)" (RSV, NAB, NEB, TEV, NIV, NJV, FrCL, GeCL). This really involves adding one letter to the traditional Hebrew text. But it has the advantage of keeping the same subject as in the preceding verses. This interpretation has much the same meaning as the one in JB above and fits more smoothly into the paragraph as a whole.

In answer to (3), those who prefer the meaning "mind" or "spirit" in (1) tend to take the word translated **guilty men** in RSV with the first part of the sentence (KJV, TOB). This fits the meaning that the Babylonians become guilty by overstepping the task God has given to them (GeCL). Most translations take "guilty men" with the second part of the verse (RSV, BJ, JB, NAB, NIV, GeCL) and take that as the explanation of the guilt.

Under (4) TEV seems to be the only English translation which follows the Dead Sea scroll. This manuscript has "set up" instead of "guilty" and gives the meaning "they set up their own power as a god." This avoids the problem of (3) but is otherwise not much different from most other translations, which assume some such word as "is" (RSV **whose own might is their god!**).

Therefore, although the main thrust of the verse is fairly clear, it is almost impossible to make firm decisions about the details. Taking the majority decision on each of the above questions, we recommend a translation model as follows: "Then they hurry on just like the wind and pass by. They are guilty men whose power has become just like a god to them" (compare FrCL). Or "Then they hurry on, just as the wind blows by and disappears. They are guilty men who worship their own power as if it were a god." Compare the second half of verse 7 with the second half of this verse.

1.12-17

RSV

12 Art thou not from everlasting,
O LORD my God, my Holy One?
We shall not die.
O LORD, thou hast ordained them as a judgment;
and thou, O Rock, hast established them for chastisement.
13 Thou who art of purer eyes than to behold evil
and canst not look on wrong,
why dost thou look on faithless men,
and art silent when the wicked swallows up
the man more righteous than he?
14 For thou makest men like the fish of the sea,
like crawling things that have no ruler.
15 He brings all of them up with a hook,
he drags them out with his net,
he gathers them in his seine;
so he rejoices and exults.
16 Therefore he sacrifices to his net
and burns incense to his seine;
for by them he lives in luxury,
and his food is rich.
17 Is he then to keep on emptying his net,
and mercilessly slaying nations for ever?

TEV
Habakkuk Complains to the LORD Again

12 LORD, from the very beginning you are God. You are my God, holy and eternal. LORD, my God and protector, you have chosen the Babylonians and made them strong so that they can punish us. 13 But how can you stand these treacherous, evil men? Your eyes are too holy to look at evil, and you cannot stand the sight of people doing wrong. So why are you silent while they destroy people who are more righteous than they are?

14 How can you treat people like fish or like a swarm of insects that have no ruler to direct them? 15 The Babylonians catch people with hooks, as though they were fish. They drag them off in nets and shout for joy over their catch! 16 They even worship their nets and offer sacrifices to them, because their nets provide them with the best of everything.

17 Are they going to use their swords forever and keep on destroying nations without mercy?

In this section Habakkuk makes his second complaint to the Lord. It seems as if he has considered the Lord's reply to his first complaint and is not satisfied with it. He admits that the wickedness of his own people needs to be punished (verse 12). However, he cannot understand how the Lord can bear to use the Babylonians, an even more wicked people, to carry out the punishment. Such a situation seems out of keeping with the Lord's holy and just character (verse 13).

The rest of the paragraph is a figurative description of the way in which the Babylonians treat other nations. It suggests that Habakkuk already had some experience of the Babylonians, and is one factor in dating this paragraph some time after the battle of Carchemish. It emphasizes the unfitness of the Babylonians to be used as the Lord's instruments, at least in Habakkuk's opinion.

Hab 1.12-17

SECTION HEADING: "Habakkuk Complains to the LORD Again"; the section heading should be recognizably parallel with the heading at verse 2 in its vocabulary and structure.

1.12

RSV

Art thou not from everlasting,
  O LORD my God, my Holy One?
We shall not die.
O LORD, thou hast ordained them as a judgment;
and thou, O Rock, hast established them for chastisement.

TEV

LORD, from the very beginning you are God. You are my God, holy and eternal. LORD, my God and protector, you have chosen the Babylonians and made them strong so that they can punish us.

The prophet begins his complaint by stating his convictions both about God and about the situation around him. The first part of the verse takes the form of a negative question, **Art thou not from everlasting ... ?** but this is really an indirect way of making a strong positive statement. See verse 2 on "rhetorical questions." TEV expresses this as a statement: "**LORD, from the very beginning you are God**" (compare NJV). In languages where rhetorical questions may be confusing, translators should follow this example.

From everlasting: translators in many languages who follow TEV's rendering "from the very beginning" as a model may be forced to state when the beginning occurred. This would make the meaning of this passage too narrow. The sense here is that the Lord has always been God, not that he started being God at a particular time. In this case the following is a legitimate rendering: "LORD, you have always been God."

The question in RSV ends with the terms of address, **O LORD my God, my Holy One**. TEV makes this a separate sentence: "**You are my God, holy and eternal.**" The words **my God** do not imply that Habakkuk owns God, but rather that he worships God. The adjective **Holy** stresses the essential being of God. It is the quality of sinlessness which separates him from sinful humanity and from other gods. The word "**LORD**" is placed at the beginning of the verse in TEV. In calling God **Holy** here, Habakkuk is laying the foundation for his question in verse 13.

The Masoretic Hebrew text next has two words which RSV translates as **We shall not die**. The second of these words is one of eighteen instances in the Old Testament which an ancient scribal tradition lists as places where the text had been deliberately altered by the scribes. The purpose of these alterations was to avoid any appearance of disrespect to God. In this case the original wording (only one letter different in Hebrew) is recorded as meaning "you do not die." The very idea that God could die was held to be disrespectful, and hence the change was made to **We shall not die**.

In this case it is very difficult to judge which possibility is more likely to be what Habakkuk originally wrote. Both make sense in the context. **We shall not die** in this setting expresses the prophet's belief that, although the Lord would punish his people, he would not let them be completely destroyed. This meaning is given in the Septuagint and Vulgate among ancient versions, in the English

Habakkuk's second question   Hab 1.13

KJV, RV, RSV, and NIV, in the French TOB, and in the German GeCL. It is also recommended in the preliminary report of HOTTP (1980).

The alternative "you do not die" (or some equivalent such as "immortal" or "eternal") is found in Mft, BJ, JB, NAB, NEB, TEV, NJV, and FrCL. It matches **from everlasting** and gives a good balance to the first half of the verse. It avoids the abruptness found in RSV and those translations which agree with it, and gives a smoother flow to the entire verse. On the whole, we recommend translators to accept this possibility. So the clause "**You are my God, holy and eternal**" may be translated "I worship you, O God. You are completely pure and do not die."

The second half of the verse consists of two parallel statements about the place of the Babylonians in the purposes of God as a means of punishing the wicked among God's own people. In RSV these statements are **thou hast ordained them as a judgment** and **thou ... hast established them for chastisement**. Each statement is accompanied by an address to God, **O Lord** in the first case and **O Rock** in the second. It is quite common in the Old Testament to refer to God as a rock (compare Deut 32.4,15,18,30,31; 1 Sam 2.2; 2 Sam 22.32; 23.3; Psa 18.2,31,46; 19.14). The meaning is that he is a source of protection, and thus TEV translates as "protector." **As a judgment** means "so that they will judge us," and **for chastisement** means "so that they will punish us."

TEV has combined into one the two parallel statements in the second half of the verse: "**you have chosen the Babylonians and made them strong so that they can punish us.**" In languages where parallel statements are natural, the translator may wish to maintain the parallel statements and translate in a way similar to the following:

> O Lord, you have chosen the Babylonians to condemn (judge) us;
>   and you, who are like a rock which protects us, have made the
>   Babylonians strong so that they can punish us.

TEV has also taken the two vocatives and placed them together at the beginning of the sentence: "**Lord, my God and protector.**" It is not clear why TEV repeats "**my God**" from the first half of the verse. In certain languages it will be necessary to put the words "you are" between **Lord** and **my God** and say, "Lord, you are my God and my protector." Another way of expressing this is "Lord, you are the God I worship, and you protect me."

1.13   RSV   TEV

RSV	TEV
Thou who art of purer eyes than to behold evil and canst not look on wrong, why dost thou look on faithless men, and art silent when the wicked swallows up the man more righteous than he?	But how can you stand these treacherous, evil men? Your eyes are too holy to look at evil, and you cannot stand the sight of people doing wrong. So why are you silent while they destroy people who are more righteous than they are?

Hab 1.13

In Hebrew the verse as a whole is a statement followed by two questions. RSV follows this order, but TEV changes it so as to put the statement between the two questions. This avoids long relative clauses which would be awkward in many languages.

The first half of the verse makes a statement in two parallel clauses, **Thou ... art of purer eyes than to behold evil and canst not look on wrong**. **Thou ... art of purer eyes** is a figure of speech called a metonym, in which the **eyes** stand for the whole person in the act of looking. Habakkuk says that the Lord's character is so pure that he cannot bear to **behold evil**. The prophet then repeats essentially the same idea in nonfigurative language in the second line, **and canst not look on wrong**. TEV retains the parallelism but expands the second part to make the implied subject clear: "**Your eyes are too holy to look at evil, and you cannot stand the sight of people doing wrong.**" Although the Hebrew word for **purer** is not the same root as the word for "holy" in the previous verse, this is a development of the same idea and forms the background to the questions which follow. Note that these questions are not really rhetorical questions, since Habakkuk is looking for an answer to them in 2.1-4. Therefore they should be translated as questions and not turned into statements. Compare comments on verse 2. In some languages it may not be possible to talk about eyes being "pure" or "sinless." In such cases translators may render this clause as "you are pure (sinless), and so you cannot look at evil . . . ."

In **why dost thou look on faithless men**, the verb **look**, as in verse 3, implies "look on, without taking action." TEV makes this a little clearer by saying "**How can you stand these treacherous, evil men?**" One may expand this line by saying "How can you watch what these treacherous and evil men do without punishing them?" The word "**treacherous**" means "untrustworthy" or "that cannot be trusted." In certain languages this meaning can be expressed idiomatically; for example, "men one cannot place one's heart in."

The last two lines make the same point in an expanded form and ask why God is **silent when the wicked swallows up the man more righteous than he**. Here **the wicked** refers of course to the Babylonians. In many languages it will be necessary to identify **the wicked** and say "So why are you silent while these wicked Babylonians destroy . . . ?" The word **swallows up** is a metaphor which TEV translates in nonfigurative language as "**destroy**." In languages where the meaning of the metaphor will be clear, translators should keep it. The word **righteous** refers to nations other than the Babylonians, but especially to Judah. Habakkuk has already admitted that his own people have done wrong and need to be punished. When he calls them **righteous** here, he means "less wicked than their enemies," not righteous in an absolute sense. In many languages the word used for "righteous" always has this absolute sense. In such cases it will be more appropriate to translate " . . . while the Babylonians destroy people who are less wicked than they are?" or " . . . destroy people who do less evil than they do?"

1.14	RSV	TEV
	For thou makest men like the fish of the sea, like crawling things that have no ruler.	How can you treat people like fish or like a swarm of insects that have no ruler to direct them?

Habakkuk's second question Hab 1.15

Verses 14-17 give a figurative description of the way the Babylonians treat their enemies. Verse 14 gives the setting, verses 15-16 describe what happens, and verse 17 states the question which the situation raises in the prophet's mind.

In verse 14, **thou makest**, Habakkuk boldly blames God for bringing about the conditions under which the Babylonians can abuse their power. In some languages it may be necessary to say "You cause men to become . . . " or "You allow men to become . . . ." He uses two comparisons: **thou makest men like the fish of the sea** and **like crawling things that have no ruler**. The point of the comparison with **crawling things** is that they have no leaders to help defend them. The point of the comparison with the **fish** is not stated here, but in the light of the following verse, it seems to be the casual way in which people kill them without worrying about it. Perhaps this can be brought out by saying "treat people as if they were only fish" or " . . . as if they were no more important than fish."

Fish of the sea is a Hebrew expression which sounds rather odd in English. Some modern translations say "fish (or fishes) in the sea" (Mft, JB, NIV), but TEV recognizes that "fish" alone is sufficient (compare TEV Zeph 1.3). Translators should consider what expression sounds natural and appropriate in their own language.

Crawling things may refer either to small "sea creatures" (NIV) or to "a swarm of insects" (TEV) such as ants or locusts. In languages which do not have a general word which equals the English word "insects" in meaning, one may say "a swarm of tiny crawling creatures," or even "a swarm of ants." The point here is that they "have no ruler" and are therefore disorganized and defenseless. This is a forceful picture of the way other nations were helpless before the Babylonian armies.

This verse is a statement in Hebrew, but TEV has turned it into a rhetorical question, "How can you treat . . . ?" as has NEB. There is no great advantage in this, and few translators will wish to do the same. However, the sense of the Hebrew in the phrase **thou makest men like** shows a direct causative action by God rather than a more passive one as in TEV's "**How can you treat people** . . . ." Therefore the following are legitimate translations: "You cause people to become . . . " or "You allow people to become . . . ." Another translation model for this verse is "You cause people to become like mere fish, or like a swarm of insects that have no ruler to direct (lead) them."

1.15	RSV	TEV

He brings all of them up with a hook, he drags them out with his net, he gathers them in his seine; so he rejoices and exults.	The Babylonians catch people with hooks, as though they were fish. They drag them off in nets and shout for joy over their catch!

He refers of course to "**the Babylonians**," as TEV makes explicit, changing the singular pronoun to a plural noun. Many translators will wish to do the same, or they may prefer to keep the noun singular, "the Babylonian." Here the Babylonians are pictured as treating other people as if they were merely fish. The comparison between people and fish was stated in the previous verse, but TEV

Hab 1.15

repeats it with **"as though they were fish."** Similar thoughts can be found in Jeremiah 16.16; Ezekiel 12.13; 17.20; 29.4; 32.3; Amos 4.2.

The second and third lines in RSV make the same statement twice but using different words: **he drags them out with his net, he gathers them in his seine**. A **seine** is a large dragnet which requires several people to pull it in a semicircle through the water. The word translated **net** probably refers to a smaller net that was cast by one person. Because **seine** is a rare word in English and will be unfamiliar to many people, TEV has run these two clauses into one and uses only the general word for a net: **"They drag them off in nets."** If different kinds of fishing nets are familiar in any particular culture, translators will have no difficulty in speaking about them. If they are not, then it will probably be best to do as TEV has done and make just one statement using a generic term for net. The comparison of the Babylonians with fishermen illustrates the ease with which they capture their prisoners.

As fishermen are happy when they catch plenty of fish, so the Babylonian **rejoices and exults**. TEV expresses this more naturally as **"shout for joy"** and makes it explicit that the "joy" is **"over their catch."** "Their catch" may also be rendered "what they have caught."

1.16   RSV   TEV

Therefore he sacrifices to his net   They even worship their nets and offer
   and burns incense to his seine;   sacrifices to them, because their nets
for by them he lives in luxury,[b]   provide them with the best of every-
   and his food is rich.   thing.

[b] Heb *his portion is fat*

Habakkuk here pictures the Babylonians as offering sacrifices to the nets as if they were gods, because of the success brought to them by their nets. There is no historical evidence that this was an actual custom of the Babylonians, so it seems best to treat this verse as figurative. When interpreted in this way, it says much the same as the last part of verse 11, which states that the Babylonians treat their own power as a god.

It will be good if the picture can be kept in translation, since it is part of the longer metaphor of the Babylonians as fishermen, which extends over verses 14-17.

The Hebrew speaks of making sacrifices and burning incense as two acts of worship. (For comments on **net** and **seine**, see verse 15.) TEV mentions only the sacrifices but makes it explicit that the purpose of the sacrifices is to treat the nets as gods: **"They even worship their nets and offer sacrifices to them."** If necessary, translators can add "as if they were gods." The nets of course stand for the weapons of war with which the Babylonians conquered other nations. An alternative translation model is "They even offer sacrifices and burn incense in honor of their nets, as if these were gods."

Incense: in some cultures the equivalent of **incense** will be "sweet-smelling substance." However, in other cultures where there is no equivalent for **incense**, translators may have to borrow a word from English or some other language and explain it in a footnote or in the glossary.

The reason the nets are worshiped is stated in two parallel clauses in RSV, **for by them he lives in luxury and his food is rich**. This is expressed in one general statement in TEV, "because their nets provide them with the best of everything." This means that military conquest gave the Babylonians a high standard of living. Another way of expressing this is "their nets enable them to live luxuriously and eat the best food."

1.17	RSV	TEV
	Is he then to keep on emptying his net, and mercilessly slaying nations for ever?	Are they going to use their swords forever and keep on destroying nations without mercy?

In the traditional Hebrew text, this verse has the form of a question. The Dead Sea Scroll of Habakkuk treats it as a statement by omitting one letter. This matches the Septuagint but is not followed by any major modern translation. A question certainly seems more appropriate in the context: Habakkuk asks how long the Lord will allow Babylonian cruelty to continue.

Emptying his net continues the picture of the Babylonian armies as fishermen from verses 14-16. Here they are described as taking the fish they have caught out of their net. The Dead Sea scroll is again one letter different from the traditional text and has "sword" instead of "net." This is followed by TEV with "**Are they going to use their swords**" (compare HOTTP, NAB, NEB, FrCL, GeCL). There is little difference in overall meaning between the two possibilities. The Dead Sea Scroll text gives in nonfigurative language the same sense that the traditional text gives in a figure of speech. The majority of modern versions (RSV, BJ, JB, TOB, NIV, NJV) follow the traditional text. This seems the best thing to do, since it is in keeping with the metaphor of the previous three verses.

The word translated **for ever** goes with the second half of the verse in the traditional Hebrew text as in RSV, but it goes with the first half in the Dead Sea Scroll, as in TEV. In a sense **for ever** goes with both halves of the verse anyway. Translators may place it in either half, according to the stylistic requirements of their language.

Slaying nations is expressed in more modern language by TEV as "destroying nations." **Mercilessly** means "without showing any pity."

Chapter 2

2.1-5

RSV

1 I will take my stand to watch,
  and station myself on the tower,
  and look forth to see what he will say to me,
  and what I will answer concerning my complaint.
2 And the LORD answered me:
  "Write the vision;
  make it plain upon tablets,
  so he may run who reads it.
3 For still the vision awaits its time;
  it hastens to the end—it will not lie.
  If it seem slow, wait for it;
  it will surely come, it will not delay.
4 Behold, he whose soul is not upright in him shall fail,
  but the righteous shall live by his faith.
5 Moreover, wine is treacherous;
  the arrogant man shall not abide.
  His greed is as wide as Sheol;
  like death he has never enough.
  He gathers for himself all nations,
  and collects as his own all peoples."

TEV
The LORD's Answer to Habakkuk

1 I will climb my watchtower and wait to see what the LORD will tell me to say and what answer he will give to my complaint. 2 The LORD gave me this answer: "Write down clearly on tablets what I reveal to you, so that it can be read at a glance. 3 Put it in writing, because it is not yet time for it to come true. But the time is coming quickly, and what I show you will come true. It may seem slow in coming, but wait for it; it will certainly take place, and it will not be delayed. 4 And this is the message: 'Those who are evil will not survive, but those who are righteous will live because they are faithful to God.'"

Doom on the Unrighteous

5 Wealth is deceitful. Greedy men are proud and restless—like death itself they are never satisfied. That is why they conquer nation after nation for themselves.

In these verses Habakkuk receives the Lord's second answer. The first verse describes his preparations for receiving the answer, and verses 2-5 give the answer itself. Verses 2 and 3 are introductory, with instructions for the prophet himself. The main part of the answer comes in verse 4. As for verse 5, it is not clear whether it should be paragraphed with verses 1-4, as in RSV and NIV, or with verses 6 and following, as in Mft, JB, TEV, and GeCL. Several versions do not have a paragraph break either before or after verse 5 (NAB, NEB, NJV, TOB, FrCL).

If verse 5 is taken with verses 1-4, it comes as rather an anticlimax after verse 4. On the other hand it does not form a particularly relevant introduction to the series of taunts against the wicked in verses 6-20. Since there are no conclusive arguments either way, we follow RSV as our base text and take verses 1-5 together.

SECTION HEADING: "**The LORD's Answer to Habakkuk**"; this heading may be translated as "The LORD replies to the prophet again" or "The LORD again answers the prophet's questions." This will balance the use of "again" in the section heading at 1.12.

The Lord's second answer

2.1 RSV | TEV

RSV	TEV
I will take my stand to watch, and station myself on the tower, and look forth to see what he will say to me, and what I will answer concerning my complaint.	I will climb my watchtower and wait to see what the LORD will tell me to say and what answer he[b] will give to my complaint. [b] *One ancient translation* he; *Hebrew* I.

The verse falls into two halves, each of which contains two statements which are parallel with each other. In the first half the two statements are **I will take my stand to watch** and **station myself on the tower**. Since the two parts are practically the same in meaning, TEV combines them into one as "**I will climb my watchtower**." Many translators will wish to follow this example. In saying "my watchtower" rather than **the tower**, TEV is following the Dead Sea Scroll text (compare FrCL, GeCL). The picture given is of a watchman climbing a tower in order to see a long way (compare 2 Sam 18.24; 2 Kgs 9.17). The prophets are often compared with watchmen elsewhere in the Old Testament (compare Isa 21.6-12; Jer 6.17; Ezek 3.17; 33.7; Micah 7.4). "My watchtower" may also be rendered as "The tower which I watch from" or "my look-out point." It is just possible that, in speaking of a watchtower, Habakkuk is speaking symbolically of waiting for a vision from God. However, it seems much more likely that he is speaking of a real watchtower (perhaps in a vineyard as in Isa 5.2; Mark 12.1), where he went to meditate.

In the second half of the verse, the parallelism is not quite as close in the Hebrew text. In the first statement Habakkuk says he will **look forth to see what he** (that is, the Lord) **will say to me**, but in the second statement he continues **and what I** (that is, the prophet himself) **will answer concerning my complaint**. **My complaint** refers to the questions raised by the prophet in 1.12-17. In the second statement the ancient Syriac translation has "what he (that is, the Lord) will answer." The Syriac seems to be based on a Hebrew text which differs from the traditional text by only one letter. It gives a better parallelism and is followed by JB, NAB, NJV, FrCL, and GeCL, as well as by TEV, which has "**What the LORD will tell me to say and what answer he will give to my complaint**." However, the traditional Hebrew text makes sense and is followed by NEB, NIV, and HOTTP. If the Hebrew text is followed, the idea is that the prophet will both wait for the Lord's answer and try to think out the problem for himself. On the whole it seems unnecessary to depart from the Hebrew text. If translators decide to follow the Hebrew text here, but wish to structure the last sentence in a way similar to TEV, they can say " . . . and what answer I will give to my complaint" or " . . . and how I will answer my criticism of the LORD." If, however, translators follow TEV's understanding of the text, one may say " . . . and how he will answer my criticism of him."

2.2 RSV | TEV

RSV	TEV
And the LORD answered me: "Write the vision;	The LORD gave me this answer: "Write down clearly on tablets what I

Hab 2.2

> make it plain upon tablets,
> so he may run who reads it.

> reveal to you, so that it can be read at a glance.

The opening words **And the LORD answered me** apply to the whole of the rest of verses 2-5 (RSV) or 2-4 (TEV). However, verses 2 and 3 contain only instructions on how to handle the message. The content of the message comes only in verse 4. The first instruction is that the prophet should **write the vision; make it plain upon tablets**. It is not often that the Old Testament records a direct command to a prophet to write his message (compare Isa 8.1; 30.8; Jer 30.2; Ezek 37.16).

For notes on the word translated **vision**, see the comments on Nahum 1.1. TEV here translates as **"what I reveal to you."** Another way of saying this is "the things I am about to tell you."

The word **tablets** does not indicate what they were made of. Clay, wood, metal, and stone are all possible. However, the word is used chiefly of the stone tablets on which the ten commandments were written (see for instance Exo 24.12). So if translators need to make a decision as to what material was involved, they may say "stone." The British edition of TEV has **"clay tablets."** Some languages have a special word for "writing" on a hard surface such as stone or clay. That word should be used here.

TEV combines the two clauses of this instruction into one: **"Write down clearly on tablets what I reveal to you."** Some translators may find it helpful to do the same. "What" in many languages will be rendered as "the things that."

The last clause says literally **so he may run who reads it**. In English this does not make clear the relationship between the verbs **run** and **read**. It may appear at first sight that the running is a result of the reading, a way of speedily obeying the message. This interpretation is found only in the NIV footnote, "so that whoever reads it may run with it." However, this seems unlikely, since the message itself does not contain any command to run. Another interpretation is that the person who reads the message reads it aloud as a professional herald, running from place to place to spread the message. This understanding is found in NEB, "for a herald to carry it with speed," and in NIV, "so that a herald may run with it." The majority of modern translations take the meaning to be "so that a man may run while reading." That is to say, the message is to be plain enough that one will not have to stop and peer at it, but can read it while still running. In this respect it would be like a large modern advertisement beside a main road. TEV expresses this interpretation well: **"so that it can be read at a glance."** Other ways of saying this are "so that it can be read easily" (NJV) or "so that one can read it easily" (NAB). This interpretation is the one recommended to translators.

2.3

RSV

> For still the vision awaits its time;
> it hastens to the end—it will not lie.
> If it seem slow, wait for it;
> it will surely come, it will not delay.

TEV

> Put it in writing, because it is not yet time for it to come true. But the time is coming quickly, and what I show you will come true. It may seem slow in coming, but wait for it; it will certainly take place, and it will not be delayed.

The Lord's second answer   Hab 2.4

After telling the prophet how to record and spread his message in verse 2, the Lord now adds a warning to him to be patient in looking for the fulfillment of it.

For indicates the relationship between this verse and the previous one. The message is to be written down because the time of its fulfillment has not yet come. TEV makes this explicit by saying "**Put it in writing, because . . . .**" In some languages this first clause may be expressed as "You must write this message down, because . . . ."

The reason is stated in RSV as **still the vision awaits its time** (better, "appointed time," as in RV, NIV). TEV expresses this much more clearly as "**it is not yet time for it to come true.**" Despite this the Lord reassures Habakkuk that the vision **hastens to the end—it will not lie**. The Hebrew word translated **hastens** can mean "to puff or pant." Thus NEB translates "it will come in breathless haste." TEV gives the meaning less vividly but more simply as "**But the time is coming quickly, and what I show you will come true.**" Note that here the negative statement **will not lie** is expressed in positive form as "**will come true.**" It may be helpful to some translators to follow this example.

The second half of the verse deals with impatience, the natural human reaction to delay: **If it seem slow, wait for it**. TEV has "**It may seem slow in coming, but wait for it.**" The word translated "wait" has overtones of hope, which are strengthened by the context here. Some languages cannot speak about "messages" or "words" coming in the sense of "happening." In such a case it may be better to translate "It may be slow in happening (occurring or coming to pass)" or "These things may be slow to happen (occur)."

The last line of the verse in effect repeats the assurance given in the second line: **it will surely come, it will not delay**. JB expresses this as "come it will, without fail." The word translated **delay** in RSV has the idea of being late, and so some versions say "it will not be late" (Mft, NAB). This may be a useful example for some translators to follow.

The last line of the verse is quoted in Hebrews 10.37, using the Septuagint translation.

An alternative translation model for this verse is:

> You must write down the things that I am showing to you, because it is not yet time for them to happen (come true). But the time is coming quickly when the things that I am showing to you will happen. Even though these things seem slow in happening, you must wait for them. They will certainly take place (occur) and will not be late.

2.4   RSV   TEV

Behold, he whose soul is not upright in him shall fail,[c] but the righteous shall live by his faith.[d]

And this is the message: 'Those who are evil will not survive,[c] but those who are righteous will live because they are faithful to God.' "

[c] Cn: Heb *is puffed up*
[d] Or *faithfulness*

[c] *Probable text* will not survive; Hebrew unclear.

Here at last the content of "the vision" referred to in verse 2 is given. It is introduced by a Hebrew word translated **Behold** in RSV. The function of this word is shown more clearly in TEV with **"And this is the message."** One may also say "Here is the message" or "This is what I want you to write."

The message itself consists of two statements, but unfortunately the first one is somewhat uncertain in meaning. Since the second statement is about **the righteous**, it is reasonable in a context like this to expect that the first statement will be in contrast to it, speaking about the wicked. Most translations fit this expectation, but the details of the statement remain uncertain.

The traditional Hebrew text is translated literally in RV as "his soul is puffed up, it is not upright in him." There is no noun for the pronouns "his" and "him" to refer to, but the general setting suggests that they refer to "the wicked" of 1.13, that is, the Babylonians. The expression "puffed up" in English usually means "full of pride" (as in TOB), and some versions have something similar to this (NAB "rash," NEB "reckless"). George Adam Smith translates "swollen, not level is his soul within him," and compares this with the everyday English expressions "swollen headed" (that is, proud of one's achievements) and "level headed" (that is, having a fair assessment of oneself and one's situation).

Some scholars prefer to change the order of two letters in one Hebrew word. This gives a translation like that of RSV, **he whose soul is not upright in him shall fail** (compare Mft, JB). **He whose soul** simply means "he." The **soul** stands for the whole person, as it often does in the Bible. TEV also accepts this change but expresses it in a clearer way as **"Those who are evil will not survive."** TEV uses the plural to express the general statement, and replaces the negative **not upright** with the single term "evil." This gives a balanced contrast with the second half of the verse, and translators are recommended to follow it. **Shall fail** ("Will not survive") may be expressed more simply as "will die."

The second statement, in its KJV form "the just shall live by his faith," is the best known text in the book of Habakkuk. RSV replaces "just" with **righteous**, which is less ambiguous (compare NEB, TEV, NIV, NJV). JB uses the more modern term "upright." In Habakkuk's time, to be "righteous" or "upright" meant to obey God's law and to treat other people fairly. So GeCL translates "whoever keeps faith with me and does what is right." A good summary of the conduct intended is given in Psalm 15. The **righteous** here are the people of Judah, or at least those of them who share Habakkuk's concerns. **Righteous** may be rendered as "good people," "straight people," "upright people," "people who obey (are loyal to) God," or even figuratively as "people with straight livers."

The word translated **faith** in RSV is more accurately "faithfulness" (RSV footnote, JB; compare **"faithful"** in Mft, NEB, TEV). This means being loyal to God and obedient to his law, even when outward circumstances make it difficult, as they did in Habakkuk's day. In modern speech we may perhaps use the word "integrity," though this does not have the religious overtones that "faithfulness" has.

TEV again uses the plural to express a general statement: **"those who are righteous."** TEV also makes the religious aspect explicit by saying **"because they are faithful to God."**

An alternative translation model for this verse is:

> This is what I want you to write: 'Those people who are evil will die, but the good people will live because they obey God (or, follow God faithfully).' "

The Lord's second answer   Hab 2.5

This verse is quoted three times in the New Testament (Rom 1.17; Gal 3.11; Heb 10.38) from its Septuagint translation. Paul makes it the basis for his doctrine of justification by faith, but in doing so he alters its meaning in two ways. First, the Greek word for "faith" does not have exactly the same components of meaning as the Hebrew word for "faithfulness." The Greek word has a stronger element of intellectual and emotional commitment and less ethical emphasis. This change of focus was caused by the very fact of translation rather than by Paul's deliberate choice. Secondly, Paul does deliberately link the words of Habakkuk together in a way different from that which Habakkuk intended. In linguistic terms, Paul uses a different immediate constituent analysis, that is, he sees a different set of semantic relationships between the words as they occur in the sentence. Whereas Habakkuk linked "by his faithfulness" with "shall live," Paul linked "by faith" with "the righteous." The contrast may be shown as "The righteous//shall live by faithfulness" (Habakkuk) as against "The righteous by faith//shall live" (Paul). In both the Hebrew and the Greek, the terms for "by faithfulness" or "by faith" come between "the righteous" and "shall live," and so the change in the analysis can be made more easily than appears from the English. (Compare RSV Rom 1.17, "He who through faith is righteous shall live," with TEV's restructuring, "The person who is put right with God through faith shall live.")

The translator of Habakkuk does not need to worry too much about Paul's theology. However, he does need to see what Paul has done, so that he can understand the difference between the meaning Habakkuk intended and the meaning Paul later drew from these words. Among Christians, Paul's teaching is much more familiar than Habakkuk's, and translators must therefore be careful not to translate in such a way that they make Habakkuk sound like Paul! Habakkuk's own meaning in its original context must be respected, and not changed to conform to the New Testament application of his words.

2.5

RSV	TEV
Moreover, wine is treacherous; the arrogant man shall not abide.[e] His greed is as wide as Sheol; like death he has never enough. He gathers for himself all nations, and collects as his own all peoples."	Wealth is deceitful. Greedy men are proud and restless—like death itself they are never satisfied. That is why they conquer nation after nation for themselves.

[e] The Hebrew of these two lines is obscure.

For the paragraph division, see the introduction to this section. RSV includes verse 5 as part of "the vision" mentioned in verses 2 and 3. It should be noted that TEV closes the quotation at the end of verse 4, but RSV includes verse 5 as part of the quotation. Either arrangement is possible.

As the RSV footnote shows, the traditional Hebrew text in the first two lines is hard to understand. The reference to **wine** seems to be completely out of place. Some scholars make a small change which gives the meaning "the traitor in his over-confidence" (NEB) or "he who boasts of being a traitor" (HOTTP). This seems to fit fairly well with the rest of the verse, understood as speaking about the Babylonians.

The Dead Sea Scroll has a word meaning "wealth" instead of the one meaning "wine." This possibility is followed by BJ, JB, NAB, FrCL, and TEV, which says "**Wealth is deceitful.**" This also fits a description of the Babylonians and probably gives the best sense available; translators are recommended to accept it. "Deceitful" here means "untrustworthy" or "something that one cannot put one's trust in."

The arrogant man shall not abide: this also speaks about the Babylonians. Some translators take this line more closely with the line that follows (**His greed is as wide as Sheol**). TEV combines the first two lines of this verse into one clause, saying "Greedy men are proud and restless." "Proud" is the TEV equivalent of **arrogant**, and "restless" is the TEV equivalent of **shall not abide**. This expression TEV takes to mean "shall not remain still or at rest," hence "restless." Compare JB "unable to rest"; NIV "never at rest."

His greed is as wide as Sheol: **Sheol** is the place where the dead were pictured as continuing their existence. It is spoken of as if it were an animal with a huge appetite. The **greed** of the Babylonians is compared with the greed of **Sheol**. In the next line, **like death he has never enough**, the meaning is almost identical. TEV combines these two lines into one with "**like death itself they are never satisfied.**" In some languages one may prefer to say "like the land of death." If translators can speak of death as being like a greedy animal, they may be able to keep the picture used in Hebrew, but in many languages it will probably be necessary to use nonfigurative language, as TEV has done. For a similar thought compare Isaiah 5.14.

In the last two lines (**he gathers for himself all nations, and collects as his own all peoples**) the application is made to the Babylonians. Just as **death** is never satisfied and is constantly taking more people, so the Babylonians are greedy for wealth and are constantly trying to conquer more nations. The fifth and sixth lines in RSV are again parallel in meaning, and again TEV combines them into one clause: "**That is why they conquer nation after nation for themselves.**"

2.6-20

RSV	TEV
6 Shall not all these take up their taunt against him, in scoffing derision of him, and say, "Woe to him who heaps up what is not his own— for how long?— and loads himself with pledges!" 7 Will not your debtors suddenly arise, and those awake who will make you tremble? Then you will be booty for them. 8 Because you have plundered many nations, all the remnant of the peoples shall plunder you, for the blood of men and violence to the	6 The conquered people will taunt their conquerors and show their scorn for them. They will say, "You take what isn't yours, but you are doomed! How long will you go on getting rich by forcing your debtors to pay up?" 7 But before you know it, you that have conquered others will be in debt yourselves and be forced to pay interest. Enemies will come and make you tremble. They will plunder you! 8 You have plundered the people of many nations, but now those who have survived will plunder you because of the murders you have committed and because of your violence against the people of the world and its cities. 9 You are doomed! You have made your

The first taunt Hab 2.6-20

earth,
to cities and all who dwell therein.
9 Woe to him who gets evil gain for his house,
to set his nest on high,
to be safe from the reach of harm!
10 You have devised shame to your house
by cutting off many peoples;
you have forfeited your life.
11 For the stone will cry out from the wall,
and the beam from the woodwork respond.
12 Woe to him who builds a town with blood,
and founds a city on iniquity!
13 Behold, is it not from the LORD of hosts
that peoples labor only for fire,
and nations weary themselves for nought?
14 For the earth will be filled
with the knowledge of the glory of the LORD,
as the waters cover the sea.
15 Woe to him who makes his neighbors drink
of the cup of his wrath, and makes them drunk,
to gaze on their shame!
16 You will be sated with contempt instead of glory.
Drink, yourself, and stagger!
The cup in the LORD's right hand
will come around to you,
and shame will come upon your glory!
17 The violence done to Lebanon will overwhelm you;
the destruction of the beasts will terrify you,
for the blood of men and violence to the earth,
to cities and all who dwell therein.
18 What profit is an idol
when its maker has shaped it,
a metal image, a teacher of lies?
For the workman trusts in his own creation
when he makes dumb idols!
19 Woe to him who says to a wooden thing, Awake;
to a dumb stone, Arise!
Can this give revelation?
Behold, it is overlaid with gold and silver,
and there is no breath at all in it.
20 But the LORD is in his holy temple;
let all the earth keep silence before him.

family rich with what you took by violence, and have tried to make your own home safe from harm and danger! 10 But your schemes have brought shame on your family; by destroying many nations you have only brought ruin on yourself. 11 Even the stones of the walls cry out against you, and the rafters echo the cry.

12 You are doomed! You founded a city on crime and built it up by murder. 13 The nations you conquered wore themselves out in useless labor, and all they have built goes up in flames. The LORD Almighty has done this. 14 But the earth will be as full of the knowledge of the LORD's glory as the seas are full of water.

15 You are doomed! In your fury you humiliated and disgraced your neighbors; you made them stagger as though they were drunk. 16 You in turn will be covered with shame instead of honor. You yourself will drink and stagger. The LORD will make you drink your own cup of punishment, and your honor will be turned to disgrace. 17 You have cut down the forests of Lebanon; now you will be cut down. You killed its animals; now animals will terrify you. This will happen because of the murders you have committed and because of your violence against the people of the world and its cities.

18 What's the use of an idol? It is only something that a man has made, and it tells you nothing but lies. What good does it do for its maker to trust it—a god that can't even talk! 19 You are doomed! You say to a piece of wood, "Wake up!" or to a block of stone, "Get up!" Can an idol reveal anything to you? It may be covered with silver and gold, but there is no life in it.

20 The LORD is in his holy Temple; let everyone on earth be silent in his presence.

This section consists of a series of five taunts against the wicked (compare Isa 5.8,11,18,20,22). In this context the wicked are best understood as the Babylonians, though some scholars think they are either the Assyrians or the corrupt leaders of Judah in the days of King Jehoiakim. The main subjects of the taunts are as follows: greed for wealth (6-8); extravagant private building (9-11); extravagant public building (12-14); misuse of liquor (15-17); and idol worship

Hab 2.6-20 — TAUNTS AGAINST THE WICKED

(18-20). Each taunt begins with the word **Woe** except the last, where the **Woe** comes in the middle (verse 19). The theme throughout is that those who do evil will themselves eventually be punished in a manner that fits their offense.

SECTION HEADING: in TEV the heading for this section is placed before verse 5 rather than before verse 6. Whichever place is preferred, the heading will have much the same content. The phrase in TEV, "**Doom on the Unrighteous**," may need to be expanded in many languages into a full sentence. One may say "Habakkuk promises that the wicked will be punished" or "Habakkuk promises that God will punish the wicked." If these are too long, "God will punish the wicked" or "God will punish people who do evil" will be sufficient.

2.6 RSV	TEV
Shall not all these take up their taunt against him, in scoffing derision of him, and say, "Woe to him who heaps up what is not his own— for how long?— and loads himself with pledges!"	The conquered people will taunt their conquerors and show their scorn for them. They will say, "You take what isn't yours, but you are doomed! How long will you go on getting rich by forcing your debtors to pay up?"

The first part of verse 6 introduces the whole series of taunts, and the first taunt proper does not begin until the second half of the verse. The first part of the verse has the grammatical form of a negative question (see RSV). This is a rhetorical question and is really a way of making a strong positive statement. TEV therefore translates as a statement, and many translators will wish to do the same.

The grammatical subject of the introduction in RSV is **all these**, which refers back to "all nations" and "all peoples" of verse 5. TEV makes this explicit by translating as "**The conquered people**." In similar manner the grammatical object **him** refers back to "the arrogant man" of verse 5. TEV again makes this explicit by translating as "**their conquerors**." In many cases translators will do well to follow the example of TEV in translating the subject and object as nouns rather than pronouns, especially if verse 6 is treated as the beginning of a new section. But in certain languages which do not use the passive, it will be necessary to say "The people who received defeat . . . " instead of "the conquered people . . . ."

The peoples whom the Babylonians had conquered will **take up their taunt** against them. The implication is that the situation of Habakkuk's own day will be reversed, and that the oppressed nations will then be in a position to repay the Babylonians for their cruelty. **Take up** may be translated as "begin."

The Hebrew word translated **taunt** here is a term with a wide range of meaning, including likeness, parable, proverb, and lament. In this context, where **scoffing** is involved, **taunt** seems the most appropriate term in English (compare Isa 14.4; Micah 2.4). In some languages there may be a specific term for this, and if so it will probably fit well here.

The Hebrew contains two more terms which help to define the meaning of **taunt** as related to mockery in this setting. RSV translates them as **in scoffing derision**, and TEV as "**show their scorn**." The Hebrew implies that the mockery

The first taunt Hab 2.6

will take the form of a brief poem or riddle, such as the second half of verse 6 is. Again, some languages may have a particular term for this.

An alternative translation model for the first part of this verse is:

The people whose lands the Babylonians have taken by force will begin to mock them and show how much they despise them, saying . . .

The second half of the verse gives the content of what the conquered people say. This opens with the words **Woe to . . .** , which also appear in the other four taunts which follow. This expression is not a wish that evil may come upon the person addressed but rather an assertion that it will come. Thus TEV translates with the statement "**you are doomed**," changing from third person to second. In languages which do not use the passive, one may say "God is going to punish you" or "You will receive punishment from God." In most of the other taunts, TEV puts these words at the beginning of the taunt, but here, because the Hebrew construction is rather awkward, TEV changes the order and puts these words later. However, TEV's use of the word "**but**" here does not seem to fit the context. The meaning of the Hebrew seems to be that the Babylonians will be punished because they have done these things. Therefore it will be more natural to translate "Because you take what isn't yours, God will punish you" or "You take what isn't yours, so God will punish you."

RSV follows the Hebrew literally—a statement in two parts with a question between them. The content of the statement is expressed in two relative clauses, **who heaps up what is not his own** and **loads himself with pledges**. TEV puts this information into two separate sentences, and links the first with the **Woe . . .** and the second with the question **how long?** TEV also changes from the third person of the Hebrew (and RSV) to a direct address in the second person. This adds vividness in English.

Thus the first sentence in TEV becomes "**You take what isn't yours, but you are doomed!**" The Hebrew refers to heaping up stolen goods, so an alternative translation model is "You take (or, seize) great quantities of things which don't belong to you, so God is going to punish you."

The question **for how long?** really applies to the whole statement, but in translation it can just as well be placed with one half or the other.

The second relative clause, **and loads himself with pledges**, may be difficult to understand. When a rich man lent money, the borrower would give him something as a guarantee of repayment. This was called a pledge. If the money was not repaid, the lender kept the pledge.

There are two ways in which the reference to **pledges** may be understood here. The first is that when the Babylonians took other people's goods by conquest, they could be thought of as borrowers giving pledges that the goods would eventually be returned. When the situation goes against the Babylonians, the other nations will hold these pledges against them and require the return of their goods. This view is shown in the translations of Mft ("loading himself with what he must repay"), NAB ("he loads himself down with debts"), and NJV ("make ever heavier your load of indebtedness").

The second possibility is to see the Babylonians as seizing pledges from their victims, and then either keeping the pledges or making their victims pay what they did not really owe. In this way they extorted goods wrongfully from those they conquered. This view is shown in NEB ("enrich yourself with goods taken in pledge"), NIV ("makes himself wealthy by extortion"), and TEV ("**getting rich by forcing your debtors to pay up**"). This second interpretation seems to be the more likely in a context which is complaining about the oppressive behavior of the Babylonians, and translators are recommended to follow it.

TEV combines the question **for how long?** with the clause about the pledges and says "**How long will you go on getting rich by forcing your debtors to pay up?**" In some cultures which do not have a technical term for "debtors," the clause "forcing your debtors to pay up" may be rendered as "forcing those who owe you money to pay it back" or "forcing those who have borrowed money from you to pay it back."

The direct quotation of the victims' words is generally taken to end at the end of verse 6. It is also possible to take the direct quotation as extending to the end of verse 8, or perhaps even verse 20. This may be the intention of JB, NAB, NJV, and TOB. However, the absence of quotation marks from these versions leaves their intention uncertain. The versions which use quotation marks all close them at the end of verse 6 (RSV, NEB, TEV, NIV). In this case the following verses are to be understood as the words of Habakkuk. Translators are recommended to follow this interpretation. GeCL closes the quotation at the end of verse 17, but this does not seem very satisfactory.

An alternative translation model for the final part of this verse is:

> They will say to the Babylonians, "You take great quantities of things that don't belong to you, so God is going to punish you. How long will you continue making yourselves rich by forcing those who owe you money to pay it back (or, pay back more than they owe)?"

2.7

RSV	TEV
Will not your debtors suddenly arise, and those awake who will make you tremble? Then you will be booty for them.	But before you know it, you that have conquered others will be in debt yourselves and be forced to pay interest. Enemies will come and make you tremble. They will plunder you!

As in verse 6, the Hebrew here has the form of a rhetorical negative question, which RSV retains. The purpose of the question is really to make an emphatic statement, and so TEV translates as a statement and breaks the verse into three sentences.

The word translated **debtors** in RSV means literally "biters." The word "to bite" also means "to pay interest," that is, to be a debtor. Here there is a play on the double meaning: those who have paid interest on unjust debts will turn and "bite" those who oppressed them, that is, take vengeance on them.

A number of versions (JB, NAB, NEB, TEV, NJV, TOB, FrCL) interpret "biters" as "creditors" rather than "debtors." This understands "bite" in the financial sense as "receive interest" rather than "pay interest." Such an understanding fits with the first possible interpretation of "pledges" discussed in verse 6 (see NAB and NJV). However, some versions which take the second interpreta-

The first taunt Hab 2.8

tion of "pledges" in verse 6 interpret "biters" as "creditors" here (see NEB and TEV "**you . . . will be in debt yourselves**"). This seems rather inconsistent. Moreover, as Driver points out in his commentary, the verb "to bite" in the tense in which it occurs here means only "to pay interest." The meaning "to receive interest" would require a different tense, as found for instance in Deuteronomy 23.20. We therefore conclude that "debtors" (as in RSV and NIV) is the more probable meaning here. (See discussion on "debtors" in verse 6.)

Whichever interpretation is adopted, it is very likely that the play on the word "bite" will be lost in other languages. Word plays can rarely be translated, and their loss has to be accepted. In this case the loss is not a major one, and it is not necessary to include a footnote to explain it.

The word translated <u>suddenly</u> in RSV is rendered as "**Before you know it**" in TEV. The rest of the sentence in TEV, "**you that have conquered others will be in debt yourselves and be forced to pay interest**," seems to be more expanded than is really necessary. If the interpretation preferred above is accepted, a translation model may be "those whose money you have taken will suddenly stand against you" or "those . . . will suddenly take vengeance on you."

In the second clause of RSV, the verb <u>awake</u> is parallel with the verb <u>arise</u> in the first clause. One can continue the translation model suggested above as "they will rouse themselves and make you tremble with fear" or " . . . and cause you to be so afraid that you tremble." See 1.7 for other ways to translate "tremble with fear."

The final clause, **Then you will be booty for them**, is translated in more natural English in TEV as "**They will plunder you!**" Another possible translation is "They will take your possessions by force" (see Nahum 2.2,9 for comments on "plunder").

2.8 RSV TEV

> Because you have plundered many nations,
> all the remnant of the peoples shall plunder you,
> for the blood of men and violence to the earth,
> to cities and all who dwell therein.

> You have plundered the people of many nations, but now those who have survived will plunder you because of the murders you have committed and because of your violence against the people of the world and its cities.[d]
>
> [d] the people . . . cities; *or* the land, the city, and those who live in it.

In this verse more details are given of the punishment that is to come upon the Babylonians. As they have greedily robbed other nations, so they in turn will be robbed. The punishment will fit the crime.

Both RSV and TEV treat the whole verse as one sentence, but many translators will find it more natural to break it into two sentences, as NIV has done.

The first two clauses in RSV state the fairness of the punishment: <u>Because you have plundered many nations, all the remnant of the peoples shall plunder you</u>. (Compare Isa 33.1.) TEV makes it explicit that **many nations** means "the people of many nations." TEV also makes it clear that <u>all the remnant of the</u>

peoples means "those who have survived" the cruelties of the Babylonians. "Those who have survived" may also be phrased as "Those who did not die."

The second half of the verse may well be translated as a separate sentence, especially since it is repeated in verse 17. One can show the relationship with the first half of the verse by beginning "This will happen because . . . ."

The blood of men in RSV is made clearer in TEV as "**the murders you have committed.**" In a similar way **violence** in RSV can be expanded to "the violence you have done." In some languages translators may need to render these two clauses as "This will happen because of all the people you have killed, and because of your cruel acts against . . . " (see 1.2 for comment on **violence**).

Those who suffered the violence of the Babylonians are stated as **the earth . . . cities and all who dwell therein**. This is not very natural English, and so TEV has expressed it in a smoother way as "**the people of the world and its cities.**" Both "the people" and the "cities" had been harmed by the Babylonian attacks. "City" here refers to a large group of houses surrounded by a strong wall (see Nahum 3.1).

The Hebrew word translated as **the earth** in RSV and "the world" in TEV may also mean "the land," as in the TEV footnote. The translation in the footnote, "the land, the city, and those who live in it," refers primarily to the land of Judah and the city of Jerusalem. However, although the words for "land" and "city" are singular in Hebrew, it seems more probable in this context that they are collective in meaning. (Compare NIV "lands and cities.") Many other countries besides Judah were attacked by the Babylonians. The translation in the text of TEV is therefore to be preferred.

An alternative translation model for this verse is:

> You have taken by force the possessions of the people of many nations, but now those who are still alive will take your possessions by force. This will happen because you have killed many people and have acted so cruelly against the people of the world and its cities.

2.9

RSV	TEV
Woe to him who gets evil gain for his house, to set his nest on high, to be safe from the reach of harm!	You are doomed! You have made your family rich with what you took by violence, and have tried to make your own home safe from harm and danger!

The second taunt begins here. As with the first one, it begins in the third person in Hebrew, **Woe to him . . .** , then changes to the second person. To avoid this change, which is rather awkward in English, TEV has used the second person throughout, starting off with "**You are doomed!**" For other ways to translate **Woe** or "doomed," see verse 6.

Him who gets evil gain for his house means people who enrich their families by unfair means. TEV states it even more explicitly as "**You have made your family rich with what you took by violence.**" We may note here that the Hebrew word for house may mean either the building or the people who live in it, the family. In this setting there seems to be a play on this double meaning. It is of

The second taunt Hab 2.10

course the people rather than the building who benefit and grow wealthy from the **evil gain**, and this is why TEV translates as "**your family**." But one of the main ways in which people showed their wealth was by building luxurious houses. In verse 11 the prophet refers to the literal parts of buildings, showing that he has had both meanings of "house" in mind. Some languages may be like Hebrew in using the word "house" with this double meaning. If so, they will be able to show the full sense of the Hebrew better than English can. However, many languages will not be able to do this, and in such languages it will be better to translate "house" as "family" here. **Gets evil gain** (TEV's "**What you took by violence**") may be rendered as "all the things you took from others by force (or, by cheating)."

The second line, **to set his nest on high**, continues the double meaning but uses a metaphor. A **nest** is the home of a bird, and a person's home can be spoken of figuratively as a nest. A bird which sets **his nest on high** builds the nest high in the mountains, where people cannot get at it. This is particularly true of eagles. But such birds are also a symbol of power and pride, and when a person is spoken of as building a **nest on high**, it implies that the person is showing pride and arrogance and will be punished. This picture is used several times in the Old Testament (see Num 24.21; Jer 49.16; Obadiah 4).

The purpose of building a **nest on high** is **to be safe from the reach of harm**. This suggests that Habakkuk also has in mind the literal building of homes in places where they can easily be fortified and defended from enemies.

It is very unlikely that the wording of this verse, if translated literally, would have in any other language all the associations which it has in Hebrew. This means that there is bound to be some loss in translation—not so much a loss of meaning as what we may call a loss of resonance. TEV has accepted this and has translated in such a way as to keep as much of the basic meaning as possible. TEV has combined the second and third lines of RSV into one clause: "**you ... have tried to make your own home safe from harm and danger.**" A possible translation model for the whole verse is:

> God is going to punish you! You made your family rich with all the things you took from others by force, and you have built luxurious and secure homes to try to protect your family from harm.

Another model is:

> You have made your family rich with the things you took from other people by force. You have built luxurious and secure homes to try to protect your family from harm. Because you have done all this, God will punish you.

2.10   RSV   TEV

You have devised shame to your house by cutting off many peoples; you have forfeited your life. | But your schemes have brought shame on your family; by destroying many nations you have only brought ruin on yourself.

The Babylonians planned to find security for themselves, but instead they will get **shame**. TEV has "**your schemes have brought shame on your family**." The word "schemes" is a good choice here in English because it often carries overtones of dishonesty which fit this context well. "Brought shame" in many languages can be translated as an idiom; for example, "caused . . . to lose face." The first sentence may then be rendered "But your schemes have caused your family to lose face."

In RSV the second line, **by cutting off many peoples**, is taken closely with the first line (compare Mft, NEB). TEV follows the punctuation of the Hebrew text and takes the second line more closely with the third: "**by destroying many nations you have only brought ruin on yourself**." This gives a cause—effect relationship between the conduct of the Babylonians towards others, and their own eventual destruction. This is very appropriate to the theme of just punishment, which is prominent in this section.

The expression **cutting off (many peoples)** is a very common Hebrew metaphor. It simply means "destroying," as TEV states in nonfigurative language. In some languages it will be possible to use some other metaphor which is natural in the language. In English, for instance, we can say "wiping out many nations" (compare Zeph 3.6 in TEV). In some languages "eating many nations" or "swallowing many nations" may be more suitable.

Because of their cruel treatment of others, the Babylonians **have forfeited** their own lives and will suffer God's punishment in due time (compare TEV "**you have only brought ruin on yourself**"). An alternative translation, then, is "you have made sure that you yourselves will be killed."

2.11	RSV	TEV
	For the stone will cry out from the wall, and the beam from the woodwork respond.	Even the stones of the walls cry out against you, and the rafters echo the cry.

Habakkuk here pictures the stone and wood of the rich houses which the Babylonians had built as speaking out against them. It is as if these materials were witnesses of the cruelty and oppression of the people who built with them.

For the stone will cry out from the wall: TEV puts this into a more natural order as "**Even the stones of the walls cry out against you**." "Cry out against you" may be translated in some languages as "cry out accusing you" or "accuse you with a loud voice."

And the beam from the woodwork respond: TEV uses the technical term "rafters" in place of **the beam from the woodwork**. TEV also translates **respond** with the expression "echo the cry," which has a stronger emotive impact.

We may note that Babylonian houses were usually built with brick rather than stone, and the prophet is describing Babylonian homes in terms of the building materials he was familiar with in Palestine. In a similar way some translators may have to speak of building materials in common use in their own areas, such as clay and wood, or wood and thatch, rather than trying to describe "rafters." So a possible alternative translation model is "and the wood (thatch, clay) in the roof cries back (echoes the cry)."

The third taunt Hab 2.13

In some languages it may not be possible to speak of building materials crying out like people. In such cases it may be possible to make the figure of speech into a simile and say "It will be as if even the stones and woodwork of your houses bore witness to your evil deeds."

2.12

RSV	TEV
Woe to him who builds a town with blood, and founds a city on iniquity!	You are doomed! You founded a city on crime and built it up by murder.

The third taunt begins here. Some scholars regard verses 12-14 as the very words of the stone and the beam mentioned in verse 11. However, no major translation treats them in this way, and it seems better to regard them as simply the next taunt in the series. See verse 6 for an alternative way to translate **Woe** or "**doomed.**"

In this case the whole taunt is in the third person, but TEV expresses it in the second person to show the relationship with the other taunts in the series.

The words of verse 12 are similar to those of Micah 3.10. The building of cities, rather than private homes, refers to official government projects rather than the work of individual citizens. A literal translation may make it sound as if **blood** and **iniquity** were building materials. In fact, **blood** stands for "bloodshed" (Mft, NAB, NEB, NIV) or "murder" (TEV), and **iniquity** stands for "crime" (TEV, Mft, JB, NIV). These were the means by which people became rich enough to build houses.

There are two things to note about the TEV rendering "**You founded a city on crime and built it up by murder.**" First, TEV has reversed the order of the clauses. This is because logically it makes more sense to speak of the foundations before the buildings which are erected upon them. Many translators will find it helpful to do the same.

Second, TEV has not completely avoided the possibility that "**crime**" and "**murder**" could be mistaken as building materials. In some languages it may be necessary to make the translation longer in order to be clear. A possible translation base is "You have committed crimes in order to get the power to found your city. You have committed murder in order to make men build your city." In this context "crimes" means "violent deeds," or in some languages it can be expressed in a way similar to RSV, as "bloody deeds."

"Crime" (or **iniquity** in RSV) refers to the general way in which the Babylonians treated other nations. "Murder" (or **blood** in RSV) may be a reference to warfare and conquest, but more likely it refers to the use of conquered peoples as slave labor on building projects. This was a common practice in ancient times, and the slaves were sometimes treated so badly that they died.

2.13

RSV	TEV
Behold, is it not from the LORD of hosts that peoples labor only for fire,	The nations you conquered wore themselves out in useless labor, and all they have built goes up in flames. The LORD Almighty has done this.

Hab 2.13

      **and nations weary themselves
for nought?**

Once again, the Hebrew has the form of a rhetorical negative question which has the force of a strong positive statement (compare verses 6, 7). TEV turns it into a statement and breaks it into two sentences. See the notes on 1.2,12 for comments on rhetorical questions.

The word **Behold** is old fashioned and has no exact equivalent in modern English (compare comments on verse 4). Its function is to draw attention to what follows (**is it not from the LORD of hosts?**). This function is achieved in TEV by placing the equivalent words, "The LORD Almighty has done this," as a separate sentence at the end of the verse. For comments on the translation of **Behold** and the phrase **the LORD of hosts**, see the notes on Nahum 2.13.

The rest of the verse consists of two lines which are parallel with each other in both form and meaning: **peoples labor only for fire and nations weary themselves for nought**. Two similar lines occur in Jeremiah 51.58, which is also speaking about Babylon. It is possible that both Jeremiah and Habakkuk are quoting or alluding to a popular proverb or saying.

The **peoples** and **nations** are those whom the Babylonians had conquered and put to forced labor as mentioned in the previous verse. Thus TEV puts the two terms together and translates as "The nations you conquered."

Labor only for fire means that all that the people were forced to build will be destroyed by burning. **Weary themselves for nought** means that they became exhausted with their work, but all they did would turn out to be purposeless. The first line, which mentions the fire, gives more of an explanation than the second line, and so TEV reverses the sequence in order to keep the fire as a climax: "**The nations you conquered wore themselves out in useless labor, and all they have built goes up in flames.**" Note that TEV makes it explicit that the "**labor**" refers to the building project ("**all they have built**"). The thought is that, as the Babylonians had destroyed other cities, so Babylon itself will be destroyed and burned.

The expression in TEV "**goes up in flames**" is rather idiomatic in English. In some languages there may be some natural expression equally vivid, but in others it may be necessary to use plain language and say "all they have built will be burned to ashes" or "completely burned."

Another translation model for this verse is:

    The nations you conquered did work which gained them nothing.
    They wore themselves out, but all the things which they built will
    be completely burned. It is the LORD Almighty who does this.

2.14   RSV   TEV

For the earth will be filled with the knowledge of the glory of the LORD, as the waters cover the sea.	But the earth will be as full of the knowledge of the LORD's glory as the seas are full of water.

This verse is very similar in thought to Isaiah 11.9, though the wording is not exactly the same. It was the Lord's will to destroy the building work of verse

The fourth taunt   Hab 2.15

13, but in contrast, here is a description of the lasting purpose of God: the earth will eventually <u>be filled with the knowledge of the glory of the Lord</u> (compare Num 14.21). <u>Knowledge</u> here means "understanding of and reverence for." <u>Glory</u> in this context refers to the "power and greatness of God."

The expression <u>the waters cover the sea</u> sounds rather odd in English. It is more natural to speak of the water filling the sea, or as TEV expresses it, the sea being "**full of water.**" In Hebrew, different words are used for <u>filled</u> and <u>cover</u>, but in English, the repeated use of the root "fill" helps to bring out the comparison between the two halves of the verse. TEV does this well with "**the earth will be as full of the knowledge of the Lord's glory as the seas are full of water.**"

Alternative translation models for this verse are "But the people of the earth will be full of knowledge about the power and greatness of the Lord, just as the seas are full of water" or "Just as the seas are full of water, so the people of the earth will . . . ." In languages in which it is difficult to speak about people being "full of knowledge," one may say "Just as the sea has a vast amount of water, so the people of the earth will have a vast amount of knowledge about the power and greatness of the Lord."

2.15   RSV   TEV

> Woe to him who makes his neighbors drink of the cup of his wrath,[f] and makes them drunk, to gaze on their shame!

> You are doomed! In your fury you humiliated and disgraced your neighbors; you made them stagger as though they were drunk.

[f] Cn: Heb *joining to your wrath*

This is where the fourth taunt begins. As with the first and second taunts (verses 6, 9), it starts in the third person and changes to second. TEV, as in the earlier cases, treats it as second person throughout. The topic in this taunt is the misuse of liquor, which is given a figurative application. The Babylonians were fond of drinking, and their parties could easily turn into shameful orgies (compare Dan 5). In verse 15 the Babylonian treatment of conquered nations is pictured in terms of such an orgy.

<u>Woe to him who makes his neighbors drink</u>: the <u>neighbors</u> stand for the surrounding nations whom the Babylonians conquered. Their forced obedience to the Babylonians is pictured as if they were forced to drink. In some languages a literal translation of <u>neighbors</u> may give the wrong meaning. In such a case it will be helpful to translate explicitly and say "the neighboring countries." For an alternative rendering of <u>Woe</u> (or "doomed"), see verse 6.

The next two words in Hebrew are of uncertain meaning. The first word may mean "pour" (RV footnote, NIV, NJV; compare NAB, NEB) or "add" (RV). The second word has a basic sense of heat, which leads to figurative meanings of either "anger, wrath" (Mft, RSV, NAB, NEB, TEV, NJV, GeCL) or "poison, venom" (RV, BJ, JB, TOB, FrCL). The second word may also be taken as coming from a different root with the meaning "wineskin" (NIV; compare KJV). The first of these two Hebrew words ends with the same letter as the second word begins with. Some scholars think this letter appears twice by a copying error, and they have suggested that it should be dropped from the end of the first word. This suggestion is followed by RSV and gives **(drink) of the cup of his wrath**, which fits the context well. Of the other possible combinations, most are used in at least one version: "addest thy venom" (RV; compare HOTTP); "pours his poison" (JB); "you pour out your wrath" (NJV; compare NAB, NEB); "pouring it from the wineskin" (NIV). All make reasonable sense in the context, but none is outstanding. Whichever one is chosen, the overall thrust of the verse remains broadly similar. We are inclined to recommend the RSV rendering as giving the best sense, and one which matches both the figure which follows in verse 16, and Old Testament usage elsewhere. As a second choice we suggest the NIV interpretation.

The result of forcing drink upon others is that he (that is, the Babylonians) **makes them drunk** or "causes them to get drunk."

The purpose of all this is **to gaze on their shame**. The word translated **shame** is literally "nakedness" (KJV, RV, JB, NAB, NJV). When people are drunk, they lose control of themselves and may expose their sexual organs, as Noah did (Gen 9.20-23; compare the story of Lot in Gen 19.30-38). This was regarded as a great disgrace. The Babylonians made people drunk in order to disgrace them in this way. TEV does not mention the nakedness but only the disgrace which it represents.

The Dead Sea scroll has a word meaning "festivals" instead of the one meaning "nakedness," but this does not make much sense and is not used in any translations.

TEV has completely restructured the verse so that it is difficult to see exactly how its parts match up with the more literal renderings of RSV. In particular the clause **"you made them stagger"** has no clear basis in the Hebrew, and no parallel in FrCL or GeCL. For this reason we cannot recommend TEV as a model in this verse. If a restructured translation base is needed, one possibility is "You are doomed! You made neighboring nations drink from the cup of wine which represents your anger. You made them drunk, then disgraced them by gazing at their naked bodies." Another possibility is "God will punish you! You made neighboring nations drink from the cup of wine which represents your anger. You made them drunk, then caused them to lose face by gazing at their naked bodies." If the last part of the verse is hard to understand when the metaphor is retained, translators may prefer to follow the example of GeCL and state the meaning in nonfigurative language. One may say "you rejoiced to see them in a powerless and shameful condition."

2.16

RSV	TEV
You will be sated with contempt instead of glory. Drink, yourself, and stagger![g] **The cup in the Lord's right hand will come around to you, and shame will come upon your glory!**	You in turn will be covered with shame instead of honor. You yourself will drink and stagger. The Lord will make you drink your own cup of punishment, and your honor will be turned to disgrace.

[g] Cn Compare Gk Syr: Heb *be uncircumcised*

The fourth taunt Hab 2.16

In keeping with the general outlook of the taunts, this verse speaks of the Babylonians being treated by God as they have treated others. The picture of drinking is continued in the description of this punishment.

The opening words **You will be sated with contempt instead of glory** keep up the picture only in the verb **sated**. JB makes this more explicit by saying "You are drunk with ignominy, not with glory." Other versions tone down the figure and say "filled with shame instead of glory" (NAB, NIV). TEV drops this figure, but instead uses a different one and says **"You in turn will be covered with shame instead of honor."** If figurative language is to be kept at all here, it seems best to make it fit with the larger figure used throughout verses 15 and 16. For this reason "filled with shame" seems better than **"covered with shame."** In some languages it may be necessary to drop the figure altogether and say "You will be disgraced instead of honored," or "People will not honor you, but will disgrace you," or " . . . cause you to receive great shame," or even " . . . cause you to lose face very much." **Glory** or **"honor"** here refers to reputation rather than to power and greatness as in verse 14.

Drink, yourself, and stagger! is a command to the Babylonians to suffer as they had made others suffer. The translation **stagger** in RSV (compare Mft, NAB, NEB, TEV, NJV) is based on the Septuagint and other ancient versions, supported by the Dead Sea Scroll. The Hebrew word in this Scroll has the same letters as the word in the traditional Hebrew text but in a different order. The traditional word means "to be uncircumcised" or "to show the foreskin" (compare KJV, RV, BJ, JB, TOB). The Babylonians did not practice circumcision. The Jews looked down on nations who were uncircumcised, and also regarded exposure of the sexual organs as disgraceful. It was therefore doubly shameful to be so drunk that one's organs were exposed, and one's lack of circumcision made obvious.

It is difficult to choose between these two possibilities. The mention of staggering fits well with the description of drunkenness and occurs in similar passages elsewhere in the Old Testament (see Psa 60.3; Isa 51.17, 22; Jer 25.15, 16; Zech 12.2). But exposure of the sexual organs fits with the reference in verse 15, and is also mentioned in connection with both drunkenness (Lam 4.21) and punishment (Nahum 3.5). On the whole it seems best to follow the traditional Hebrew text and speak of exposure (compare HOTTP).

In some languages it may not be acceptable to refer explicitly to the foreskin or to the sexual organs in general. In such cases it will be necessary to find some suitable euphemism such as "private parts." Or else one can follow a model similar to NIV and FrCL and say "people will see you naked," or "people will see you with your body completely uncovered," or "people will see you with no clothes on."

The second half of the verse speaks more explicitly of punishment as being forced to drink. This time the Lord is named as the one who causes the punishment: **The cup in the LORD's right hand will come around to you**. There are several Old Testament passages in which a cup of wine is used as a symbol of punishment. The figure is most fully developed in Jeremiah 25.15-29 and is found also in Psalm 75.8; Jeremiah 49.12; and Obadiah 16. Since this is a common picture and is related to wine, one of the central features of Palestinian culture, it is desirable to keep it in translation if at all possible. This may be a problem in areas where wine is not known, or a cup has not been used before with a symbolic meaning. Translators will have to decide whether a new figure of speech will be acceptable and understandable to the readers. For further comments see the notes on Obadiah 16 in *A Translator's Handbook on the Books of Obadiah and Micah*. TEV retains the figure but makes its meaning explicit by saying "**The LORD will make you drink your own cup of punishment.**" One may also say "The LORD will make you drink a cup of punishment yourself." In some cultures, however, it will be necessary to dispense with the figure and say "The LORD will punish you severely."

The cup in the LORD's right hand: in some languages it may be better to express this as "the cup which the LORD is holding."

The cup . . . will come around to you means that the Babylonians will have to take a turn at drinking, just as they had forced others to drink. To make the participants clear, one may say "the cup which the LORD is holding, he will pass around to you."

Shame will come upon your glory: the Hebrew word here translated **shame** is a word related to the one translated **contempt** at the beginning of the verse. There is perhaps a play on words here. The Hebrew word may also be read as two words with the meaning "vomit of disgrace" (NJV footnote; compare HOTTP, "shameful vomiting"; KJV "shameful spewing"). The mention of vomiting would be a continuation of the comparison of punishment with drinking. Just as drunkenness causes vomiting, so the Lord's punishment produces disgrace.

In some languages it may be helpful to restructure the verse so as to put the events mentioned into a more logical order. One possibility is "The cup of punishment which the LORD holds in his right hand he will pass to you. You yourself will have to drink from it. You will get drunk and people will see you naked. Instead of honoring you, they will despise you and you will be disgraced." However, in cultures which cannot retain all this figurative language, a possible translation model is the following: "The LORD will punish you just like forcing you to drink a cup of bitter wine. It will be as if you got drunk and people will see you naked. Instead of honoring you, they will . . . ."

2.17

RSV	TEV
The violence done to Lebanon will overwhelm you; the destruction of the beasts will terrify you,[h] for the blood of men and violence to the earth, to cities and all who dwell therein.	You have cut down the forests of Lebanon; now you will be cut down. You killed its animals; now animals will terrify you. This will happen because of the murders you have committed and because of your violence against the people of the world and its cities.[d]
[h] Gk, Syr: Heb *them*	[d] the people . . . cities; *or* the land, the city, and those who live in it.

This verse gives the reason for the punishment pictured in verses 15 and 16. This is first of all the destruction carried out on the forests of Lebanon and on the wild animals that lived in them.

The violence done to Lebanon: **Lebanon** is probably best understood as referring to the area more or less the same as that occupied by the modern country of Lebanon. In particular, it refers to the Lebanon mountain range which in ancient times was covered with thick forest (see comments on Nahum 1.4). The trees, especially the cedars, were highly valued as timber for building. Ancient

The fifth taunt Hab 2.18

inscriptions agree with the Old Testament in recording that both the Assyrians (Isa 37.24) and the Babylonians (Isa 14.8) carried out large scale logging operations there. Cutting down forests means that the soil is eroded and the land becomes barren. These results justify the description of the Babylonian activities as **violence done to Lebanon**.

Will overwhelm you: in keeping with the theme of the taunts that the punishment of the Babylonians will fit their crime, TEV translates "**You have cut down the forests of Lebanon: now you will be cut down**." One may also say "You have cut down (destroyed) ... now people will cut you down (destroy you)." If some similar word link can be found in other languages, it will be good to use it.

The destruction of the beasts will terrify you: the forests of Lebanon were a favorite place for hunting parties. When the forests were cut down, the wild animals were robbed of their homes and sources of food, and so diminished in number. This kind of thoughtless behavior by men was hateful to God, and the Babylonians were to be punished for it. TEV expresses this in a manner roughly parallel to the first part of the verse: "**You killed its animals: now animals will terrify you**."

The RSV footnote indicates that the words **terrify you** follow the ancient Greek and Syriac translations. TEV and almost all modern versions do the same, and translators into other languages should do so as well (compare HOTTP).

The rest of the verse speaks of a further reason for the punishment of the Babylonians: they had killed people and destroyed cities. The words used are the same as in the second half of verse 8. See comments on verse 8.

2.18	RSV	TEV
	What profit is an idol when its maker has shaped it, a metal image, a teacher of lies? For the workman trusts in his own creation when he makes dumb idols!	What's the use of an idol? It is only something that a man has made, and it tells you nothing but lies. What good does it do for its maker to trust it—a god that can't even talk!

In this fifth taunt the prophet mocks idols and those who make and worship them. This theme occurs in several other passages (compare Psa 115.4-8; 135.15-18; Isa 44.9-20; 46.6-7; Jer 10.2-16; Baruch 6 [also called the Letter of Jeremiah]). The Babylonians were a very idolatrous people, and in that respect the prophet is mocking them.

Each of the previous taunts began with the words **Woe to him** (verses 6, 9,12,15). In the case of this last taunt, these words do not occur until verse 19. It may be that in the final taunt of the series, the prophet reserves these words till later as a kind of climax. However, many scholars think that verses 18 and 19 have been reversed accidentally, and that verse 19 should come before verse 18. Some translations print verse 19 first, such as Mft, BJ, JB, and NAB. This has the advantage of giving the last taunt the same structure as the other four, as well as presenting the content of verses 18 and 19 in a more convincing order. However, if translators wish to do this in other languages, it will probably be better to put the verses together and number them 18-19 rather than print the numbers separately in the wrong order. In this Handbook comments will follow the traditional order.

The verse opens with a rhetorical question, **What profit is an idol when its maker has shaped it . . . ?** As in previous examples (verses 6,7,13) this is a way of making a strong statement. In languages which do not use rhetorical questions, the first clause may be rendered as "An idol is useless!" or "An idol is a useless object!" TEV, however, keeps the question form with "What's the use of an idol?" and then turns the rest of the sentence into an answer to the question. This makes it clear that "**an idol**" is no "**use**."

The subordinate clause **when its maker has shaped it** can be taken to mean "that its maker should carve it" (NAB; compare JB, NJV). If taken in this way, the clause is better treated as part of the question, as in NAB. TEV makes it the answer to the question: "**It is only something that a man has made.**"

The Hebrew text mentions two different kinds of image (**idol** and **metal image** in RSV). For the distinction between them, see the comments on Nahum 1.14. Since English vocabulary does not offer a convenient way to make this distinction, TEV drops it and translates both Hebrew words under the general term "idol." In some languages translators will have various terms for different types of idol, but in others they will need to follow the example of TEV or perhaps say "an idol made of wood or metal" (compare GeCL).

The idol once completed is only **a teacher of lies**. TEV turns this into a separate clause: "**it tells you nothing but lies.**" One may also say "it lies to you continually."

In Hebrew the second half of the verse is a statement: **For the workman trusts in his own creation when he makes dumb idols!** TEV makes it parallel with the first half by translating as another rhetorical question with the answer following: "**What good does it do for its maker to trust it—a god that can't even talk!**" Some translators may wish to use a statement here rather than a rhetorical question. In such a case one may say "It is useless for its maker to trust it, because it is a false god that can't even talk!" This sentence is ironic, and TEV shows the irony in English by adding the word "even." The irony is the prophet's way of ridiculing the Babylonians. Translators should use irony in their own language if at all possible. Another way of introducing irony is to use a figurative expression and say something like this: "It is just like chasing the wind, for an idol's maker to trust a false god that can't even talk."

2.19 RSV TEV

Woe to him who says to a wooden thing, Awake; to a dumb stone, Arise! Can this give revelation? Behold, it is overlaid with gold and silver, and there is no breath at all in it.

You are doomed! You say to a piece of wood, "Wake up!" or to a block of stone, "Get up!" Can an idol reveal anything to you? It may be covered with silver and gold, but there is no life in it.

The opening words **Woe to him . . .** are parallel with the opening words of the other taunts (verses 6, 9, 12, 15). In this case the whole taunt is in the third person in Hebrew and RSV, but TEV treats verse 19 as second person to keep it

The fifth taunt   Hab 2.20

the same as the earlier taunts. Translators may treat it as second person or third, according to how they handled the other taunts.

The first part of the verse mocks idol worshipers in two parallel clauses: **Woe to him who says to a wooden thing, Awake; to a dumb stone, Arise!** TEV retains the parallel structure: **"You say to a piece of wood, 'Wake up!' or to a block of stone, 'Get up!'"** In some languages it may be necessary to combine the two clauses into one and say "You say to a dumb idol made of wood or stone 'Wake up! Get up!'" In many languages it will be necessary to use polite forms of speech in addressing a supposed god, so that one will say "... 'Please wake up! Please get up!'" The words **Awake** and **Arise** are a cry for help to the Lord, the living God, in Psalm 35.23; 44.23; 59.4. Such use elsewhere emphasizes the stupidity of speaking in the same terms to man-made idols which can give no help.

In some languages the direct quotation of the words of the worshiper may need to be changed to indirect speech. One can say "You tell dumb idols of wood or stone to wake up and stand up."

In the second half of the verse, there is a rhetorical question, **Can this give revelation?** followed by a statement which gives an implied answer to the question. TEV treats the verse in the same way but makes it explicit that **this** refers to "an idol." In some languages it may not be sufficient to leave the answer to the question implicit. In such cases it will be better to say "Can an idol reveal anything to you? Of course not!" In other languages which do not use rhetorical questions, one may say, for example, "An idol cannot reveal anything to you."

In the last sentence the two parts give a sharp contrast between the appearance of an idol and its power. The word **Behold** helps to point out the contrast. TEV expresses the contrast in a different way by saying "**It may be ... but ....**" Another possibility is to say "Even though ... nevertheless ...."

Gold and silver were used as a kind of skin laid over the surface of idols, especially wooden ones. They gave a fine outward appearance but nothing else. The idol could give no help to the worshiper because **there is no breath at all in it**. Here **breath** may stand for "life"; TEV says "**but there is no life in it**" (compare Psa 135.17; Jer 10.14, 51.17). It is also possible that **breath** is related to speech and implies an answer to the question **Can this give revelation?** Those who understand it this way translate "but it can't say a thing."

An alternative translation model for this verse is:

> God will destroy you! You say to a piece of wood or a block of stone, "Wake up! Get up!" Can an idol tell you anything? Even though people have covered it with silver and gold, yet it cannot say anything.

2.20   RSV   TEV

But the LORD is in his holy temple; let all the earth keep silence before him.

    The LORD is in his holy Temple; let everyone on earth be silent in his presence.

Hab 2.20

The taunt ends with a statement about the true God, which sharply contrasts with the description of useless man-made idols in the previous two verses. The contrast is indicated by the opening word **But**, and many translators will wish to show this contrast in a similar way. TEV, however, does not use this word but shows the contrast by setting this verse out as a separate paragraph. One may also express the contrast by saying "As for the Lord, he is . . . ."

The Lord is in his holy temple: this refers primarily to the Lord's "temple" in heaven rather than to the Temple built by Solomon in Jerusalem (compare Psa 11.4; Micah 1.2). So **his holy temple** in this context means "the temple in heaven which belongs to the Lord."

The appropriate response from man to the holy God is silence: **let all the earth keep silence before him**. TEV makes it explicit that **all the earth** means "everyone on earth," and that **before him** means "in his presence." In certain languages it will be necessary to translate in an idiomatic way; for example, "before his face." (For similar expressions of reverence, see Zeph 1.7; Zech 2.13.)

This verse forms a fitting link between the taunts of chapter 2 and the prayer of chapter 3.

Chapter 3

3.1-19

RSV

TEV
A Prayer of Habakkuk

1 A prayer of Habakkuk the prophet, according to Shigionoth.
2 O LORD, I have heard the report of thee,
and thy work, O LORD, do I fear.
In the midst of the years renew it;
in the midst of the years make it known;
in wrath remember mercy.
3 God came from Teman,
and the Holy One from Mount Paran.
His glory covered the heavens,
and the earth was full of his praise.
Selah
4 His brightness was like the light,
rays flashed from his hand;
and there he veiled his power.
5 Before him went pestilence,
and plague followed close behind.
6 He stood and measured the earth;
he looked and shook the nations;
then the eternal mountains were scattered,
the everlasting hills sank low.
His ways were as of old.
7 I saw the tents of Cushan in affliction;
the curtains of the land of Midian did tremble.
8 Was thy wrath against the rivers, O LORD?
Was thy anger against the rivers,
or thy indignation against the sea,
when thou didst ride upon thy horses,
upon thy chariot of victory?
9 Thou didst strip the sheath from thy bow,
and put the arrows to the string.
Selah
Thou didst cleave the earth with rivers.
10 The mountains saw thee, and writhed;
the raging waters swept on;
the deep gave forth its voice,
it lifted its hands on high.
11 The sun and moon stood still in their habitation
at the light of thine arrows as they sped,
at the flash of thy glittering spear.
12 Thou didst bestride the earth in fury,
thou didst trample the nations in anger.
13 Thou wentest forth for the salvation of thy people,
for the salvation of thy anointed.
Thou didst crush the head of the wicked,

1 This is a prayer of the prophet Habakkuk:
2 O LORD, I have heard of what you have done,
and I am filled with awe.
Now do again in our times
the great deeds you used to do.
Be merciful, even when you are angry.
3 God is coming again from Edom;
the holy God is coming from the hills of Paran.
His splendor covers the heavens,
and the earth is full of his praise.
4 He comes with the brightness of lightning;
light flashes from his hand,
there where his power is hidden.
5 He sends disease before him
and commands death to follow him.
6 When he stops, the earth shakes;
at his glance the nations tremble.
The eternal mountains are shattered;
the everlasting hills sink down,
the hills where he walked in ancient times.
7 I saw the people of Cushan afraid
and the people of Midian tremble.
8 Was it the rivers that made you angry, LORD?
Was it the sea that made you furious?
You rode upon the clouds;
the storm cloud was your chariot,
as you brought victory to your people.
9 You got ready to use your bow,
ready to shoot your arrows.
Your lightning split open the earth.
10 When the mountains saw you, they trembled;
water poured down from the skies.
The waters under the earth roared,
and their waves rose high.
11 At the flash of your speeding arrows
and the gleam of your shining spear,
the sun and the moon stood still.
12 You marched across the earth in anger;
in fury you trampled the nations.
13 You went out to save your people,
to save your chosen king.

Hab 3.1-19   HABAKKUK'S PSALM OF PRAYER

	laying him bare from thigh to neck.		You struck down the leader of the wicked
	Selah		and completely destroyed his followers.
14	Thou didst pierce with thy shafts the head of his warriors,	14	Your arrows pierced the commander of his army
	who came like a whirlwind to scatter me,		when it came like a storm to scatter us,
	rejoicing as if to devour the poor in secret.		gloating like those who secretly oppress the poor.
15	Thou didst trample the sea with thy horses,	15	You trampled the sea with your horses,
	the surging of mighty waters.		and the mighty waters foamed.
16	I hear, and my body trembles,	16	I hear all this, and I tremble;
	my lips quiver at the sound;		my lips quiver with fear.
	rottenness enters into my bones,		My body goes limp,
	my steps totter beneath me.		and my feet stumble beneath me.
	I will quietly wait for the day of trouble to come upon people who invade us.		I will quietly wait for the time to come when God will punish those who attack us.
17	Though the fig tree do not blossom,	17	Even though the fig trees have no fruit
	nor fruit be on the vines,		and no grapes grow on the vines,
	the produce of the olive fail		even though the olive crop fails
	and the fields yield no food,		and the fields produce no grain,
	the flock be cut off from the fold		even though the sheep all die
	and there be no herd in the stalls,		and the cattle stalls are empty,
18	yet I will rejoice in the LORD,	18	I will still be joyful and glad,
	I will joy in the God of my salvation.		because the LORD God is my savior.
19	GOD, the Lord, is my strength;	19	The Sovereign LORD gives me strength.
	he makes my feet like hinds' feet,		He makes me sure-footed as a deer
	he makes me tread upon my high places.		and keeps me safe on the mountains.
	To the choirmaster: with stringed instruments.		

This chapter is quite different from the rest of the book in both form and content. It resembles a psalm in many ways, and if translators have tried to put the Psalms into poetry, then they should try to do the same with this chapter. For a discussion of the principles involved, see *A Translator's Guide to Selected Psalms*, pages 1-2, as well as the introduction to the forthcoming Handbook on the Psalms.

It is not easy to make paragraph divisions within the chapter, and modern versions are all different in this respect. Verse 2 is in the form of a petition to the Lord in the first person, and verses 16-19 are also in the first person, stating the prophet's response to the Lord. Verses 3-6 are in the third person, and verses 8-15 are in the second person. (There is one first-person verb in verse 7 and one first-person pronoun suffix in verse 14.) Verses 3-15 give a poetic and figurative description of the Lord appearing in great power to help his people. Within this section the best points for breaks are at verses 8, 9, and 13. For a more detailed discussion of the problems involved, see the comments on verse 8. New paragraphs, then, are recommended at the beginning of verses 2, 3, 8, 9, 13, and 16.

SECTION HEADING: "**A Prayer of Habakkuk.**" TEV places a new section heading before verse 1. Many translators will have no difficulty with this, but some may need to turn it into a full sentence and say "Habakkuk prays a prayer," " . . . prays to the LORD," or something similar, such as "Habakkuk expresses his trust in the LORD."

HABAKKUK'S PSALM OF PRAYER

3.1

RSV

A prayer of Habakkuk the prophet, according to Shigionoth.

TEV

This is a prayer of the prophet Habakkuk:[e]

[e] *Hebrew has an additional phrase, the meaning of which is unclear.*

In Hebrew this verse is a title for the rest of the chapter, just as 1.1 serves as a title for chapters 1 and 2. Some psalms have a similar title (Psa 17, 86, 90, 102, 142), and translators may wish to treat this verse in the same way as they have treated the titles of those psalms. TEV has made the verse into a full sentence, "**This is a prayer . . . ,**" and many translators will need to follow this example. One may also translate "The prophet Habakkuk prayed this prayer."

For notes on **Habakkuk the prophet**, see comments on 1.1.

The final words in RSV, **according to Shigionoth**, are mentioned only in the footnote in TEV. **Shigionoth** is just a transliteration of a Hebrew word whose meaning is unknown. The singular form of this word occurs in the heading of Psalm 7. Probably the word was intended as some kind of instruction about the music which should accompany the psalm. Some modern versions attempt to translate it. Mft has "in dithyrambic measure"; JB has "tone as for dirges"; NAB has "To a plaintive tune"; but these are all guesses. It is better for translators to do as TEV has done, that is, to omit the word and state in a footnote that its meaning is no longer known.

3.2

RSV

O LORD, I have heard the report
  of thee,
and thy work, O LORD, do I
  fear.
In the midst of the years renew
  it;
in the midst of the years make
  it known;
in wrath remember mercy.

TEV

O LORD, I have heard of what
  you have done,
and I am filled with awe.
Now do again in our times
  the great deeds you used to do.
Be merciful, even when you are
  angry.

This verse is the only one in the whole chapter which is a prayer in the sense of a request to God to do something. Verses 3-15 can be seen as a record of the prophet's vision of God's answer to this request.

The RSV expression **I have heard the report of thee** is old-fashioned English. TEV expresses this in modern terms as "**I have heard of what you have done.**" The word "**what**" may also be rendered as "the things that."

The second line, **and thy work, O LORD, do I fear**, TEV renders as "and I am filled with awe." The meaning of **thy work** has already been included in the phrase "**what you have done.**" This is a reference to the activity of God on behalf of his people at the time of the exodus from Egypt. This activity became in later years a kind of standard against which people measured the evidence of God's presence in the events of their own day. Translators should note that **fear** in English may mean either "terror" or "reverence, awe." In this context the second meaning is clearly intended, and TEV has made this explicit. An alternative translation model for these first two lines is "O LORD, people have told me about the things you have done, and this causes me to reverence you greatly."

TEV uses the vocative "**O LORD**" once at the beginning of the verse and does not repeat it in the second line. Translators may include it once or twice according to the natural usage of their language.

In the second half of the verse, Habakkuk asks the Lord to act to help his people, just as he had in times past. This request is expressed in three ways, **renew it**, **make it known**, and **remember mercy**. The first two of these clauses are parallel with each other, and both contain the rather odd expression **in the midst of the years**. This refers to Habakkuk's own times, which he pictures as many years away from the great events of the exodus, and also many years away from God's final intervention in history. The word **it** in **renew it** and **make it known** is not in the Hebrew but is a legitimate addition in this context. It refers to **thy work** in the first half of the verse. TEV takes these first two requests together and expresses their meaning as "**Now do again in our times the great deeds you used to do.**" This loses some of the meaning of the second request. One could translate more fully and say "Do again . . . used to do; make people acknowledge them (or, recognize them)" (compare FrCL); or "Make your people experience them again" (compare GeCL). In some languages the imperative "**do again**" in TEV needs to be softened somewhat; for example, "Please do again . . . " or "Let your people experience again . . . ."

It is also possible to understand the second request as "make yourself known" (compare Septuagint, Mft, NEB). In this case it would then be necessary to keep the two clauses separate and say "Now in our times do great deeds again; make your presence known again now in our times." However, the majority of translations adopt the same interpretation as RSV, and translators are recommended to follow it.

The final request is **in wrath remember mercy**. This can be understood in three ways: (1) "even while you are angry with us, restrain your anger and show mercy to us"; (2) "while you are angry with our enemies, yet remember to show mercy to us"; (3) "though you are angry with us, show mercy to us by punishing our enemies." The third possibility does not seem very likely, but either of the other two will fit the context satisfactorily. TEV's "**Be merciful, even when you are angry**" is ambiguous. If a language requires the translators to make explicit with whom God is angry and to whom he shows mercy, then they should choose between the first two possibilities given above. On the whole the first one seems to be more probable. One may say, for instance, "Even if you have reason to be angry with us, still show mercy to us" (compare FrCL).

3.3	RSV	TEV
	God came from Teman, and the Holy One from Mount Paran. His glory covered the heavens, and the earth was full of his praise. *Selah*	God is coming again from Edom; the holy God is coming from the hills of Paran. His splendor covers the heavens, and the earth is full of his praise.

Verses 3-15 describe a theophany, or an appearance of God in great power and glory. This is to be seen as the answer to the prophet's request in verse 2. The theophany is pictured in traditional language drawn from such natural occurrences as a thunderstorm in the mountainous desert area of the Sinai Peninsula. In the Old Testament impressive events in nature such as thunderstorms, earthquakes, and volcanic eruptions are often associated with the special presence of the Lord (compare Exo 19.16-20; Psa 18.7-15, 29.3-10; 97.1-5; Micah 1.3-4; Nahum 1.4-5). Mention of such occurrences often has overtones of reference back to the dramatic events of the exodus and the giving of the Law on Mount Sinai. This is the case here also.

One difficulty in this whole passage is to decide whether to translate the verbs as past, present, or future. In Hebrew many of the verbs are in a tense that describes events which are complete, or which happened repeatedly in the past. However, this is probably the so-called "prophetic perfect," in which the prophet describes future events with such certainty that he speaks of them as if they had already happened. Some translations (KJV, RSV, NIV) put the verbs mostly in the past, while others (JB, NAB, NEB, NJV, FrCL, GeCL) put them mostly in the present. In English the present tense can sometimes be used to describe events which are in the near future, and that is the effect here. TEV puts verses 3-6 in the present tense, and verses 7-15 in the past. That is because TEV understands verses 7-15 to be alluding to what God has done in the past to help his people.

In one sense, however, it hardly matters what various European language versions have done. Translators must consider the effect on the reader that various tenses will have in their own languages, and then decide whether past, present, or future will be most appropriate to indicate an event yet to take place. In languages where the verb system does not lay emphasis on time distinctions, verb forms which are neutral with regard to time may be appropriate.

God came from Teman, and the Holy One from Mount Paran: these two clauses are obviously parallel with each other and are broadly similar in meaning. The Hebrew word for **God** here is an archaic form which reminded the readers of God's previous acts to help his people. TEV helps to bring this out by saying "God is coming again." In languages which have special words for showing the direction of the action, the word used here should have the action coming toward the prophet.

Teman was a district of Edom, a country to the southeast of Judah. It stands for Edom as a whole, and so TEV translates as "**Edom**." In many languages one must say "the country of Edom" or "the land of Edom."

The Holy One is a title for God (compare Isa 1.4; 6.3; 40.25) which is particularly relevant in the book of Habakkuk in the light of 1.12. TEV makes it clear that this is a reference to God by translating "**the holy God**." See the comments on 1.12 and 13 for a discussion on "holy."

Mount Paran refers to the mountainous and barren area in the Sinai Peninsula west of the Gulf of Aqaba. Because it is an area rather than one particular mountain, TEV translates as "**the hills of Paran**." "The hills of Paran" may also be expressed as "the hills in the district of Paran."

Teman and **Paran** together are to the south of Judah. God is pictured as coming from the south, from the area where he made himself known to his people in the giving of the Law and the wandering in the desert. Thus even the place names point back to the past acts of God and help to add to the feeling of reverence for the majesty of God. (For similar use, see Deut 33.2; Judges 5.4-5; Psa 68.7-8.) The area of Paran also had some association with King David (1 Sam

25.1). The Gulf of Aqaba, Edom, and Paran may be located on the map entitled "Egypt and Sinai" in American editions of TEV, and on the map entitled "Liberation from Egypt, the Route of the Exodus" in British editions of TEV.

The second half of the verse also consists of two parallel lines which have similar meaning. **His glory covered the heavens**: **glory** here probably refers to the bright shining light which is associated with the presence of God. This fits with the mention of lightning in verse 4. TEV translates as "**splendor**."

The earth was full of his praise: here **praise** does not mean the sounds men make when praising God, but rather the qualities in God that make men want to praise him. Similar usage is found in Isaiah 60.18; 62.7; Jeremiah 51.41. One can put the two lines together and say "The heavens and the earth are filled with God's splendor that makes people all over the earth praise him." In languages which do not use the passive, one may say "God's bright shining light fills the heavens (skies) and the earth, causing people everywhere to praise him."

These two lines form an introduction to the description of the thunderstorm that follows in verses 4-6.

The word **Selah**, which comes at the end of the verse in RSV, actually comes in the middle of the verse in Hebrew (compare NIV, NJV). Except here and in verses 9 and 13, it occurs only in the Book of Psalms. Its meaning is no longer known, but it is probably some kind of instruction relating to the musical accompaniment or the liturgical use of the passages in question. Some versions translate it as "Pause" (JB, TOB, FrCL), but many others simply omit it (Mft, NAB, NEB, TEV, GeCL), and translators are recommended to do the same. See *A Translator's Guide to Selected Psalms*, page 42 (on Psa 24.6).

3.4

RSV	TEV
His brightness was like the light, rays flashed from his hand; and there he veiled his power.	He comes with the brightness of lightning; light flashes from his hand, there where his power is hidden.

His brightness was like the light is ambiguous. Some scholars think that it refers to the way light spreads across the sky at sunrise, and they compare it with Psalm 19.5-6. Thus NEB translates "He rises like the dawn," and NIV "His splendor was like the sunrise." Other scholars link the first line more closely with the second and interpret it as a reference to the way lightning flashes across the sky. Thus Mft translates "his radiance is a lightning blaze," and TEV "**He comes with the brightness of lightning**." This second interpretation seems to fit the context better and is recommended to translators. This clause may also be rendered "as he comes, he shines brightly like lightning."

Rays flashed from his hand: the word here translated **rays** is the word usually translated "horns," and its presence here has led some scholars to think that there is some copying mistake in the Hebrew. However, the same root in a verbal form is used of Moses' face shining in Exodus 34.29-30, and there is no strong reason why the noun could not have a related meaning in a poetic passage like this one. The Hebrew word is dual in form, and NEB reflects this by translating "twin rays" (compare TOB). Translators may do something like this, if it would add to the poetic feeling of the passage in their language. But there seems to be no particular emphasis on the dual meaning, and many translators will prefer to treat it as a plural, as most English versions do (JB, NAB, NIV, NJV). TEV treats **rays** as standing for "light" and translates "**light flashes from his hand.**" This line is best understood as referring to lightning.

Some scholars think that the words **from his hand** should be translated as "at his side" (NEB; compare Mft, NAB, NJV). However, the normal meaning of the word is "hand," and this makes perfectly good sense here (compare Deut 33.2).

There he veiled his power: **there** refers to the Lord's hand, which is sometimes pictured as the location of his power (compare 2 Sam 24.14). TEV turns the sentence into a passive and renders "**there where his power is hidden.**" In languages which do not use the passive, translators may say, for example, "there where he hides his power." The picture seems to say that God's power is hidden behind the flashes of lightning. This is a little awkward, and some scholars think there are some words missing from the text (a gap is marked in Mft's translation). NEB places here some words found in verses 6 and 7 in Hebrew. However, the majority of English translators consider that the Hebrew text as it stands makes adequate sense, and this view can safely be followed in other languages.

An alternative translation model for this verse is "As he comes he shines brightly like lightning, and rays of light flash out from his hand, the place where he hides his power."

3.5   RSV   TEV

> Before him went pestilence,
>   and plague followed close be-
>   hind.

> He sends disease before him
>   and commands death to follow
>   him.

Some scholars think that here **pestilence** and **plague** are personified and spoken of as if they were the Lord's attendants whose work was to punish his enemies. Diseases were thought of as one of the accompaniments of war (compare 2 Kgs 19.35), and the Lord was often pictured as punishing his enemies with disease (Lev 26.25; Deut 32.24; 2 Sam 24.15-16) or saving his own people from it (Psa 91.3, 6). Such a picture is in keeping with the wider context of verses 3-15. God is still being thought of as directing his actions toward the prophet, and then more widely toward the rest of the world's inhabitants as they watch him acting in the skies above. Possible translation models in languages which must show the direction of actions are the following: "He sends disease (coming) before him," or "He causes disease to come (down) before him."

The word translated **plague** is originally a darting flame and can be used of lightning (Psa 78.48). Fever, the disease which makes people feel hot, was thought to be caused by such flames.

The terms translated **pestilence** and **plague** do not refer to any of the specific illnesses known to modern medicine. They are general terms and should be translated by generic words like "disease" or "illness" rather than by specific terms like "malaria" or "typhoid." TEV renders them as "**disease**" and "**death.**" "Death" indicates that the illness is fatal.

TEV has also restructured the sentence to show that God is the agent who is in control of the diseases ("**He sends . . . and commands**"). In certain languages it will be helpful to expand this verse slightly and say "He sends disease to go in front of him, and commands death to follow close behind him."

3.6 RSV | TEV

RSV	TEV
He stood and measured the earth; he looked and shook the nations; then the eternal mountains were scattered, the everlasting hills sank low. His ways were as of old.	When he stops, the earth shakes; at his glance the nations tremble. The eternal mountains are shattered; the everlasting hills sink down, the hills where he walked in ancient times.

The prophet now speaks of the effect of God's presence on the world. The description mingles language appropriate to a thunderstorm with language appropriate to an earthquake. This kind of mixture is acceptable in Hebrew poetry, which sees God's presence in all the major events in the world of nature.

He stood is ambiguous. It may refer either to standing up from a sitting position (JB "When he stands up") or to standing still in contrast with moving (NAB "He pauses," NEB "He stands still"). Since the previous verse implied that God was moving, the second possibility seems much more apt. TEV accepts it and translates unambiguously as **"When he stops."** In some languages it will be necessary to indicate what action was completed or stopped. In such a case one may say "When he stops moving . . ." or "When he stops walking . . ." (compare FrCL).

Measured the earth: the word translated **measured** in RSV is doubtful in meaning. Many scholars think that the Hebrew form comes from a different verb which means "to shake" (Mft, JB, NEB, NIV, NJV, FrCL, GeCL; compare the Septuagint). TEV accepts this interpretation and renders **"the earth shakes."** This fits the context better and is recommended to translators.

He looked and shook the nations: the second line is parallel to the first but extends its thought to include the effect of God's presence on people. TEV expresses this from the point of view of the people concerned and says **"at his glance the nations tremble."** "At his glance" will be difficult to translate in certain languages. An alternative translation is "When he looks . . . ." **"The nations"** will be rendered in certain languages as "all the people of the world."

The next two lines say the same thing twice in different words: **then the eternal mountains were scattered, the everlasting hills sank low.** The language here is drawn from the effect of an earthquake (compare Micah 1.4). The Hebrew verb translated **scattered** in RSV is taken by TEV to come from another root meaning "to shatter." "Scatter" means to be dispersed or to move away from something (in the case, from the Lord), and "shatter" means to break into little pieces. Major translations are evenly divided between them. "Scatter" or something similar is found in RSV, Mft, BJ, JB, TOB, and FrCL, while "shatter" or the like occurs in NAB, NEB, TEV, NIV, NJV, and GeCL. Both meanings fit the context well, and it makes little difference to the overall effect of the verse which one is chosen.

The words translated **eternal** and **everlasting** do not imply that the mountains and hills were not created by God. Rather they refer to the apparent permanence and stability of the mountains in contrast with the brief span of a human life. It may perhaps be better to use terms like "ancient mountains" and "age-old hills" (NIV; compare Gen 49.26; Deut 33.15). In languages which do not use the passive, one may say "He causes the ancient mountains to shatter into pieces (or, to scatter) and the hills to sink down."

The last line, **His ways were as of old**, may be understood in two ways. First, it may be taken as a separate statement about God (compare NIV "His ways are eternal"). Second, it may be taken as in apposition to the previous statement about the mountains and hills. **His ways** then refers to the mountains and hills as the route by which God moves over the earth. This would be another allusion to the giving of the Law, when the Lord appeared to Moses at the top of Mount Sinai amidst storm and earthquake (Exo 19.16-20). This second interpretation fits the context better and is preferable. TEV accepts it and translates "**the hills where he walked in ancient times**" (compare JB, FrCL, GeCL). Some translators will prefer to begin a new sentence with this final clause: "These are the hills where he walked . . . ." See Nahum 1.5 for an alternative translation of "mountains."

An alternative translation model for this verse is:

> When he stops walking, the earth shakes; as he looks, all the people of the earth tremble. He causes the ancient (very old) mountains to shatter into pieces (or, to scatter) and the hills to sink down (low), the hills (high ground) where he walked in times long ago.

3.7

RSV	TEV
I saw the tents of Cushan in affliction; the curtains of the land of Midian did tremble.	I saw the people of Cushan afraid and the people of Midian tremble.

Verse 7 takes up the theme of the second line of verse 6 and speaks of the effect of God's presence on specific peoples. There is no justification for starting a new paragraph at this point, as TEV does.

I saw the tents of Cushan in affliction: the verb translated **I saw** is the only one in the first person in verses 3-15. Its occurrence reminds the reader that the description the prophet is giving is a kind of vision which he had in answer to his prayer of verse 2.

Cushan as the name of a tribe, a nation, or a region does not occur anywhere else in the Old Testament. Some scholars link it with the name Cush, which refers to an area including most of Sudan and part of modern Ethiopia (see comments on Nahum 3.9 and Zeph 1.1). Others regard it as referring to some small and otherwise unknown group of people living in the Sinai Peninsula (FrCL footnote). It may be an alternative name for the people of Midian mentioned in the second half of the verse, or perhaps a name for some clan among the Midianites. Some slight support for this view can be claimed by comparing Exodus 2.16-21 with Numbers 12.1. It is possible that Moses' Midianite wife Zipporah is the same person referred to as a Cushite in Numbers 12.1 (compare GeCL footnote), but this cannot be proved. Translators should keep the name

Cushan in the form in which it appears here, and not change it to a more familiar form like "Cushite." In languages which need to identify **Cushan**, one may say "the people from the clan of Cushan."

The tents of Cushan refers to the dwellings of the people. As inhabitants of the desert, these people were nomads and lived in tents made of goat skins or cloth woven from goat hair.

In affliction is ambiguous and can be understood in two ways. It may be taken physically as referring to the damage or destruction of the tents in the storm and earthquake. Thus NAB translates "the tents of Cushan collapse" (compare NJV, TOB, GeCL). Or it may be taken psychologically as referring not just to the tents but to the people who live in them. Thus JB translates "I have seen the tents of Cushan terrified." TEV follows this interpretation. However, the TEV translators thought that readers might not understand the idea that the tents represent the people living in them (a figure of speech called metonymy). Therefore TEV does not mention the tents but states the meaning in nonfigurative language as "**I saw the people of Cushan afraid**" (compare FrCL).

The curtains of the land of Midian did tremble: the tents of the desert dwellers were often divided by curtains placed across them. This provided a private section for the women behind the curtain in the inner part of the tent. Here the word is used as a parallel to the tents in the previous line (compare Isa 54.2; Jer 4.20; 10.20; 49.29), and there is no special emphasis on the curtains as such. Some versions translate as "pavilions," which is really no more than another word for tents (JB, NAB, NJV).

Again the line may be interpreted either physically or psychologically. If it is taken physically, it refers to the tents enduring the fierce winds of the storm. Thus NEB translates "the tent-curtains of Midian flutter" (compare TOB). If taken psychologically it speaks of the people of Midian trembling in fear at the presence of God. Thus JB translates "I have seen . . . the pavilions of the land of Midian shuddering." TEV follows this interpretation but again drops the metonymy and states the meaning in nonfigurative language as "**the people of Midian tremble**." This interpretation has a parallel in Exodus 15.15, where neighboring nations are spoken of as in panic when they hear what the Lord has done for his people.

The land of Midian lay on the east side of the Gulf of Aqaba, but the Midianites also lived on the west side in the Sinai Peninsula. This is the area near "the hills of Paran" mentioned in verse 3. The mention of it strengthens the associations which the passage has with the events of the Book of Exodus.

In cultures where tents are commonly used, translators may render this verse as "I saw the people who live in tents in Cushan show great fear, and those people who live in the land of Midian tremble with terror" or "I saw the people of Cushan very much afraid in their tents, and the people of Midian trembling with terror in their homes."

3.8	RSV	TEV
	Was thy wrath against the rivers, O LORD? Was thy anger against the rivers,	Was it the rivers that made you angry, LORD? Was it the sea that made you furious?

or thy indignation against the sea, when thou didst ride upon thy horses, upon thy chariot of victory?	You rode upon the clouds; the storm cloud was your chariot, as you brought victory to your people.

The prophet turns from his description of the theophany to address the Lord directly and ask what was the purpose of it all. The questions occur in verse 8, but then verses 9-12 turn back to describing the theophany. Only in verse 13 comes the answer to the questions of verse 8. But the fact that the answer comes at all shows that the questions in verse 8 are not rhetorical. In translation, therefore, they should be kept as questions and not changed into statements. It may seem confusing to have the answer such a long way from the questions, but it is one of the features of poetry, that different themes and ideas may be interwoven in a way which does not seem very logical. If the separation of question and answer here will cause a serious problem of understanding, translators may consider the following ways of overcoming the problem:

(1) They can rearrange the order of verses and put verse 8 after verse 12, so that the questions come immediately before the answer.

(2) They can put the first half of verse 13 between verse 8 and verse 9, and perhaps repeat it in its normal place.

(3) They can give verses 9-12 a different degree of indentation than the other verses in the chapter. If verse 13 is at the same degree of indention as verse 8, the reader will have a clue that those verses are to be linked.

There are advantages and disadvantages to each of these suggestions. The first is simple but leaves the verse numbers in the wrong order. This can easily confuse the readers. The second is also fairly simple, but if it is adopted, a footnote should be included to explain what has been done, especially if the first half of verse 13 is included twice. Repetition of this kind may fit well with poetic style in some languages but may offend the readers in others.

The third suggestion keeps the text in the traditional order but may be too complicated to help many readers. Moreover, if this solution is adopted, it will mean looking at the indentation of the whole chapter, and not just verses 8-13. For instance, one may decide to have verses 8 and 13-15 at one degree of indentation, verses 3-7 and 9-12 at another, and verses 2 and 16-19 at a third. This can be arranged as follows:

```
    2                    or          2
      3-7                               3-7
        8                                 8
      9-12                              9-12
        13-15                           13-15
    16-19                             16-19
```

The British edition of TEV has done something like this in Proverbs 6.16-19; 30.16,19,23,31, but it is easier to do in Bibles with a single column of print on the pages, like JB, NJV, and some editions of NEB.

To sum up, then, we cannot offer any particular solution as the best one for all situations. Translators will have to decide which of the various possibilities is likely to cause the fewest problems in their own situation.

Was thy wrath against the rivers, O LORD? In some languages it may be necessary to put the vocative **O LORD** at the beginning of the sentence. Some scholars think that one Hebrew letter should be dropped from the word translated **the rivers**, so that it would mean "the mountains." Among available English translations, only Mft follows this idea. It gives a good connection with verse 6, but the Hebrew makes sense as it stands, and there is no pressing need to alter it.

The second line **Was thy anger against the rivers?** repeats the first line in slightly different words. Because these lines are so similar, some scholars think there is a copying mistake in the traditional Hebrew text, and that the line is repeated wrongly. Some versions accept this view and translate the line only once (JB, NEB). TEV translates "Was it the rivers that made you angry, LORD?" Probably TEV has run the two lines into one as a matter of translation principle rather than by assuming a copying mistake in the Hebrew.

The third line, **or thy indignation against the sea**, is parallel in thought with the second. TEV makes this a separate sentence and says "Was it the sea that made you furious?" In ancient Near Eastern usage waters such as the rivers and the sea were symbols of the powers that resisted God, especially in the creation. This kind of thinking may underlie this verse, as it does certain other Old Testament passages (Job 26.12; Psa 74.13-15; 77.16-20; 89.9-11; 114.3-5; Isa 50.2; 51.9-10). However, in the light of the answer to these questions given in verse 13, it seems that here the rivers and the sea are symbols of "the wicked" (3.13), and that the prophet has in mind the Babylonians rather than cosmic forces of evil.

However, translators should keep the references here to **the rivers** and **the sea** and not replace them by "the Babylonians." If necessary a footnote can be included to explain the symbolism. Other translation models for this first section are "LORD, was it the rivers that made you angry or stirred up your rage? Was it the sea that made you furious?" or "LORD, was it with the rivers that you were furious? Did they make you angry? Was it the sea that put you in a rage?" See Nahum 1.6 for other ways to translate "angry" or "furious."

When thou didst ride upon thy horses, upon thy chariot of victory: again we have two lines which are closely parallel with each other in thought. **Horses** were used only for military purposes in the ancient world, and the mention of **horses** and a **chariot** here create the impression of the Lord as a warrior going to battle. For notes on **chariot**, see comments on Nahum 2.3. Translators may prefer to borrow the English word "chariot" and describe it in more detail in a footnote or in the word list.

Just as the rivers and the sea had a symbolic meaning in the first part of the verse, so have the **horses** and **chariot** in the second part. As a soldier may ride a horse or chariot in battle, so the Lord is pictured as riding on the clouds in various parts of the Old Testament (see Deut 33.26; Psa 18.10-11; 68.33; 104.3-4; Isa 19.1). The **horses** and **chariot** stand for the clouds, and so TEV translates as "You rode upon the clouds; the storm cloud was your chariot" (compare FrCL). This makes clear the connection with the description of the thunderstorm in the earlier verses, especially verse 4. Some translators may wish to say "the storm cloud was like a chariot for you," or even render the final part of the verse as "You rode on the storm clouds as if they were your chariot, as you brought victory to your people (or, caused your people to be victorious)."

TEV also expands the **victory** of RSV to make the participants explicit: "**as you brought victory to your people.**" It will be helpful in many languages to follow this example. One may also render this clause as "as you caused your people to be victorious over their enemies."

3.9	RSV	TEV

**Thou didst strip the sheath from thy bow,
and put the arrows to the string.**[i]   *Selah*
Thou didst cleave the earth with rivers.

[i] Cn: Heb obscure

You got ready to use your bow, ready to shoot your arrows.[f]
Your lightning split open the earth.

[f] *Probable text* ready to shoot your arrows; *Hebrew unclear*.

In general terms, this verse continues to describe the Lord's activity in the storm by using symbolic language.

Thou didst strip the sheath from thy bow means that the Lord took his bow from its protective cover, ready for use. JB puts it more simply as "You uncover your bow," and TEV explains the meaning of this action by saying "**You got ready to use your bow.**"

And put the arrows to the string: in this line the three Hebrew words of the traditional text are a serious problem. The first two words have different possible meanings, but no combination of the various possibilities makes much sense or shows much connection with the context. Probably the best one is found in the RV: "The oaths to the tribes were a sure word." This can be taken to mean that the Lord had promised to act on behalf of his people, to save them (compare verse 13).

However, after the mention of a bow in the first line, one expects some mention of arrows in the second line. The word translated "tribes" in RV may also mean "rods, sticks," which can stand symbolically for arrows. The word translated "oaths" in RV may be read with different vowels with the meaning "you filled." One manuscript of the Septuagint has a translation "you filled your quiver with arrows"; this involves assuming that the third Hebrew word is different from the one in the traditional text, but it does give a meaning which fits the context. This possibility is accepted by some modern versions: NAB has "filled with arrows is your quiver," and NEB "charge thy quiver with shafts."

Other scholars prefer to assume a different change in the third Hebrew word and translate as **put arrows to the string** or "you ply its string with arrows" (JB).

TEV feels the importance of mentioning arrows in this context but does not indicate whether it prefers to understand "quivers" or "strings." TEV has translated with a general statement, "**ready to shoot your arrows,**" which gives a good parallel with the first line.

NIV tries to obtain sense without changing the traditional Hebrew text. To do this its translators have accepted a third possible meaning for the first of the three Hebrew words, namely, "sevens," that is, "many." NIV thus translates "you called for many arrows." Yet another possibility that retains the traditional Hebrew text is found in the French TOB, "the words of oaths are arrows" (compare NJV, FrCL, GeCL, HOTTP).

With so many possibilities to be found in reputable translations (and many other suggestions in scholarly writings), how are translators to decide what to do? Their first and most important duty is to say something that makes sense, and in this case it seems that this is best achieved by accepting that the traditional Hebrew text needs to be changed. The change followed by NAB and NEB has at least some ancient manuscript support and therefore seems to offer the best possibility available. We therefore suggest as a translation base for these first two lines "You drew your bow from its case and filled your quiver with arrows." It is also acceptable to express this meaning in more general terms, as TEV has done. "Quiver" in certain languages will be expressed as "container for arrows."

It remains to note that the **arrows** here are symbolic and stand for the flashes of lightning that in ancient thinking were shot from the hand of God (compare Psa 29.7; 77.18; Hab 3.4).

The second line in Hebrew ends with the word **Selah**. See comments on verse 3.

The third line, **Thou didst cleave the earth with rivers**, is expressed in more modern language by NIV as "you split the earth with rivers." TEV has linked this with the earlier part of the verse, understanding an implied cause—effect relationship, and at the same time has made explicit that the arrows stand for lightning flashes: "**Your lightning split open the earth.**" It is not clear why TEV, unlike FrCL and GeCL, has failed to mention the rivers. There seems to be no good reason for this. In mountainous desert areas the rare and fierce thunderstorms do indeed quickly produce roaring torrents of water which can change the landscape considerably (compare Judges 5.21). An eyewitness account of such a storm in the Sinai Peninsula is given in Driver's commentary, pages 99-100. The mention of God making rivers reminded the original readers of the way he provided water in the desert for the people of Moses' day (Exo 17.6; Num 20.11; compare Psa 74.15; 77.17-18; 78.15-16). One possible translation model is "As your lightning flashes, rivers split the earth." Other possibilities are "The earth opens and rivers gush out" (FrCL) or "You split the earth and streams spurt forth" (GeCL).

3.10   RSV   TEV

    The mountains saw thee, and writhed;
      the raging waters swept on;
    the deep gave forth its voice,
      it lifted its hands on high.

    When the mountains saw you, they trembled;
    water poured down from the skies.
    The waters under the earth roared,
    and their waves rose high.

The description of the storm and its effect continues, in terms very similar to those of Psalm 77.16-18. **The mountains saw thee and writhed**: the Hebrew word translated "writhe" is often associated with the movements a woman makes in childbirth (compare GeCL, "like a woman who lies in birth pangs"). Other terms used in English versions are "shiver" (JB), "tremble" (NAB), and "rock" (NJV). This movement may refer either to an earth tremor accompanying the storm, or more probably to the effect of flash floods running down the mountain sides. Many languages have a term that refers to the movements of a woman in labor, and if such a term does not sound strange when applied to mountains, it may be good to use it here for poetic effect.

The raging waters swept on: this refers to the newly formed streams dashing down the mountains, or to the "torrent of rain" (NAB, NJV) as it falls from the sky. TEV takes this second interpretation and says "**water poured down from the skies.**" Compare FrCL "torrential rains flood the earth."

The deep gave forth its voice: the Hebrew word translated **the deep** is the same word as that used in Gen 1.2. It has overtones of cosmic forces opposed to God (compare verse 8). In the Hebrew world view, **the deep** referred to "**the waters under the earth,**" and TEV translates in these terms. However, it is possible that in this context the prophet is thinking of the sea roaring as the flooded rivers pour into it (compare FrCL, NAB "the ocean," NEB "the deep sea").

The last line, **it lifts its hands on high**, fits well with the interpretation of **the deep** as the ocean. **Its hands** then refers to the waves rising high in the storm. TEV states this meaning in nonfigurative language as "**their waves rose high**" (compare NIV). An alternative translation model for these two lines is "the sea roared, and its waves rose high" or "the sea made a roaring sound and its waves bubbled up and frothed." For cultures which live in the mountains far away from any sea, one may have to say something like this: "the huge lake made a roaring sound . . . " or "the great expanse of water made a roaring sound . . . ."

3.11

RSV	TEV
The sun and moon stood still in their habitation[j] at the light of thine arrows as they sped, at the flash of thy glittering spear.	At the flash of your speeding arrows and the gleam of your shining spear, the sun and the moon stood still.

[j] Heb uncertain.

The sun and moon stood still in their habitation: as the RSV footnote indicates, there are some uncertainties in the Hebrew text of this line. The sun and the moon are both mentioned, but the verb is in the singular. Some scholars have suggested that there should be a second verb to complete the line, and have tried to supply this verb by linking **the sun** with the last line of the previous verse. Such a course of action requires some changes in the last line of the previous verse but is followed by NAB ("The sun forgets to rise, the moon remains in its shelter") and NEB ("The sun forgets to turn in his course, and the moon stands still at her zenith"). This has some support from certain manuscripts of the Septuagint. However, it is not necessary to accept this change in order to make sense of the Hebrew, and translators are recommended to follow the traditional Hebrew text as represented by RSV and TEV (compare HOTTP).

TEV translates "**the sun and the moon stood still**" and puts this main clause at the end of the verse, following the two prepositional phrases, and in many languages this will be the best translation option. **In their habitation** has no equivalent in TEV, but NIV makes it clear that this means "in the heavens." In many languages which cannot talk about the sun and moon "standing still," this clause may be expressed as "The sun and moon stopped moving through the sky." JB has "Sun and moon stay in their houses."

The reference to the **sun and moon** standing still may be an allusion to the story of Joshua's long day (Josh 10.12-13).

The second and third lines in RSV are parallel to each other and say similar things in different words: **at the light of thine arrows as they sped, at the flash of thy glittering spear**. TEV has "At the flash of your speeding arrows and the gleam of your shining spear." The **arrows** and the **spear** are further symbolic references to the lightning of the thunderstorm. It is as though the sun and moon are hiding from God's power demonstrated in the storm (compare JB "avoiding the flash of your arrows, the gleam of your glittering spear"). In natural terms, they were hidden by the clouds (compare verse 8), and their normal brightness was surpassed by the dazzling brightness of the lightning. In some languages the expression **at the flash of** will be difficult to translate. In such cases one may render these lines as "When your speeding arrows flashed and your shining (glittering) spear gleamed . . . ."

3.12

RSV	TEV
Thou didst bestride the earth in fury, thou didst trample the nations in anger.	You marched across the earth in anger; in fury you trampled the nations.

The description moves on from the natural world to its inhabitants and thus provides an introduction to the purpose of the entire theophany given in verse 13. (See comments on the theophany in verse 3.)

Thou didst bestride the earth in fury is expressed in modern terms in TEV as "You marched across the earth in anger." For the idea of God marching, compare Psalm 68.7. For alternative ways to translate **in anger** or **in fury**, see the comment on Nahum 1.3.

The second line is parallel in form to the first line: **thou didst trample the nations in anger**. Again TEV puts this into modern speech: "**in fury you trampled the nations.**" The Hebrew word translated **trample** is frequently used of threshing crops like wheat or barley. This was usually done by having an ox walk round and round in a pit, treading the sheaves of grain with his feet to separate the ears of grain from the stalks (compare Deut 25.4). Sometimes the ox would drag a sledge with sharp stones or knives on the bottom to help the process. This operation was sometimes used in a figurative way to speak of punishment (see Isa 41.15; Amos 1.3; Micah 4.13). This is the case here also. When God is spoken of as trampling the nations, the meaning is that he is punishing them for their wickedness. In some languages it may be necessary to state this in plain language. Two alternative translation models are the following:

When you were angry, you marched across the earth.
When you were furious, you trampled on the nations.

Or:

You marched angrily across the earth,
and trampled furiously on the nations.

In some languages it will be necessary to combine the two clauses and say "You were furious, so you marched across the earth and trampled on all the people in the world." See Nahum 1.6 for comments on the translation of "furious."

3.13

RSV

Thou wentest forth for the salvation of thy people,
for the salvation of thy anointed.
Thou didst crush the head of the wicked,[k]
laying him bare from thigh to neck.[l]   Selah

[k] Cn: Heb *head from the house of the wicked*
[l] Heb obscure

TEV

You went out to save your people,
to save your chosen king.
You struck down the leader of the wicked
and completely destroyed his followers.[g]

[g] *Probable text* completely ... followers; *Hebrew unclear.*

Here at last is the answer to the questions of verse 8. For a discussion of various ways to help the reader understand that this is indeed the answer, see comments on verse 8.

The first part of the verse says the same thing twice in different words. The first line, **Thou wentest forth for the salvation of thy people**, is clear enough. The Hebrew word here translated **salvation** is a form of the same root as that translated "victory" in verse 8. TEV expresses the meaning in modern English as "You went out to save your people."

The second line is not quite so clear. RSV translates literally **for the salvation of thy anointed**. Anointing someone was a sign that the person was specially chosen by God. Thus TEV often translates as "chosen." The question is, to whom does **thy anointed** refer? It is a term often used of the king, either the particular individual, or the kings in general as the descendants of David (as in Psa 89.38,51). TEV accepts this interpretation and translates as "**to save your chosen king**" (compare FrCL, GeCL). However, in this context, where **thy anointed** is parallel with **thy people**, it seems more likely that it refers to the nation of Israel as a whole. If this interpretation is accepted, a translation base can be "to save your chosen nation," or even "to save your chosen nation Israel." This interpretation has some support from the Septuagint, which understood **anointed** collectively and translated as a plural. Compare the usage in Psalm 28.8, where the words "his people" and "his anointed" are again parallel with each other. In languages which do not use the passive, one may say "You went out to save the nation which you have chosen." **Salvation** ("save") in some languages will need to be rendered as a phrase; for example, "help ... to escape from their enemies."

The rest of the verse gives more detail about the way God saves his people, namely, by destroying their enemies. It contains problems both in the text itself and in its interpretation. Either it speaks directly about a person who is leader of the forces opposed to God, or else it speaks of this person through the figure of a building. The ultimate reference is the same either way, but the translator must make two decisions:

(1) Is the Hebrew using figurative language?
(2) If so, is it better to keep it or to drop it in translation?

A literal translation is found in RV: "Thou woundedst the head out of the house of the wicked, laying bare the foundation even unto the neck." As in 2.9, the basic question is whether the word "house" stands for a building or a family. The presence of the word "foundation" in the last line suggests that "house" is intended as a building; compare Mft, BJ, JB, NEB, NJV. (BJ and JB drop the word for "head," though this is hardly necessary.) To wound the head of a house must then be a figurative way to describe damaging or removing the roof (compare GeCL, "You tear off the roof of your enemy's palace"). The last line then goes on to describe the complete destruction of the house. The idea of laying bare the foundations as a sign of complete destruction occurs also in Micah 1.6. If this is the correct interpretation, the main problem lies in the words "even unto the neck" (RV). One would expect some term that refers to the other end from the head, such as foot. Some scholars have suggested dropping one letter from the Hebrew word for neck. This gives a word meaning "rock." To speak of "laying bare the foundations even unto the rock" would make good sense in itself and would also fit the context very well. The change of "neck" to "rock" is accepted by BJ, JB, and NEB.

RSV **laying him bare from thigh to neck** has taken a different interpretation, and has understood the passage to speak directly of the enemy leader as a person. This view has led RSV to drop the word "house" altogether (compare NAB) and apparently to change the word for "foundation" to another word meaning **thigh**. This necessitates changing three letters out of four in the Hebrew word for "foundation" and cannot be judged very convincing.

TEV has adopted the first interpretation discussed above, including the change from "neck" to "rock," but has dropped the figurative language. TEV has made it explicit that the building is a symbol for a group of people, the roof standing for the leader and the rest of the building for the followers. Thus TEV translates "**You struck down the leader of the wicked and completely destroyed his followers**" (compare FrCL). In the context of Habakkuk, this is best taken to refer to the Babylonians.

To sum up, we recommend that translators (1) interpret the passage as speaking of a building which is a symbol for people, and (2) accept the change from "neck" to "rock." In most cases, it will also be helpful to follow the example of TEV, that is, to drop the symbolism and to state clearly that the passage refers to wicked people. But if translators prefer to keep the figurative language, an alternative translation model is the following: "You removed the roof of the house of the wicked, exposing the foundation right down to the rock."

The verse ends with **Selah**; see comments on verse 3.

3.14	RSV	TEV
	Thou didst pierce with thy[m] shafts the head of his warriors,[n] who came like a whirlwind to scatter me, rejoicing as if to devour the poor in secret.	Your arrows pierced the commander of his army when it came like a storm to scatter us, gloating like those who secretly oppress the poor.[h]

ᵐ Heb *his*
ⁿ Vg Compare Gk Syr: Heb uncertain

ʰ *Verse 14 in Hebrew is unclear.*

The description of the defeat of God's enemies continues, and as in the previous verse, there are some problems with the text.

Thou didst pierce with thy shafts the head of his warriors: the Hebrew word translated **thy shafts** in RSV is literally "his own staves" (RV). It is the same word as that translated "arrows" in verse 9 and can be interpreted in the same way here. Many modern versions change one letter of this Hebrew word to alter the possessive suffix and have **"your arrows"** instead of "his arrows" (Mft, BJ, JB, NAB, NEB, TEV, NJV). This has the support of one manuscript of the Septuagint. However, the traditional Hebrew text also makes good sense (RV, TOB, NIV, FrCL, GeCL, HOTTP) and supplies an element of poetic justice, and even makes the punishment fit the crime in a manner similar to that which occurred frequently in the taunts of 2.6-20.

The word **head** may be taken literally (NAB, NIV, NJV, TOB) but is usually understood to mean "leader" (Mft, RSV, BJ, JB, NEB, TEV, FrCL, GeCL), and this seems to fit the context better, especially if verse 13 is understood as in the comments above.

The Hebrew word translated **warriors** in RSV occurs nowhere else, and its meaning is uncertain. The rendering **warriors** is based on the understanding shown in the ancient Latin Vulgate version. It is accepted in most modern versions and makes good sense.

TEV **"Your arrows pierced the commander of his army"** accepts the change from "his" to "your," and with the word **"commander"** makes it clear that it understands "head" in the sense of "leader." Since **warriors** is rather old-fashioned, TEV uses the modern term **"army."** However, in languages which do not have a collective word for army, translators may express the final phrase as "leader (commander) of his soldiers."

Who came like a whirlwind to scatter me translates the traditional Hebrew text (compare RV, TOB, HOTTP), which makes good sense. Some scholars change one letter of the Hebrew to read **"us"** instead of **me** (Mft, BJ, JB, TEV, NIV, FrCL, GeCL). However, **me** can be interpreted as a collective singular, like "anointed" in verse 13, and rendered as the exclusive pronoun "us" on translational grounds rather than by changing the text (Driver, Lehrman).

Other scholars have suggested more extensive changes, so that NEB, for instance, translates "their leaders are torn from them by the whirlwind." NAB omits the line altogether. All this seems quite unnecessary. TEV **"When it came like a storm to scatter us"** expresses the meaning clearly and simply and is an adequate translation model. The words **"to scatter us"** imply a comparison with grain husks which are blown away by the wind of the **"storm."** If translators need to use the word "soldiers" rather than a collective word meaning "army," it is possible to translate the second line as "when they (the soldiers) came like a storm to scatter us." **Scatter** can be rendered as "cause to go in all directions."

The last line adds to the description of the wicked, speaking of their attitude toward God's people: **rejoicing as if to devour the poor in secret**. In this setting the **rejoicing** is for bad reasons, and TEV shows this by the word **"gloating"** (compare NIV; and see Obadiah 12-13; Micah 7.8 in TEV).

To devour is figurative and implies a comparison with wild animals. TEV expresses this in nonfigurative language as **"oppress."** Some versions try to keep the figure of speech in English, but they express it by translating **in secret** as "in their lair" (JB, NAB). "Lair" in English is used primarily of the home of a fierce wild animal (see Nahum 2.11 on the translation of "lair" or "den"). **"Oppress"** may be expressed in some languages as "treat cruelly," "rob," or "plunder."

The Hebrew word for **the poor** meant originally those in physical need. Later it came to be applied to the godly minority, since they were often oppressed by those in power (compare Zeph 3.12). Here the word probably has these religious overtones, but its main reference is to physical need. This is shown by the terms used in various versions: "some poor wretch" (JB); "the wretched" (NAB, NIV); "their wretched victims" (NEB). **Poor** can also be rendered "poor people," or even "powerless people." However, in languages spoken by marginal peoples where most of the population is termed poor by the rest of the world, there may not be precise terms for distinguishing between poor and rich people. In such cases translators will find it helpful to use phrases such as "people who have no possessions" or "people who have only one animal." Alternative translation models for this final clause are "gloating like those who secretly treat poor people cruelly," or in the case of translators who wish to follow RSV's figurative language, "gloating as if they would devour (eat) poor people, as a wild animal does in its den."

3.15   RSV   TEV

Thou didst trample the sea with thy horses, the surging of mighty waters.

You trampled the sea with your horses, and the mighty waters foamed.

The section ends with a general statement which sums up the victory of God. It does not say any more about his human opponents but speaks in terms of nature, as do verses 9-12. It is also similar to Psalm 77.19.

Thou didst trample the sea with thy horses: the expression **trample the sea** reminds readers of the crossing of the Red Sea at the time of the exodus. The **horses** probably stand for the clouds as in verse 8. **The sea**, also as in verse 8, is probably an allusion to powers opposed to God. TEV rephrases with modern grammar as "**You trampled the sea with your horses.**" The various subtle allusions which were understood by the original readers are almost always lost in translation. This is one of the difficulties of translating poetry, but it simply has to be accepted.

RSV takes the second line, **the surging of mighty waters**, to be in apposition to **the sea** in the first line (compare JB). However, in other versions the fact that the waters surge is taken as the result of the treading (NEB, NIV, NJV). This may be stated as a cause—effect relationship, or just as two simultaneous events. TEV does the latter: "**and the mighty waters foamed.**" In this way the cause—effect relationship is implied but not stated explicitly. In some languages it may be necessary to be more explicit and say "You trampled the sea with your horses and made the mighty waters foam" or "You rode your horses over the sea, and they trampled it and made the mighty waters foam."

3.16

RSV

I hear, and my body trembles,
 my lips quiver at the sound;
rottenness enters into my bones,
 my steps totter° beneath me.
I will quietly wait for the day of trouble
 to come upon people who invade us.

° Cn Compare Gk: Heb *I tremble because*

TEV

I hear all this, and I tremble;
 my lips quiver with fear.
My body goes limp,
 and my feet stumble[i] beneath me.

I will quietly wait for the time to come
when God will punish those who attack us.

[i] *Probable text* my feet stumble; *Hebrew* I am excited, because

Just as verse 2 introduced the theophany with a prayer in the first person, so verse 16 concludes the theophany with a statement of the prophet's response, again in the first person. This link is also explicit in the repetition of the verb **hear** in verses 2 and 16. For possible ways of indicating the relationship between the two verses, see the discussion of indentation at verse 8.

I hear, and my body trembles: the object of **I hear** is the sound of the storm which accompanied the presence of God (verses 3-15). TEV makes this clear by saying "I hear all this." The trembling is the result of the hearing, the involuntary reaction of a human being to the deep experience of God's majesty and power. In some languages one may need to say "I hear all this, and so I tremble" or "I hear the sounds of the storm, and so I tremble."

The Hebrew word translated **body** in RSV is literally "belly" (KJV, RV, NEB). Because this sounds undignified in English, RSV has used the more general term **body** (compare JB, NAB), while TEV simply says "I." In some languages it may be perfectly natural to speak of the "belly" here. In others, perhaps some other organ such as the heart, liver, or kidneys will be more natural. It certainly helps to make the passage sound more vivid and poetic if some specific part of the body is mentioned. NIV does this in English with "my heart pounded." NJV attempts it with "my bowels quaked," but this is both old fashioned and rather coarse. Translators should avoid any expression like this which makes it sound as if Habakkuk had a sudden attack of diarrhea!

My lips quiver at the sound: TEV makes the cause explicit by saying "my lips quiver with fear." Again, if necessary, one can substitute some similar action which is considered to show fear, such as "my teeth chatter." In some languages translators may need to say "I am so afraid that my lips quiver (my teeth chatter)" or "my fear makes my lips quiver."

The words **at the sound** have no equivalent in TEV, because their meaning is included in the "all this" of the previous line.

Rottenness enters into my bones is another expression which is natural in Hebrew (compare Pro 12.4; 14.30) but which may sound strange if translated literally into other languages. Most English versions mention **bones**, but the thought is really of the bones as the framework for the body. If the bones are rotten, the body has no support and loses its shape. TEV expresses this meaning in plain language as "My body goes limp." A more idiomatic expression in

English is "my bones turn to jelly." Some translators may be able to find a natural expression in their own language which is of equivalent force.

The last symptom of the prophet's fear is **my steps totter beneath me**. This translation depends on changing three letters of the traditional Hebrew text and has some support from the Septuagint. TEV accepts this change also and says "**my feet stumble beneath me**" (compare JB and NAB). In some languages it may not be necessary to translate the words **beneath me**, since it will be understood that the feet are below the rest of the body. NEB makes a change involving only one Hebrew letter and comes out with a very similar meaning, "my feet totter in their tracks." The traditional Hebrew text is translated "I trembled in my place" (RV) or "I trembled where I stood" (NJV), so that the difference in meaning between the various possibilities is not very great. The problem with the traditional text is that it necessitates a close connection between this clause and the next, which makes awkward sense. As the footnotes indicate, this would mean translating "I tremble because I will quietly wait . . . " (RSV) or "I am excited because I will quietly wait . . . " (TEV). Some versions try to lessen the problem by translating as "yet" instead of "because" (Mft, NIV, NJV). On the whole, however, it seems better to accept the change in the traditional text and translate as RSV and TEV.

The second half of the verse gives a different kind of reaction to the theophany. It is as though the prophet's physical fear passes, and he sees the implication of God's ability and willingness to help his people as he did in ancient times. This implication is that God's people do not need to worry about the political situation, however bad it may seem, because God will never abandon them. When the realization of this has penetrated the prophet's fear, he can say **I will quietly wait for the day of trouble to come upon people who invade us**. Here at last is an answer to the problem of 1.13. Though God may punish his own people's sins by using other nations whose sins are even greater, nevertheless he will not overlook the sins of these other nations but will bring **the day of trouble** upon them also in due time. TEV gives the same meaning but makes it explicit that God is the one who is responsible for punishing the enemy: "**I will quietly wait for the time to come when God will punish those who attack us.**" In certain languages this sentence may be expressed as "I will wait with a quiet heart for the day . . . ."

There are some difficulties in deciding the exact meaning of the traditional Hebrew text, but all available modern versions except one give the same sense as RSV and TEV. The exception is NJV, which has "yet I wait calmly for the day of distress, for a people to come to attack us." This can also be seen as a response of faith to the problems of 1.13, but it seems less appropriate than the alternative. We therefore recommend that translators follow the sense given in RSV and TEV.

3.17-18 RSV   TEV

17 Though the fig tree do not blos-   17 Even though the fig trees have
      som,   no fruit
    nor fruit be on the vines,   and no grapes grow on the
    the produce of the olive fail   vines,
      and the fields yield no food,   even though the olive crop fails
    the flock be cut off from the   and the fields produce no
      fold   grain,

and there be no herd in the stalls,	even though the sheep all die and the cattle stalls are empty,
18 yet I will rejoice in the LORD, I will joy in the God of my salvation.	18 I will still be joyful and glad, because the LORD God is my savior.

These two verses form one long sentence in Hebrew and also in most English translations. Verse 17 contains a series of six clauses introduced by **Though** (RSV), and verse 18 gives two more clauses introduced by **yet**. There are two problems that must be resolved before we discuss the details: (1) how is this sentence related to its context; and (2) how is the translator to handle such a long sentence as this?

(1) Some scholars understand that verse 17 describes a series of facts rather than a series of possibilities. This has led them to regard the verse as a kind of side remark which is not closely related to the preceding and following verses. Thus JB puts verse 17 in brackets, and implies that verse 18 both follows on from verse 16 and develops the expression of faith with which verse 16 ends. This makes verses 16-19 as a whole rather disjointed and robs verse 17 of any real relevance.

Even if verse 17 does describe facts rather than possibilities, in the context of this psalm, it is very reasonable to interpret them as possibilities which seem so vivid to the prophet that he describes them as if they had already happened. On this interpretation it is legitimate to translate verse 17 as a series of possibilities, to which verse 18 gives the prophet's reaction. This makes verse 17 stand apart from verse 16, but gives a cohesion to the whole of verses 17-19 which enables them to be seen as a fitting climax to the psalm, and indeed to the whole book.

This second interpretation is found in most versions (KJV, RV, RSV, Mft, NAB, NEB, TEV, NIV, NJV) and is definitely to be recommended to translators.

(2) If the above interpretation is accepted, there still remains the problem of how to handle such an unusually long and complex sentence. The **Though** of RSV introduces no less than six clauses, before the **yet** of verse 18 introduces the balancing half of the sentence. Most English versions simply accept this, and indeed the structure remains clear in English, even in RSV. Several versions repeat the word "though" at the beginning of the third and fifth clauses (NAB, TEV, NIV, NJV). This helps to make the structure even clearer and also indicates that the clauses go together as pairs in Hebrew.

One alternative is to do as the French TOB has done, that is, to make verse 17 a separate sentence ("Yes, the fig tree does not blossom" and so on), then to begin again in verse 18 with "As for me, I will nevertheless rejoice in the Lord . . ." (compare FrCL).

Another alternative is as follows: As already noted, the six clauses of verse 17 go together in pairs. In some languages it may be clearer to give the first line of verse 18 after each of the first two pairs of clauses in verse 17. This will necessitate combining the verses into one and numbering them as 17-18. It will also lead to some repetition which is not in the Hebrew. However, such repetition may help to increase the poetic effect in some languages. If this suggestion has to be adopted, a possible translation model for the two verses is:

¹⁷⁻¹⁸ Even if there are no figs on the fig trees and no grapes on the vines, yet I will be joyful because of the LORD. Even if there

are no olives on the olive trees, and no grain grows in the fields, yet I will be joyful because of the LORD. Even if there are no sheep in the sheep pens and no cattle in the cattle stalls, yet I will be glad because God protects me.

Once translators have decided how to handle the overall structure of the sentence, they can begin to examine the details. The verse is speaking of complete economic disaster, but it does so in the specific terms of the economy of Palestine. This was based on patterns of agriculture and animal use which may be unfamiliar in many cultures. However, the prophet is here speaking of things which are central features of his own culture, and these should be retained in translation if at all possible. If there is no way to speak of particular items like figs, grapes, olives, or grain, translators should not substitute other items (such as bananas, oranges, pineapples, and rice) which would have been unknown in Palestine in Habakkuk's time. In such cases translators may have to use generic terms and perhaps combine each pair of clauses into one. A possible translation model in this kind of situation is:

17-18 Even if the fruit trees do not bear any fruit and the gardens (or, fields) do not have any crops, yet I will be happy because of the LORD. Even if the animals that provide meat all die, yet I will be joyful and glad because God protects me.

In situations where it is possible to speak of the specific items of Palestinian culture, translators should note that the food items listed here seem to be mentioned in ascending order of importance. Figs were perhaps the most luxurious items in the list. They were important as a source of sugar but were not essential. See Nahum 3.12 for a detailed discussion on the translation of **fig tree**, which will also apply to other fruit trees. "Grapes" produced wine, the normal daily drink. To be without it was a hardship but would not kill anyone. "Olives" gave oil which was used for cooking and lighting, and the lack of this oil would be a serious inconvenience. "Grain" (primarily wheat and barley) provided the staple food for the entire population, and the loss of the grain crop would mean starvation on a large scale (compare Gen 42.2).

The death of all the "**sheep**" and goats would mean no meat, since these were the animals most often eaten. It would also mean no wool from the sheep, with which to make warm clothes for the winter, and no milk or other dairy products like butter and cheese from the goats. "**Cattle**" were eaten rarely and only as a luxury, but without them there would be no help with plowing to prepare the ground for a crop the following year.

Though the fig tree do not blossom: TEV instead of **blossom** translates "have no fruit." This appears to follow the Septuagint and implies a change of one letter in the traditional Hebrew text. But there is no real difference in meaning since, if the trees have no flowers, they cannot bear any fruit. The TEV wording may have been chosen for translation reasons and may not in fact follow the Septuagint.

Nor fruit be on the vines: TEV mentions the specific fruit that is to be expected on vines, namely, "**grapes**" (compare NIV); but many languages will translate in a similar way to RSV and say, "and the vines produce no fruit." In cultures where grape vines do not exist, one may need to use a generic word for vines or vine-like plants, along with the English word "grape." However, when choosing a word for a vine-like plant, one must avoid terms which may give the reader the wrong picture. One should identify the grape vine as a vine which produces fruit, and avoid types of vine which produce such things as pumpkins.

The produce of the olive is expressed more simply as **"the olive crop"** in TEV (compare Mft, NEB, NIV, NJV). In many languages this will be expressed as "there is no fruit on the olive tree."

The fields yield no food: this is a generic statement which in this context obviously refers to the main crops grown in the fields, wheat and barley. These were the most important items of diet and were used in making bread. TEV makes the meaning of **food** explicit by saying **"grain"** (British edition "corn"). In many languages the generic term for food will be identical with the name of the staple crop, such as rice, yam, sago, or sweet potato.

The flock be cut off from the fold: the word **flock** was used in Hebrew of both sheep and goats. Some English versions retain the ambiguity by keeping the word **flock**, which may refer to both sheep and goats (RSV, Mft, NAB, NEB). Other versions give the name of one particular animal; all the available English versions which do this say **"sheep"** (TEV, JB, NIV, NJV). Presumably this is because sheep are much more common than goats in English-speaking countries. In areas where goats are more common, there is no reason why translators should not say goats rather than sheep, or else "goats and sheep."

Be cut off is a common Hebrew expression for death or destruction (compare Nahum 1.12,14,15; 2.13; 3.15; Zeph 1.3,4,11; 3.6; and many other Old Testament passages). TEV translates the plain meaning as **"even though the sheep all die."**

The fold ("pen" in NIV and NJV) was a walled enclosure where sheep and goats were kept at night for safety from wild animals and robbers. In areas where this method of looking after sheep and goats is not known, there is no need to mention the fold (compare TEV).

And there be no herd in the stalls: the term **herd** refers to **"cattle"** (TEV, JB, NEB, NIV, NJV). This means mainly cows and oxen, and in languages with no generic term equivalent to **"cattle,"** it may be necessary to mention by name whichever species is better known.

Stalls were places where cattle could be kept and fed. As most people possessed few cattle, the stalls were often near, or even inside, the house where the family lived. Again the emphasis is on the animals rather than their accommodation, and in areas where **stalls** are unknown, there is no need to mention them. Compare the two possible translation models suggested above for variation in this respect.

In the Hebrew verse 18 says the same thing twice in different words: **I will rejoice in the LORD, I will joy in the God of my salvation**. Most English versions retain this parallel structure, as it has some poetic value in English. However, in some languages this may not be desirable. TEV has restructured the verse as **"I will still be joyful and glad because the LORD God is my Savior."**

The God of my salvation (compare Psa 18.46; 24.5; 25.5; 27.9; Isa 17.10; Micah 7.7) is expressed in TEV as **"God is my Savior."** In some languages this may need to be expressed with a verb such as "the God who saves me," "the God who protects me," or "the God who delivers me" (compare NEB, NJV).

3.19

RSV

GOD, the Lord, is my strength;
he makes my feet like hinds' feet,
he makes me tread upon my high places.

To the choirmaster: with stringed^P instruments.

TEV

The Sovereign LORD gives me strength.
He makes me sure-footed as a deer
and keeps me safe on the mountains.

^P Heb *my stringed*

GOD, the Lord, is my strength: the Hebrew here has both YHWH, the personal name of God, and the title *adonai* (lord). This is why **GOD** is spelled with capital letters in RSV (compare Zeph 1.7). For a fuller discussion, see the comments on Obadiah 1 in *A Translator's Handbook on the Books of Obadiah and Micah*. TEV translates this expression as "**The Sovereign LORD**" (compare NIV).

Is my strength means "is my source of strength." TEV restructures this as "gives me strength." It may also be expressed as "causes me to be strong."

The second half of the verse contains the same thought as 2 Samuel 22.34 and Psalm 18.33, though the words in Hebrew are not identical.

He makes my feet like hinds' feet: **hinds** are female deer and can run very swiftly. Some species of deer can also climb steep and rocky places safely. The point of the comparison here may be either speed (NAB) or sure-footedness (Mft, TEV). Since the context speaks of moving among **high places** (TEV "mountains"), it seems more likely that sure-footedness is in view. TEV has "**He makes me sure-footed as a deer**," and NEB has "makes my feet nimble as a hind's." Several modern versions (RSV, NIV, NJV, BJ, TOB) fail to show what the point of the comparison is. In many languages this point will not be obvious, and so translators should take care to make it explicit, as TEV has done by adding "**sure-footed**."

He makes me tread upon my high places: the meaning is expressed clearly in TEV as "keeps me safe upon the mountains." The Hebrew expression for **tread upon my high places**, like several earlier parts of the psalm, has overtones of reference to the Lord's actions in the days of Moses (compare Deut 32.13; 33.29). It is also used of the Lord's triumphant movement over the earth in Amos 4.13; Micah 1.3. All who, like Habakkuk, have learned to trust the Lord in times of trouble, will be given the privilege of sharing in his eventual triumph (compare 2 Tim 2.12). An alternative translation model for the last two lines of this verse is "He helps me to run over the high mountains (or, hills) without stumbling, just as a deer does."

The Hebrew text ends with two words translated in RSV **To the choirmaster: with stringed instruments**. This is another musical instruction such as appears at the beginning of several psalms (Psa 4; 6; 54; 55; 61; 67; 76). It relates to the use of the psalm in the liturgical worship of the temple and is not part of the words of the prophet. For this reason it is printed in different type in some Bibles (Mft, NAB, TOB, FrCL) and is omitted in others (NEB, TEV). Translators should include or omit these words according to what they have done in the psalms listed above. If the Book of Psalms has not yet been translated, then it is probably best to set the example here of omitting the musical instruction, since it is not relevant to modern readers. Alternatively, it can be mentioned in a footnote (compare the comments on "Shigionoth" in verse 1).

Translating the Book of Zephaniah

Zephaniah is probably the earliest of the prophets who brought the message of the Lord to the people of Judah in the seventh century B.C. Most commentators agree with the statement in the Introduction to Zephaniah in TEV which places his work in the years shortly before the great reform carried out by King Josiah in 621 B.C. For more details about this, see 2 Kings 22—23 and 2 Chronicles 34—35.

Zephaniah was convinced that the day was near when the Lord would act to judge all the nations. It is possible that the background to this belief lay in an invasion from the north by a fierce nomadic nation of horsemen called the Scythians. According to the Greek historian Herodotus, the Scythians swept as far south as the borders of Egypt. So far as is known they did not attack or pass through Judah, but traveled through the coastal plains occupied by the Philistines. If the invasion of the Scythians took place about 627 B.C., Zephaniah's prophetic work would most likely date from shortly after this.

Some scholars have felt that certain parts of the book come from a later time than the seventh century B.C., but there is little general agreement. Such questions are rarely of concern to translators and therefore are not discussed in this handbook.

Outline

The outline of the book given in TEV will be followed in this handbook, namely:

      1.1—2.3   The day of the Lord's judgment
      2.4-15   The doom of Israel's neighbors
      3.1-20   Jerusalem's doom and redemption

Many commentators would prefer to divide chapter 3 into more than one section, and indeed, TEV itself treats 3.14-20 as separate from the earlier part of the chapter by giving this paragraph a separate section heading and setting it out as poetry.

* * * * * * *

In an article published too recently to be available when the main body of this Handbook was being prepared, Ivan J. Ball, Jr. has proposed an analysis of the whole book of Zephaniah which is quite different from that found in the TEV Outline of Contents. It is based on a detailed study of the Hebrew text, and although it is not represented in any modern English translation, it deserves careful consideration by people who are translating into other languages.

Ball takes Zephaniah 2.1-7 as the starting point for his analysis and maintains that these verses form a unit. (If he is correct, then a major break between sections after 2.3 in TEV is in the wrong place.) He sees 2.1-7 as composed internally of three smaller units which may be set out as follows:

TRANSLATING THE BOOK OF ZEPHANIAH

    (a) 2.1-3   Warning of the coming Day of the Lord
    (b) 2.4   Destruction of the enemy
    (c) 2.5-7   Woe and salvation

He supports this view with many arguments based on the Hebrew which cannot be repeated here. A significant point in his favor is that he handles the traditional Hebrew text without suggesting any alterations, even where it is hard to understand, as in 2.2.

Then he goes on to claim that the structure of 2.1-7 is a miniature picture of the structure of the whole Book of Zephaniah. He analyzes the complete book as follows:

    (A) 1.2-18   Warning of the coming Day of the Lord
     (2.1-7   Analyzed as above)
    (B) 2.8-15   Destruction of the enemy
    (C) 3.1-20   Woe and salvation

He is able to point out many similarities of wording in Hebrew between paragraphs, as follows:

    (a) 2.1-3   and   (A) 1.2-28
    (b) 2.4   and   (B) 2.8-15
    (c) 2.5-7   and   (C) 3.1-20

If translators wish to follow this analysis, then they will need to think carefully about an outline and section headings. It may be best to use two levels of section headings, as TEV already does in a few places such as Amos 1.3—2.5. One way of setting this out is:

    The day of the LORD's judgment, 1.1-18
    Summary of the prophet's message, 2.1-7
        (a) The day of the LORD's judgment, 2.1-3
        (b) The LORD will destroy his enemies, 2.4
        (c) The LORD will judge foreign enemies and bless his own people, 2.5-7
    The LORD will destroy his enemies, 2.8-15
    The LORD will judge his enemies in Jerusalem and bless those who obey him, 3.1-20

Section headings in the text can be mostly the same as in this outline, though some translators may not wish to use the subheadings in the outline above as section headings. It may also be helpful to split chapter 3 into two sections. One heading may appear at 3.1 as "The LORD will judge his enemies in Jerusalem," and a second probably at 3.9 as "The LORD will bless those who obey him."

SECTION 1: THE DAY OF THE LORD'S JUDGMENT
(Chapters 1.1–2.3)

Chapter 1

This section falls into three main units:

1.1 Introduction
1.2-18 The announcement of the Lord's punishment
2.1-3 A call to repentance

The middle unit also has three parts:

1.2-3 God's universal judgment
1.4-16 God's judgment on Judah
1.17-18 God's universal judgment

In a Hebrew structure of the kind found in this middle unit, where the first part and the last part parallel each other, and the middle part is different, the focus is often on the middle part. That appears to be the case here, since Zephaniah's main interest is in God's judgment on the people of Judah.

1.1 RSV

The word of the Lord which came to Zephaniah the son of Cushi, son of Gedaliah, son of Amariah, son of Hezekiah, in the days of Josiah the son of Amon, king of Judah.

TEV

This is the message that the Lord gave to Zephaniah during the time that Josiah son of Amon was king of Judah. (Zephaniah was descended from King Hezekiah through Amariah, Gedaliah, and Cushi.)

The word of the Lord is a common way of introducing a prophecy (compare Jer 1.2; Hos 1.1; Joel 1.1; Jonah 1.1; Micah 1.1; Hag 1.1; Zech 1.1; Mal 1.1). TEV makes a full sentence ("**This is the message that the Lord gave**"), and many translators will need to do the same. Some may need to say "This is the message that the Lord sent (or, spoke) to Zephaniah." See Nahum 1.1 for other ways to translate this clause.

The name **Zephaniah** means "The Lord has hidden" and may perhaps refer to God's protection from persecution at the time of Zephaniah's birth during the reign of the evil king Manasseh.

The father of Zephaniah was called **Cushi** (compare Jer 36.14). Elsewhere in the Old Testament this name is usually found as an ethnic label, meaning a person from Cush, the Upper Nile region which included most of modern Sudan

Zeph 1.1   THE DAY OF THE LORD'S JUDGMENT

and part of Ethiopia. Here it may mean that Zephaniah's father was an African, and that Zephaniah himself was a black man. This possibility gains some support from the fact that in his short prophecy Zephaniah twice (2.12; 3.10) mentions the land or people of Cush (translated "Ethiopia" in RSV and "Sudan" in TEV). A Cushite dynasty had ruled Egypt 715-663 B.C., and this no doubt led to increased familiarity with Cushites in Judah, and perhaps to some intermarriage with them. It was quite possible for a Cushite to settle in Jerusalem at this period. Indeed we know that a few years later, Jeremiah was rescued by Ebedmelech, the God-fearing eunuch from Cush (Jer 38.7-13; 39.15-18). See also comments on Nahum 3.9.

The book of Zephaniah is unique in that the family of Zephaniah is named for four generations, going back to a **Hezekiah**. The only reason that can be suggested for this unusual amount of detail is that the **Hezekiah** in question was in fact the king of that name. TEV makes this explicit by saying "**King Hezekiah**." If the prophet Zephaniah was indeed descended from King Hezekiah, then he was a relative of King Josiah. This would fit well with certain parts of his prophecy, as he shows a detailed knowledge of Jerusalem (verses 10-11) and of the conduct of court officials (1.8-9; 3.3). Translators should follow the way genealogies are handled in their own languages, rather than simply copying the Hebrew pattern (RSV) or TEV's ordering of names. Alternative renderings of this genealogy are "King Hezekiah was the ancestor of Zephaniah. Zephaniah's father was Cushi, his paternal grandfather was Gedaliah, and his paternal great-grandfather was Amariah the son of Hezekiah" or "King Hezekiah was the ancestor of Zephaniah. Zephaniah's father was Cushi, his father's father was Gedaliah. Gedaliah was the son of Amariah who was the son of Hezekiah."

Zephaniah prophesied **in the days of Josiah the son of Amon, king of Judah**, that is, 640-609 B.C. **In the days of Josiah** means "during the time that Josiah . . . was king," as TEV puts it. **Josiah** was **the son of Amon**, who had been king of Judah 642-640 B.C. He was thus the grandson of Manasseh, who reigned from 687-642, and the great-grandson of King Hezekiah. Josiah was only a boy of eight when he became king (2 Kgs 22.1), and so did not have full authority during the early years of his reign. Zephaniah's prophetic work was probably begun about the time that King Josiah reached full adult status. In some languages translators may render **king** as "the great chief" or "the great one." One should avoid borrowing the English word if at all possible. Another way to translate this clause is "during the time when Josiah the son of Amon ruled Judah."

1.2-18

RSV

TEV
The Day of the LORD's Judgment

2 "I will utterly sweep away everything
      from the face of the earth," says the
      LORD.
3 "I will sweep away man and beast;
      I will sweep away the birds of the air
      and the fish of the sea.
   I will overthrow the wicked;
      I will cut off mankind
      from the face of the earth," says the
      LORD.
4 "I will stretch out my hand against

2 The LORD said, "I am going to destroy everything on earth, 3 all human beings and animals, birds and fish. I will bring about the downfall of the wicked. I will destroy all mankind, and no survivors will be left. I, the LORD, have spoken.

4 "I will punish the people of Jerusalem and of all Judah. I will destroy the last trace of the worship of Baal there, and no one will even remember the pagan priests who serve him. 5 I will destroy anyone who goes up on the roof and

The announcement of the Lord's punishment   Zeph 1.2-18

      Judah,
        and against all the inhabitants of Jerusalem;
      and I will cut off from this place the remnant of Baal
      and the name of the idolatrous priests;
5   those who bow down on the roofs
        to the host of the heavens;
      those who bow down and swear to the LORD
      and yet swear by Milcom;
6   those who have turned back from following the LORD,
      who do not seek the LORD or inquire of him."

7   Be silent before the Lord GOD!
      For the day of the LORD is at hand;
      the LORD has prepared a sacrifice
      and consecrated his guests.
8   And on the day of the LORD's sacrifice—

      "I will punish the officials and the king's sons
      and all who array themselves in foreign attire.
9   On that day I will punish
      every one who leaps over the threshold,
      and those who fill their master's house with violence and fraud."

10   "On that day," says the LORD,
      "a cry will be heard from the Fish Gate,
      a wail from the Second Quarter,
      a loud crash from the hills.
11   Wail, O inhabitants of the Mortar!
      For all the traders are no more;
      all who weigh out silver are cut off.
12   At that time I will search Jerusalem with lamps,
      and I will punish the men
      who are thickening upon their lees,
      those who say in their hearts,
      'The LORD will not do good,
      nor will he do ill.'
13   Their goods shall be plundered,
      and their houses laid waste.
      Though they build houses,
      they shall not inhabit them;
      though they plant vineyards,
      they shall not drink wine from them."

14   The great day of the LORD is near,
      near and hastening fast;
      the sound of the day of the LORD is bitter,
      the mighty man cries aloud there.
15   A day of wrath is that day,
      a day of distress and anguish,
      a day of ruin and devastation,
      a day of darkness and gloom,
      a day of clouds and thick darkness,
16   a day of trumpet blast and battle cry
      against the fortified cities
      and against the lofty battlements.

17   I will bring distress on men,
      so that they shall walk like the blind,
      because they have sinned against the LORD;

worships the sun, the moon, and the stars. I will also destroy those who worship me and swear loyalty to me, but then take oaths in the name of the god Molech. 6 I will destroy those who have turned back and no longer follow me, those who do not come to me or ask me to guide them."

7 The day is near when the LORD will sit in judgment; so be silent in his presence. The LORD is preparing to sacrifice his people and has invited enemies to plunder Judah. 8 "On that day of slaughter," says the LORD, "I will punish the officials, the king's sons, and all who practice foreign customs. 9 I will punish all who worship like pagans and who steal and kill in order to fill their master's house with loot.

10 "On that day," says the LORD, "you will hear the sound of crying at the Fish Gate in Jerusalem. You will hear wailing in the newer part of the city and a great crashing sound in the hills. 11 Wail and cry when you hear this, you that live in the lower part of the city, because all the merchants will be dead!

12 "At that time I will take a lamp and search Jerusalem. I will punish the people who are self-satisfied and confident, who say to themselves, 'The LORD never does anything, one way or the other.' 13 Their wealth will be looted and their houses destroyed. They will never live in the houses they are building or drink wine from the vineyards they are planting."

14 The great day of the LORD is near—very near and coming fast! That day will be bitter, for even the bravest soldiers will cry out in despair! 15 It will be a day of fury, a day of trouble and distress, a day of ruin and destruction, a day of darkness and gloom, a black and cloudy day, 16 a day filled with the sound of war trumpets and the battle cry of soldiers attacking fortified cities and high towers.

17 The LORD says, "I will bring such disasters on mankind that everyone will grope about like a blind man. They have sinned against me, and now their blood will be poured out like water, and their dead bodies will lie rotting on the ground."

18 On the day when the LORD shows his fury, not even all their silver and gold will save them. The whole earth will be destroyed by the fire of his anger. He will put an end—a sudden end—to everyone who lives on earth.

>   their blood shall be poured out like dust,
>   and their flesh like dung.
> 18 Neither their silver nor their gold
>   shall be able to deliver them
>   on the day of the wrath of the LORD.
>   In the fire of his jealous wrath,
>   all the earth shall be consumed;
>   for a full, yea, sudden end
>   he will make of all the inhabitants of
>   the earth.

SECTION HEADING: "**The Day of the LORD's Judgment.**" The heading to this section may need to be expanded into a full sentence such as "The day is coming when the LORD will judge people." The "people" here refers to all people on earth (see verses 3 and 17), not just the Lord's own people, though these are of course included (verses 4-13).

The section is broken into five paragraphs in RSV (verses 2-6, 7-9, 10-13, 14-16, 17-18). TEV has paragraph breaks in all these places, but also has extra breaks beginning with verses 4, 12, and 18. In other languages it will generally be more convenient to follow the shorter paragraphs of TEV.

1.2-3

RSV

2 "I will utterly sweep away everything
    from the face of the earth,"
    says the LORD.
3 "I will sweep away man and beast;
    I will sweep away the birds of the air
    and the fish of the sea.
  I will overthrow[a] the wicked;
    I will cut off mankind
    from the face of the earth,"
    says the LORD.

[a] Cn: Heb *the stumbling blocks*

TEV

2 The LORD said, "I am going to destroy everything on earth, 3 all human beings and animals, birds and fish. I will bring about the downfall of[a] the wicked. I will destroy all mankind, and no survivors will be left. I, the LORD have spoken."

[a] *Probable text* I will bring about the downfall of; *Hebrew* the stumbling blocks.

These two verses go closely together. The first is a general statement of judgment, and the second is an expansion of it which gives specific details of the form that the judgment will take. The words used echo the flood story of Genesis (see Gen 6.7; 7.4,21-23; and compare also Hos 4.3; Ezek 38.19-20).

The words translated **utterly sweep away** in RSV are not figurative in Hebrew. However, **sweep away** is a figure of speech that sounds very natural in English. The same phrase occurs in JB, NAB, and NIV, and NEB is also similar. Such a figurative term adds vividness to the effect, and if translators have some such term which is natural in their own language, this will be a good place to use it. In Hebrew the verb root is repeated to intensify the meaning, and this is why RSV inserts **utterly**. TEV has no equivalent to this, but in some languages it may be good to say "I will completely sweep away (or, destroy) ...." If some figurative word other than **sweep** is more natural, such as perhaps "eat up" or "wipe out" (compare verse 18), then this will be the better term to choose. TEV

The announcement of the Lord's punishment   Zeph 1.2-3

expresses the meaning in nonfigurative language as "**destroy**." In some languages one may say "kill." Although God is the one initiating the "destroying," or "killing," others actually carry out the action. Therefore in many other languages it will be helpful to say "I will cause every living creature to die."

The face of the earth means simply "the earth," which here refers to the whole world, not just the land of Judah.

In Hebrew each verse ends with the words translated **says the LORD** in RSV. TEV changes the order so as to put "**The LORD said**" at the beginning of verse 2, and thus it makes the speaker explicit right from the start. The phrase at the end of verse 3 which is identical in Hebrew becomes in TEV "**I, the LORD, have spoken.**" This is more appropriate in English, both to avoid dull repetition and to mark the close of this subsection. Some languages normally mark the end of a speech in a way similar to that of Hebrew; for example, "I, the LORD say it like this."

The general word **everything** in verse 2 clearly does not refer to inanimate things, but only to living beings. Verse 3 gives more detail with four categories of creature, **man and beast . . . the birds of the air and the fish of the sea**. The words **of the air** and **of the sea** are standard forms of expression in Hebrew which go with **birds** and **fish** respectively. They add nothing to the meaning and need not be translated if they sound unnatural. TEV omits them and says only "**human beings and animals, birds and fish.**" In some languages it will be helpful to say "all living things on earth."

As the footnote shows, the translation **I will overthrow** is based on a slight change in the traditional Hebrew text. This change is accepted by most modern translators into English and underlies the English of RSV, JB, NAB, NEB, and TEV. The Hebrew text as it stands is translated in NIV "The wicked will have only heaps of rubble," but a footnote in that version admits that the meaning of the Hebrew is uncertain. It is better for translators to accept the change in the text and translate as do RSV and TEV.

The point being made here is that it is the deeds of **the wicked** which are the basic reason for the Lord to judge and punish the world. **I will overthrow the wicked** will be rendered in many languages as "I will cause the wicked to be completely defeated," or in some languages which do not favor the passive, the following is possible: "I will cause people to overthrow (conquer) those who do evil." The mention of **the wicked** is the central point and climax of the verse, and the last part of the verse, **I will cut off mankind from the face of the earth**, repeats and summarizes what was said in verse 2 and the opening part of verse 3. **The wicked** may also be rendered as "the bad people," "the people who are evil," or "people who do evil things."

The verb **cut off** is a dead metaphor in Hebrew, that is, a metaphor which is so common that it has virtually ceased to be recognized as figurative. So TEV translates in nonfigurative language as "**destroy**" (compare Nahum 1.15; 2.13; 3.15). If the verb **cut off** is used figuratively with the right meaning in the translator's language, then it can be kept here, but if not, then it will be better to translate the nonfigurative meaning as TEV does.

From the face of the earth is repeated from verse 2. Here it has been translated in TEV as "**no survivors will be left**"; this may also be expressed as "no one will be left alive" or "I will not let anyone stay alive anywhere on the earth."

An alternative translation model for this final sentence is:

I will cause people to conquer those who do evil. I will wipe out everyone, so that no one will be left alive anywhere in the world. I, who am the LORD, say this.

1.4

RSV

"I will stretch out my hand against Judah,
and against all the inhabitants of Jerusalem;
and I will cut off from this place the remnant of Baal
and the name of the idolatrous priests;[b]

TEV

"I will punish the people of Jerusalem and of all Judah. I will destroy the last trace of the worship of Baal there, and no one will even remember the pagan priests who serve him.

[b] Compare Gk: Heb *idolatrous priests with the priests*

Verses 4-6 form a unit in Hebrew which consists of a long list of different classes of people in Judah and Jerusalem who will be singled out for punishment. For a comparable list, see 2 Kings 23.5. Since it is not natural in English to have the long list of noun phrases in verses 4 to 6 dependent on a single verb in verse 4, as in RSV, TEV has split the list into several sentences and repeated the clause "I will destroy" in each sentence.

At the beginning of verse 4 in Hebrew there is a figure of speech which is retained in RSV, <u>I will stretch out my hand against</u> (compare 2.13). This figure is not normal usage in English, and TEV therefore drops it and gives the meaning in nonfigurative language with **"punish."** In other languages, however, this figure of speech may well be acceptable, and translators should consider whether they can keep it in their own language. <u>Punish</u> may be restructured as "cause to suffer" (see comments under Nahum 1.2).

The opening part of verse 4 also shows a repetitive structure in Hebrew which can be seen in the RSV wording <u>against Judah, and against all the inhabitants of Jerusalem</u>. TEV makes the English clearer by reversing the order of the place names to give **"the people of Jerusalem and of all Judah."** This also has the effect of putting the main focus on Jerusalem, which is what the Hebrew does by mentioning Jerusalem last. Since this is the first mention of Jerusalem in Zephaniah, it will be helpful for many translators to identify it as a city or town. An alternative translation base for this first sentence is "I will cause all the people in the city of Jerusalem and in the land of Judah to suffer." For comments on the translation of "city," see notes on Nahum 3.1

TEV's **"I will destroy"** translates the Hebrew verb for <u>cut off</u>, as in the previous verse. See verse 3 for comments on the translation of <u>cut off</u> or "destroy."

The remnant of Baal means "every vestige of idol worship" (Lehrman) and is expressed in TEV as **"the last trace of the worship of Baal."** This may need to be expressed in some languages as "every single person who worships Baal." This is the first time the god **Baal** has been mentioned in these three prophetic books. In many languages translators will need to identify **Baal** as a male god and as a false god (see Nahum 1.14 for a discussion on the translation of "god").

The announcement of the Lord's punishment　　　　　　　　　　　　　　Zeph 1.5

In Hebrew the verb **cut off** also governs a second object, which is rendered in RSV **the name of the idolatrous priests**. These are of course the priests involved in the cult of Baal, and TEV makes this explicit with its "**the pagan priests who serve him.**" The Hebrew expression **cut off . . . the name** means "cause people to forget," and this is the meaning expressed nonfiguratively in TEV, "**no one will remember.**"

The Hebrew text contains two more words, translated **with the priests** in the RSV footnote. The ancient Greek translation omits these words, and many modern versions do the same, including RSV, Mft, JB, NEB, TEV, and FrCL. However, the word used suggests that the second group are priests of the Lord who have turned away from him to serve Baal. One can therefore translate "no one will remember the pagan priests or the priests who have turned away from the Lord."

1.5

RSV	TEV
those who bow down on the roofs to the host of the heavens; those who bow down and swear to the Lord and yet swear by Milcom;	I will destroy anyone who goes up on the roof and worships the sun, the moon, and the stars. I will also destroy those who worship me and swear loyalty to me, but then take oaths in the name of the god Molech.

In Hebrew verse 5 continues the sentence begun in verse 4. RSV keeps the Hebrew sentence structure, but TEV, as mentioned above, repeats "**I will destroy**" here to begin a new sentence and so produce a more natural structure in English. Many translators will wish to do likewise.

People would easily be able to go **on the roofs** of their houses, because in Palestine house roofs were normally flat. In cultures where houses do not have flat roofs, a footnote or a note in the word list will be helpful. It will be preferable in many languages to translate this clause as "goes up on the roof of a house and worships," similar to TEV. The objects of their worship are called in RSV **the host of the heavens**, which follows the form of the Hebrew expression. The plain meaning of this phrase is made explicit by TEV with "**the sun, the moon, and the stars.**" However, in many languages translators may wish to use more general expressions similar to the Hebrew; for example, "the heavenly bodies." One advantage of going onto the roof to worship these heavenly objects was that from there the worshiper had a clear and unbroken view of his so-called gods in the sky.

The second half of verse 5 deals with people whose loyalties are divided between the Lord and other gods. On the one hand they **bow down and swear to the Lord**, and on the other hand they also **swear by Milcom**. **Swear** in this context has nothing to do with using bad language. To **swear** to or **by** a god meant to partake in the worship of that god. The meaning is well expressed in TEV as "**who worship me and swear loyalty to me**" and "**take oaths in the name of the god Molech.**" The clause **swear to the Lord** ("swear loyalty to me") may be expressed as "promise that they will be loyal to me," or even "give a strong promise that they will serve me faithfully."

The Lord is the speaker in verses 4-6 but refers to himself in the third person as **the Lord** once in verse 5 and twice in verse 6. Since this is unnatural

Zeph 1.5 THE DAY OF THE LORD'S JUDGMENT

in English, TEV translates as **"me"** on all three occasions. Many translators will wish to do the same.

The actual name of the false god here is somewhat uncertain. The consonants of the Hebrew text are *mlkm*, and in the Hebrew manuscripts the vowels added give the word *malkam*, which means "their king." This wording is followed in the KJV and RV and is taken as a proper name, Malcham (KJV) or Malcam (RV). Ancient translations, however, gave different vowels to the consonants *mlkm* and translated as "Milcom," the god of the Ammonites. This is the wording followed by RSV, JB, NAB, NEB, FrCL, GeCL, and the 1976 printing of TEV. Another and more common form of this name is "Molech," as found in the 1979 printing of TEV, and in NIV. This is probably formed by writing the consonants *mlk* with the vowels of the Hebrew word *bosheth* "shame," thus dishonoring a false god. The reason TEV now prefers the form "Molech" is that there are several other references to the worship of Molech in Judah in the period when Zephaniah was alive, such as 2 Kings 23.10; Jeremiah 32.35. The majority of modern versions retain the form Milcom. Whichever form of the name is used, the meaning of the verse remains the same, being a reference to the worship of a false god.

1.6

RSV

those who have turned back from
  following the LORD,
who do not seek the LORD or
  inquire of him."

TEV

I will destroy those who have turned back and no longer follow me, those who do not come to me or ask me to guide them."

Again RSV keeps the Hebrew sentence structure, continuing the sentence begun in verse 4. TEV begins a new sentence and once more repeats the verb "**I will destroy**" from verse 4.

The people condemned this time are those who, while they may not have taken up the worship of other gods, are no longer active in the worship of the Lord; they **have turned back from following the LORD**. In many languages one cannot speak of **following** a person in the sense of "serving." In such a case translators may say "going with the LORD" or "serving the LORD." The whole sentence may be restructured as "I will destroy those who have stopped serving me." For the Lord's reference to himself in the third person, see comments on verse 5. (For comments on "**destroy**" see verse 3).

In the second half of the verse, RSV translates literally the rather technical terms of the Hebrew, **seek the LORD** and **inquire of him**. These are expressed in clearer language in TEV's "**come to me**" and "**ask me to guide them.**" In certain languages it will be helpful to make these last two clauses into a separate sentence and say "These people do not come to me or ask me to guide them."

1.7

RSV

Be silent before the Lord GOD!
For the day of the LORD is at
  hand;

TEV

The day when the LORD will sit in judgment is near; so be silent in his presence. The LORD is preparing to

The announcement of the Lord's punishment   Zeph 1.8

the LORD has prepared a sacrifice and consecrated his guests.	sacrifice his people and has invited enemies to plunder Judah.

This verse is an introduction to a long section of direct speech from the mouth of the Lord covering verses 8-13. It sets forth the topic of the following verses, namely, **the day of the LORD**.

To be **silent** in the presence of God is a sign of reverence and is mentioned elsewhere in this connection (Hab 2.20; Zech 2.13). The clause **Be silent before the Lord GOD** may be expressed idiomatically in certain languages as "Be silent in front of the face of the Lord GOD," or "Do not say anything when you are in front of the Lord GOD's face," or "Do not say anything when you are in the place where the Lord GOD is."

For the spelling of **GOD** with capital letters, see the comments on Habakkuk 3.19.

The day of the LORD: TEV expands this expression to make the full meaning clear by saying "The day when the LORD will sit in judgment." Other possible translation models are " . . . sit to judge people" or " . . . cut judgment against the people of the world." **The day . . . is at hand** may also be expressed as "The day when . . . will come very soon" or "The time when . . . will come very soon." TEV also reverses the order of the first two clauses in Hebrew, giving the reason (the nearness of judgment) before the command which follows from it, "**so be silent in his presence.**"

The second half of verse 7 uses the technical language of sacrificial ritual. The Hebrew roots underlying the words **sacrifice**, **consecrate**, and **guests** all appear in 1 Sam 16.5, but whereas there a literal sacrifice is being described, here the terms have a figurative meaning. The judgment of God is pictured as a **sacrifice** in which God's own people are slaughtered by their enemies. When guests at a sacrifice were **consecrated**, this involved ritual purification and also constituted official invitation. Here the focus is on the invitation, and so TEV translates "**has invited.**" The **guests** in this case are enemies who will punish the people of Judah, and TEV "**enemies**" makes this meaning explicit. TEV makes the identification of all the participants clear by saying "**The LORD is preparing to sacrifice his people and has invited enemies to plunder Judah.**" One can also make the event or action implied in the word sacrifice more explicit by saying "to slaughter his people as animals are killed in sacrifice." (Compare with Jehu's slaughter of the worshipers of Baal in 2 Kgs 10.18-27.)

1.8   RSV   TEV

And on the day of the LORD's sacrifice— "I will punish the officials and the king's sons and all who array themselves in foreign attire.	"On that day of slaughter," says the LORD, "I will punish the officials, the king's sons, and all who practice foreign customs.

On the day of the LORD's sacrifice: RSV takes the first phrase to be introductory, whereas TEV takes the Lord's words to start at the beginning of the verse. Probably the TEV interpretation is better, since the phrase "**On that day**" is repeated at the beginning of verses 9 and 10, and the similar phrase "At that time" comes at the beginning of verse 12. Each time, the phrase is part of the Lord's words. Presumably RSV interprets as it does in order to avoid having the Lord speak of himself in the third person. This is not unusual in Hebrew, but it sounds odd in English and many other languages. TEV maintains a natural English structure by dropping the third-person reference and saying "On that day of slaughter." It is also possible to turn this phrase into a clause with a first-person reference and say "On that day when I have my people slaughtered" or " . . . when I cause their enemies to slaughter my people."

I will punish the officials and the king's sons: **the officials** are the leaders of the court and government. **The king's sons** refers to the royal family in general, not just the princes, and in most languages it will be helpful to indicate this by saying "the king's family." The fact that the king himself is not mentioned is taken by some scholars as evidence that this passage dates from the time when King Josiah was still a child. If Zephaniah was indeed related to the king, he would have been well acquainted with the conduct of people in high places. Another translation model for this sentence is "I will punish the king's (chief's) advisors and the members of his family."

All who array themselves in foreign attire: foreign clothes showed that those who wore them were sympathetic to foreign customs, which usually involved the worship of foreign gods. Perhaps this is a reference to clothes used particularly in such worship. Compare with 2 Kings 10.22; 2 Maccabees 4.12. TEV omits the reference to clothes and translates in general terms as **"all who practice foreign customs."** In certain languages one may say "all who follow foreign customs," or "all who follow the customs of foreigners (foreign people)," or "all who worship foreign gods."

1.9	RSV	TEV
	On that day I will punish every one who leaps over the threshold, and those who fill their master's house with violence and fraud."	I will punish all who worship like pagans and who steal and kill in order to fill their master's house[b] with loot. [b] their master's house; *or* the temple of their god.

On that day: In many languages it will be helpful to repeat this phrase at the beginning of verses 9 and 10, as RSV does (compare also "At that time" in verse 12).

The expression **every one who leaps over the threshold** is of uncertain meaning. It has usually been interpreted in the light of 1 Sam 5.4-5 as a practice associated with pagan religion (compare NIV "all who avoid stepping on the threshold"). In this sense it has some parallels in other parts of the world. TEV follows this understanding and makes it explicit by saying **"all who worship like pagans."** "Pagans" may be expressed in many languages as "people who worship false gods."

However, there are other possible interpretations. One interpretation takes **threshold** to refer to the homes of the poor and thus pictures the servants of the rich rushing madly into the homes of the poor in order to rob them. This understanding fits well with the second half of the verse.

A third possibility is that the word translated **threshold** in RSV actually means a raised platform on which the king's throne stood, and that the word translated **leaps** means "climbs." This understanding seems to be behind the JB rendering "all those who are near the throne."

NEB also interprets **threshold** to mean a raised platform but takes it to refer to a part of the temple where the altar was situated ("the temple terrace"). The word for **leaps** is taken to refer to dancing, and the whole clause is translated "all who dance on the temple terrace." This is a reference to pagan worship, as in the interpretation followed by TEV.

The way in which the second half of the verse is to be understood depends on the way in which the first part was taken. **Their master's house** may refer to the royal palace which the wicked officials fill with goods acquired by **violence and fraud**. The TEV footnote gives as an alternative "the temple of their god," understanding "master" to refer not to the king but to a pagan god. NEB and FrCL show the same two possibilities, giving "their master's house" in the text and the alternative in a footnote. JB follows the same interpretation but gives no footnote for an alternative; it shows that it understands "master" to refer to the king by translating **house** as "palace" (compare GeCL). NIV, on the other hand, gives only the second possibility and says "who fill the temple of their gods with violence and deceit." On the whole "their master's house" seems the more probable interpretation.

The abstract nouns **violence and fraud** refer to acts of beating people up or killing them, and acts of stealing by deception or cheating. The phrase **with violence and fraud** is somewhat ambiguous. To speak of filling a house with violence and fraud may mean that crimes of violence and cheating take place in the house. This is probably the meaning intended by NEB, "who fill their master's house with crimes of violence and fraud." However, it seems more likely that the Hebrew refers to filling the master's house with goods obtained as a result of crimes of violence and fraud. TEV accepts this interpretation and makes it explicit with **"who steal and kill in order to fill their master's house with loot."** Note that TEV has reversed the order of **violence and fraud** by putting "steal" before "kill." This is because killing is a more serious crime and so makes a more effective climax in English. Another translation model can be based on FrCL, "all those who fill their master's house with riches acquired through [crimes of] deception and violence."

Some scholars regard verses 8 and 9 as an example of a chiasmus, that is, a structure of the pattern "a-b-b-a." With this understanding, the first part of verse 8 goes with the second part of verse 9, and the second half of verse 8 goes with the first half of verse 9. This has the advantage of closely linking the two clauses that deal with foreign customs. It also takes the last part of verse 9, the part about violent behavior, to be a description of the court officials mentioned at the beginning of verse 8. This view is the one behind Mft: "8 I will punish the officials and the royal house, who by their violence and fraud enrich the palace; 9 I will punish all who leap across the threshold, and all arrayed in foreign garb."

A chiasmus is a common feature of Hebrew writing, and it seems quite likely that verses 8 and 9 are indeed an example of it. If translators wish to adjust the order of the clauses to bring together those which are related in theme, they should number the verses at the beginning as "8-9" rather than change the order of clauses, as Mft did, without indicating what they have done.

It is not certain whether the text in these verses is speaking of two groups of people, (a) violent officials and (b) those who indulge in pagan worship, or whether the officials are the same people who adopt pagan ways. On the whole, the latter seems more probable, since in prophetic writings it is often those who turn away from the Lord who also turn to violence. A possible alternative translation model for verses 8 and 9 (similar to Mft's) is:

> 8-9 On that day when I cause my people to be slaughtered, I will punish the officials and the king's family members who steal and kill in order to fill their master's house with things they have taken by force. I will punish them because they follow the customs of foreigners and worship like those who honor false gods.

1.10

RSV	TEV
"On that day," says the LORD, "a cry will be heard from the Fish Gate, a wail from the Second Quarter, a loud crash from the hills.	"On that day," says the LORD, "you will hear the sound of crying at the Fish Gate in Jerusalem. You will hear wailing in the newer part of the city and a great crashing sound in the hills.

Verses 10 and 11 go together and describe a scene in which Jerusalem is being captured by an enemy army. This continues the theme of the Lord punishing his people, as is suggested by the repetition of the phrase **On that day** at the beginning of verse 10.

A cry will be heard from the Fish Gate: TEV avoids the passive and supplies a subject, saying "**you will hear the sound of crying.**" The **cry** is the noise made by people shouting in distress, and in some languages it will be necessary to make this explicit and say "you will hear people (or, the sound of people) crying out." The site of **the Fish Gate** can no longer be identified, but it was on the north side of the city (Neh 3.3), the side on which an enemy would attack. In some languages **the Fish Gate** may be expressed as "the gate named Fish." It may also be helpful to identify the city as Jerusalem (TEV).

A wail from the Second Quarter: a **wail** is also a sound expressing distress, but it is probably not intended as a contrast with the word translated **cry**. Rather the two words are in parallel with each other, and if translators can find two words in their own language with similar meanings, that will probably give much the same effect as the Hebrew. A **wail** may be translated as "you will hear people wailing."

The Second Quarter: this was a district on the northern side of the city, near the Fish Gate (2 Kgs 22.14). As it had been built more recently than other areas, TEV translates as "**the newer part of the city.**" One may also say "the new part of the town nearby (or, near the Fish Gate)."

In some languages it may be helpful to combine the two parallel clauses and say "you will hear the sound of people shouting and crying in distress at the Fish Gate and in the newer part of the city."

The **loud crash from the hills** is caused by the fall of buildings being destroyed by the enemy army. In certain languages this will need to be made explicit by saying "the noise of buildings crashing down on the hills." The **hills**

The announcement of the Lord's punishment   Zeph 1.12

refers to the hills on which Jerusalem was built, so one may say "from the hills in (or, of) Jerusalem."

1.11	RSV	TEV

> Wail, O inhabitants of the Mortar!
> For all the traders are no more;
> all who weigh out silver are cut off.

> Wail and cry when you hear this, you that live in the lower part of the city, because all the merchants will be dead!

Inhabitants of the Mortar: a mortar is a vessel in which food or other substances can be pounded. A particular area of Jerusalem was known as **the Mortar**. It is not certain exactly where this area was, but from its name, scholars assume it was in a hollow somewhere within Jerusalem. Many have suggested the northern part of the Tyropoeon Valley, and this fits the context well, since it is near the Second Quarter and thus in the same general area as the places mentioned in verse 10. It was also a market area, and this fits with the mention of **traders** in the second part of the verse. TEV translates the general meaning without mentioning any district by name: "**you that live in the lower part of the city.**"

The words of TEV "**when you hear this**" have no basis in the Hebrew text and are best omitted (compare FrCL, GeCL).

For all the traders are no more; all who weigh out silver are cut off: the parallel structure of the Hebrew can be seen from the literal translation of the RSV. The term rendered **traders** is literally "people of Canaan" (RV; compare JB). It may refer to foreign traders, most likely Phoenicians, but probably the expression is more general and refers also to Jews. The last line of the Hebrew speaks of the traders as those **who weigh out silver**. Since coinage was not in use at this time, it was necessary in each transaction to weigh the metal that served for money. Since this procedure is virtually unknown today, it will probably be better for most translators to follow the example of TEV and express these two parallel lines as one: "**because all the merchants will be dead.**" For **traders** ("merchants") see comments on Nahum 3.16; for **cut off** see comments on verse 3.

1.12	RSV	TEV

> At that time I will search Jerusalem with lamps,
> and I will punish the men who are thickening upon their lees,
> those who say in their hearts,
> 'The LORD will not do good,
> nor will he do ill.'

> "At that time I will take a lamp and search Jerusalem. I will punish the people who are self-satisfied and confident, who say to themselves, 'The LORD never does anything, one way or the other.'

Verses 12 and 13 go together as the third section of the direct speech of the Lord, which covers verses 8-13. This section is introduced by the phrase **At that time**, which is parallel to "On that day" in verses 9 and 10.

I will search Jerusalem with lamps: the word for **search** implies a very thorough search by the enemy invaders, to find any hidden treasure or any people trying to escape. The word for **lamps** implies small clay lamps held in the hand. It is not the same as the word for torches in Nahum 2.4. In some languages this clause will be expressed as "I will use lamps to search Jerusalem."

I will punish the men who are thickening upon their lees: the Hebrew metaphor is drawn from the process of wine-making. When the wine has fermented, it has to be poured from one vessel to another to separate the wine from the sediment which is called **lees**. This process is described in Jeremiah 48.11. If this is not done, the wine becomes too sweet and spoils. The verb translated **thickening** means "condense" or "congeal." **The men who are thickening upon their lees** are people who have enjoyed uninterrupted wealth for too long and have thus become "self-satisfied and confident" (TEV). "Self-satisfied" can be rendered idiomatically in many languages; for example, "filled-up-breast-filled-up-heart." "Confident" can be translated as "trusting in oneself completely." Material prosperity has made such people forgetful of God and led them to **say in their hearts** that the Lord has no interest in them. In cultures where wine-making is a well-known process, one may be able to keep the Hebrew figure of speech. Otherwise it will be better to follow the example of TEV and use nonfigurative language.

Say in their hearts is expressed in more natural English in TEV as "**say to themselves**." In certain languages this idea is more naturally expressed as "think in their hearts" or merely "think."

These people think that **The LORD will not do good, nor will he do ill**: that is, he will not take action at all, either for good or for bad. These are the people that the invading enemy will search out and punish, and then they will realize how wrong their views about the Lord were. An alternative translation model for this final sentence is "The LORD will do nothing to us, whether for our good, or to hurt us."

1.13	RSV	TEV
	Their goods shall be plundered, and their houses laid waste. Though they build houses, they shall not inhabit them; though they plant vineyards, they shall not drink wine from them."	Their wealth will be looted and their houses destroyed. They will never live in the houses they are building or drink wine from the vineyards they are planting."

Their goods shall be plundered and their houses laid waste: the material goods on which the people relied will be taken away from them. In languages which do not use the passive, translators may say "Their enemies will take away all their possessions, and will destroy their houses."

The last part of the verse gives in traditional language a picture of people being disappointed in their hope for things which they would have expected to enjoy in the normal course of events: **Though they build houses, they shall not**

The announcement of the Lord's punishment Zeph 1.14

inhabit them; though they plant vineyards, they shall not drink wine from them. TEV expresses the meaning more simply by doing away with the subordinate clauses and saying "**They will never live in the houses they are building or drink wine from the vineyards they are planting.**" The same picture is used to describe punishment in Deuteronomy 28.30; Amos 5.11; Micah 6.15. **Vineyards** may be rendered as "places for growing grape vines" or "gardens where grape vines are grown." See Habakkuk 3.17 for further comments on the translation of "grape vines."

1.14 RSV TEV

The great day of the LORD is near,	The great day of the LORD is near—very near and coming fast!
near and hastening fast;	That day will be bitter, for even[c] the bravest soldiers will cry out in despair!
the sound of the day of the LORD is bitter,	
the mighty man cries aloud there.	[c] That day . . . even; *or* Listen! That terrible day is coming when even.

Verses 14-16 take up again the theme of the nearness of the day of the Lord first mentioned in verse 7. They are best taken as a comment by the prophet himself before the direct words of the Lord begin again in verse 17, though NIV takes them as continuing the quotation begun in verse 2.

The great day of the LORD is near: the words in Hebrew are the same as in verse 7, with the addition of **great**, and the same event is meant. In some languages it will be helpful to repeat the words from verse 7 and say, for example, "The day when the LORD will judge people is near." **Near** may be expressed in many languages as "coming very soon." **Near and hastening fast** means "near and quickly coming nearer."

The second half of the verse is difficult in Hebrew and is translated literally in RSV: **The sound of the day of the LORD is bitter, the mighty man cries aloud there**. Various scholars have suggested ways of improving the sense. One of these suggestions involves changing only the word divisions of the Hebrew without altering any of the letters, and this suggestion seems to be behind the NEB translation "no runner so fast as that day, no raiding band so swift." However, the traditional Hebrew text is intelligible, and TEV gives its sense clearly with "**That day will be bitter, for even the bravest soldiers will cry out in despair.**" The alternative given in the TEV footnote does not involve changing the text of the Hebrew, but only dividing the sentence into clauses differently. "**That day will be bitter**" may also be rendered as "That day will be full of tragedy," or "That day will bring only sorrow," or "That day will cause people to receive great sorrow." Translators may be able to express this meaning in their languages by means of an idiom or figure of speech.

It is possible that the cry given by **the mighty man** is not to be understood as one of "**despair**," as in TEV, but rather as a battle cry. This understanding is shown by JB "the warrior shouts his cry of war," and probably by NIV "the shouting of the warrior." However, the general emphasis of the paragraph is on the trouble that people will suffer on the day of the Lord, and for this reason it seems best to follow the understanding of TEV. In some languages "**cry out in** despair" may be expressed as "cry out because there is no hope of receiving help."

An alternative translation model for this verse is:

> The day when the LORD will judge people is near—very near. It is coming very soon. That day will cause people to receive great sorrow, and even brave soldiers will cry out because they have no hope of receiving help.

1.15-16

RSV

15 A day of wrath is that day,
    a day of distress and anguish,
    a day of ruin and devastation,
    a day of darkness and gloom,
    a day of clouds and thick darkness,
16 a day of trumpet blast and battle cry
    against the fortified cities
    and against the lofty battlements.

TEV

15 It will be a day of fury, a day of trouble and distress, a day of ruin and destruction, a day of darkness and gloom, a black and cloudy day, 16 a day filled with the sound of war trumpets and the battle cry of soldiers attacking fortified cities and high towers.

These two verses form one sentence in Hebrew and are composed of short, vivid, and poetic descriptive phrases with no main verb stated. The verb "to be" is implied and is used in all major English translations, as in RSV **A day of wrath is that day**. **Wrath** or "fury" refers to the anger of God. So one may translate "It will be a day when God displays his fury (terrible anger)," or in a more figurative way, "It will be a day when God shows a terribly hot heart." See Nahum 1.2 for other ways to translate "anger."

A day of distress and anguish: in Hebrew there is a play on the sounds of the two nouns used. The second has some sounds similar to the first but has an extra syllable at the beginning. A similar structure would be produced in English by translating "a day of stress and distress" (Mft), but this is not in keeping with patterns of poetic usage in English. If translators can use some kind of play on sounds that fits their own language patterns, that will be very suitable here. In some languages translators may need to expand this sentence and say "a day when people will be troubled and distressed" or "a day when people will receive trouble and experience terrible difficulties."

A day of ruin and devastation: a similar play on the sounds of the Hebrew words is used here, and again it will be appropriate to use a play on sounds in a translation, if it can be done according to the patterns of the language. No major English version succeeds in making a play on the sounds, in this case. This phrase also occurs as "dry and desolate ground" in Job 30.3; 38.27. In some languages it will be necessary to show the subject of the events of **ruin** and **destruction**; for example, "a day when the enemies will cause ruin and destruction."

A day of darkness and gloom, a day of clouds and thick darkness: there are no wordplays in these phrases, but a translator should feel free to include them here instead of (or as well as) in the previous phrases, if it is easier to do so. These phrases occur also in Joel 2.2. As with the previous sentences, translators

The announcement of the Lord's punishment Zeph 1.17

may need to structure this sentence in a slightly different way; for example, "a day full of darkness and gloom, a day full of clouds." **Gloom** is similar to **darkness**. Perhaps it can be expressed as "complete darkness."

A day of trumpet blast: blowing a trumpet was the traditional way to call soldiers to prepare for battle (see Judges 3.27; 6.34). The trumpets were actually made of rams' horns, and many translators will have terms in their languages for some similar instrument. The same type of description is found in Amos 2.2. In many languages one may say "A day when they blow the war trumpets (rams' horns)," or even "A day when people hear the sound of the war trumpet."

And battle cry against the fortified cities and against the lofty battlements: this last part of the verse in Hebrew consists of three phrases. The first of them is closely linked with the earlier part of the sentence, and the other two are parallel to each other in structure. All this can be seen clearly from the literal translation of RSV. TEV has made the relationships between the different parts explicit by stating that the **battle cry** is "**of soldiers attacking**." In many other languages this information will also need to be made explicit. The **fortified cities** of ancient times usually had a strong stone wall around them and were strengthened with **lofty battlements**, or as TEV puts it more simply, "**high towers**" at the corners. In some languages, of course, these cities will need to be described as "large groups of houses surrounded by strong walls with high towers at the corners," or some similar phrase. The whole of this passage may be based on the events at the time of the Scythian raid mentioned in the introduction, "Translating the Book of Zephaniah."

Translators should notice, in tackling a passage like this, that part of the meaning comes from the cumulative effect of having phrase heaped upon phrase. In some languages it may be difficult to find words exactly equivalent to those in the Hebrew, especially where the Hebrew uses pairs of words very close together in meaning, as in verse 15. In such languages the translator should not worry too much about matching the number of terms in the original, but rather about matching the overall effect in building a picture of terror and panic. The fact that a number of phrases in these verses occur elsewhere in the Old Testament as noted above suggests that the language is partly traditional, making use of established expressions. Translators may therefore be able to use similar traditional expressions in their own language to create a similar effect, even if the individual words are not identical in meaning with those of the Hebrew. They should be careful, however, not to introduce into the translation any element that would have been culturally or historically impossible in Israel in the seventh century B.C.

1.17	RSV	TEV
	I will bring distress on men, so that they shall walk like the blind, because they have sinned against the LORD; their blood shall be poured out like dust, and their flesh like dung.	The LORD says, "I will bring such disasters on mankind that everyone will grope about like a blind man. They have sinned against me, and now their blood will be poured out like water, and their dead bodies will lie rotting on the ground."

At this point the Hebrew goes back to the first person, and TEV marks this by the introductory words **"The LORD says,"** to identify the speaker. The question arises whether verses 17 and 18 continue to speak of the Lord's judgment on the people of Judah only, or whether they speak of all mankind. The wording is capable of either interpretation, but these verses close an entire section, and it is very much in keeping with Hebrew structure to refer at the end to the same theme as was mentioned at the beginning. In verses 2-3 the theme was universal judgment, and most English translations take that to be the theme again here.

I will bring distress on men, so that they shall walk like the blind: the word here translated **distress** is a form of the same Hebrew root that occurred in verse 15. **Men** here means not just males, but **"mankind"** (TEV). **I will bring distress on men** may also be rendered as "I will cause people to undergo such disasters (terrible difficulties) that . . . ."

They shall walk like the blind: the idea of punishment by the Lord being like blindness is found also in such passages as Deuteronomy 28.29 and Isaiah 59.10. Its meaning is that, when the Lord acts, people will be helpless and unable to find a way of escape. In certain languages the construction **"such . . . that"** is difficult to match literally. In such cases one may render this first sentence as "I will cause people everywhere to undergo terrible disasters, and as a result everyone will grope about . . . ." One may also express this as "I will cause mankind to receive terrible disasters until they grope about . . . ."

Because they have sinned against the LORD: the Lord here refers to himself in the third person, but since this is unnatural in English, TEV keeps first-person references throughout the verse. RSV and most other English translations follow the Hebrew punctuation of the verse and take this clause with those that preceded. TEV takes it with what follows, but the overall meaning of the verse is hardly affected. Either way, this clause states the cause, and the rest of the verse states the effects arising from it.

Their blood shall be poured out like dust: **like dust** seems unnatural in English because it does not sound appropriate to compare a liquid with a solid. TEV therefore drops the original comparison and uses another one, **"like water."** This is both natural in English and is also found elsewhere in the Old Testament (Psa 79.3). Most important, it conveys the same meaning as the original, namely, worthlessness. But although this is appropriate in English, it may not be so in other languages, especially in areas where water is scarce and precious. Translators should consider carefully what will be appropriate and natural in their own language. Some may find it natural to retain the expression **like dust**, or perhaps to say "like sand." In languages which do not use the passive, alternative translation models are the following: "Their enemies will pour out their blood like . . . " or "Their enemies will cause their blood to flow like . . . ."

And their flesh like dung: the comparison of flesh with rotting waste matter shows that the flesh is the flesh of dead people. TEV makes the meaning clear by dropping the figure of speech and translating in nonfigurative language: **"and their dead bodies will lie rotting on the ground."** If a translator has made the previous sentence active, this sentence may be rendered as "and leave their dead bodies to rot on the ground." It may also be possible to restructure the two sentences together without mentioning an agent, by saying "their blood will flow like dust (or sand, or water), and their dead bodies will lie on the ground and rot."

The announcement of the Lord's punishment   Zeph 1.18

1.18   RSV   TEV

Neither their silver nor their gold shall be able to deliver them on the day of the wrath of the LORD. In the fire of his jealous wrath, all the earth shall be consumed; for a full, yea, sudden end he will make of all the inhabitants of the earth.	On the day when the LORD shows his fury, not even all their silver and gold will save them. The whole earth will be destroyed by the fire of his anger. He will put an end—a sudden end—to everyone who lives on earth.

RSV apparently takes this verse to be a continuation of the direct quotation in verse 17, and it is also taken as such, for instance, by NIV. If a translator regards verse 18 as a continuation of the quotation, he will probably need to retain first-person references to the Lord throughout the verse. In view of the parallel theme between verses 2-3 and verses 17-18, this seems the most probable interpretation. However, TEV takes the verse to be a comment by the prophet, as does FrCL.

Neither their silver nor their gold shall be able to deliver them: this may be another reference to the Scythian invasion. According to Herodotus, when the Scythians reached the borders of Egypt, they were bribed by the Pharaoh to turn back and not to attack his land. Zephaniah here makes the point that no amount of money can buy escape from the punishment of the Lord. **Their** and **them** refer to mankind in the previous verse. In some languages it will therefore be helpful to say "not even all the silver and gold of mankind will save them." In cultures where silver and gold are not used or even known, one may say "How ever rich they are, their money will not help them to escape."

On the day of the wrath of the LORD: TEV changes the order of the Hebrew phrases so as to put this time phrase first, which it translates as "**On the day when the LORD shows his fury.**" This follows a more natural order in English and also matches verses 8, 10, 12, and 14, all of which begin with a time phrase.

In the fire of his jealous wrath, all the earth shall be consumed: this whole clause is repeated in 3.8. It is common in the Old Testament to speak of the Lord's **wrath** as being like **fire** (for example Psa 79.5; 89.46; Isa 30.30; 66.15; Jer 15.14; 17.4; Nahum 1.6), and if possible this figure of speech should be kept in translation. It may be expressed more easily in some languages as a simile or comparison than as a metaphor. The word translated **jealous wrath** refers to the Lord's concern for the honor which is rightly his. It does not have the sense common in ordinary English conversation, of envious desire for that which rightly belongs to someone else. See also comments on Nahum 1.2.

As mentioned in the discussion of verse 17, RSV understands this verse to refer to a universal judgment by God, and therefore uses the term **earth** rather than "land," as NEB. "Land" would refer only to Judah.

The verb translated **consumed** is literally "eaten." TEV drops this metaphor and renders as "**destroyed**," but some translators may be able to keep it, if it is natural in their language to speak of fire eating things. In languages which do not use the passive, alternative translation models are "The LORD will destroy the whole world (earth) with the fire of his anger," or "The LORD is so angry that he will destroy the whole world as if by fire," or even "The LORD's heart is hot just like a fierce fire and will burn up the whole world."

For a full, yea, a sudden end he will make of all the inhabitants of the earth: there is probably another play on the sounds of the Hebrew words here translated as **full (end)** and **sudden end**. In many languages it will be impossible to reproduce this play on sounds in Hebrew. In such cases one may say, for example, "he will suddenly kill every person who lives on earth." This clause is the climax to the lengthy description of the Lord's judgment, which has taken up most of chapter 1.

Chapter 2

2.1-3

RSV

1 Come together and hold assembly,
   O shameless nation,
2 before you are driven away
   like the drifting chaff,
   before there comes upon you
   the fierce anger of the LORD,
   before there comes upon you
   the day of the wrath of the LORD.
3 Seek the LORD, all you humble of the land,
   who do his commands;
   seek righteousness, seek humility;
   perhaps you may be hidden
   on the day of the wrath of the LORD.

TEV
A Plea for Repentance

1 Shameless nation, come to your senses 2 before you are driven away like chaff blown by the wind, before the burning anger of the LORD comes upon you, before the day when he shows his fury. 3 Turn to the LORD, all you humble people of the land, who obey his commands. Do what is right, and humble yourselves before the LORD. Perhaps you will escape punishment on the day when the LORD shows his anger.

This paragraph draws a conclusion from the message of judgment in chapter 1. The conclusion is that the people of Judah should repent in the hope that the Lord will spare them.

Some scholars take this paragraph with the verses that follow as a call to the Philistines to repent, but this seems unlikely for two reasons. Firstly, the paragraph follows a section in which Judah is the object of the Lord's anger (1.4-16), and secondly, there is no mention of the Philistines or anything connected with them until 2.4.

SECTION HEADING: "**A Plea for Repentance**." The TEV section heading may need to be expanded into a full sentence in some languages. It can be expressed as "The prophet calls the people to repent" or something similar. Translators who prefer to follow Ball's analysis (as described in "Translating the Book of Zephaniah") will need a heading such as "The prophet sums up his message," to cover 2.1-7.

2.1-2

RSV

1 Come together and hold assembly,
   O shameless nation,
2 before you are driven away
   like the drifting chaff,[c]
   before there comes upon you
   the fierce anger of the LORD,

TEV

1 Shameless nation, come to your senses 2 before you are driven away like chaff blown by the wind, before the burning anger of the LORD comes upon you, before the day when he shows his fury.

> before there comes upon you
> the day of the wrath of the
> LORD.

^c Cn Compare Gk Syr: Heb *before a decree is born; like chaff a day has passed away*

The verbs translated **Come together** and **hold assembly** are forms of the same root in Hebrew. The root is derived from a word for "stubble" and is used elsewhere of gathering straw (Exo 5.7, 12) or sticks for firewood (Num 15.32; 1 Kgs 17.10). This fits a setting in which the Lord's anger has been compared to fire (1.18), but the allusion can hardly be kept in translation. The meaning of neither form of the root is certain, nor is it clear whether any difference is intended between them. Some translations render both forms identically, and some give them different meanings. JB leaves a blank space in its translation and lists the various possibilities in a footnote. These are stated as "assemble together," "enter into yourselves," "bow down," and "heap yourselves up" (that is, for the threshing mentioned in verse 2). The first interpretation for both Hebrew verbs is followed by RSV, NAB, NEB, NIV, and NJV (usually using the English verb "gather"), though it is not easy to see how this is relevant to the context. Mft seems to give the first meaning to the first verb ("huddle") and the third meaning to the second verb ("cower"). GeCL gives the second meaning ("enter into yourselves") to the first verb, and the third meaning ("bow down") to the second verb. Presumably the action of cowering or bowing down is seen as a symbol of repentance, which fits the context quite well. BJ and TOB follow the fourth possibility ("heap yourselves up"). TEV and FrCL give the second meaning to both verbs. FrCL translates "take the trouble to consider (the situation), take hold of yourselves." TEV understands the verbs to have the meaning expressed idiomatically in English as "pull yourselves together" and translates only once, saying in plain language **"come to your senses."** This fits the context of a call to repentance and is probably the course which most translators will want to follow. In some languages the clause **"come to your senses"** may have to be expanded to "think about the evil things you have done, and repent . . . ."

The term translated **shameless** (RSV, TEV; compare NAB "without shame" NIV "shameful") may perhaps mean "without desire" and is translated thus in JB. It would have to mean "without desire for God," but the problem is that God is not mentioned. The ancient Greek and Syriac translations understood it differently again, and their understanding is apparently followed in NEB, "you unruly nation." All these translations fit the context fairly well, but translators should probably follow the majority of English versions in understanding the meaning as **shameless** (compare FrCL, GeCL). **Shameless** does not mean "having no cause for shame" but rather "having reason to be ashamed, but failing to show shame." In certain languages it will be necessary to render this phrase as "you people who have no shame," "you people who will not admit your evil deeds," or idiomatically in certain languages as "you hard-faced people" or "you thick-faced people."

The term translated **nation** is a word which in Hebrew normally refers to non-Jewish nations. It has been argued above that this paragraph is addressed to

Judah, and if this is true, then the use of this word may imply that the people of God have become no different from heathen nations.

The opening words of verse 2 are very difficult to understand. A literal translation of the traditional Hebrew text is given in the RSV footnote, "before a decree is born; like chaff a day has passed away." The first part of this, "before a decree is born," can perhaps be taken to mean "before the events decreed by the Lord take place" (compare HOTTP). This interpretation seems to underlie NIV, "before the appointed time arrives." Many modern translations make a change in the Hebrew text and obtain a meaning similar to that in RSV, **before you are driven away like the drifting chaff** (JB, NAB, NEB). Earlier editions of TEV at this point followed the Septuagint and rendered "before you wither and die like a flower," which makes good sense in the context. However, later editions of TEV are closer to RSV and have "**before you are driven away like chaff blown by the wind**," with no footnote.

The second half of verse 2 says the same thing twice in almost identical words: **before there comes upon you the fierce anger of the LORD, before there comes upon you the day of the wrath of the LORD**. TEV also uses two clauses in English but varies the wording slightly to make the expressions more natural: "**Before the burning anger of the LORD comes upon you, before the day when he shows his fury.**" Translators should consider what is natural in their own language before deciding how to translate. Some will perhaps follow the example of TEV in having two clauses with variant words. Others will prefer to stay closer to the Hebrew structure and say the same thing twice in very similar words. Others again may prefer to avoid repetition and put the two clauses into one which expresses all the distinctive material from both, such as "before the day when the burning anger of the LORD comes upon you" or "before the day when the LORD shows his great anger by punishing you the way a fire burns" (see comments on "wrath" in 1.18 for ways to translate "burning anger").

An alternative translation model for the two verses is:

[1] You people (nation) without shame, think about your sins and repent [2] before you are driven away like chaff blown by the wind, before the day comes when the LORD shows his great anger and punishes you just as a fire burns everything in front of it.

2.3 RSV TEV

Seek the LORD, all you humble of the land, who do his commands; seek righteousness, seek humility; perhaps you may be hidden on the day of the wrath of the LORD.

Turn to the LORD, all you humble people of the land, who obey his commands. Do what is right, and humble yourselves before the LORD. Perhaps you will escape punishment on the day when the LORD shows his anger.

Verses 1 and 2 give the negative, warning side of the call to repentance. Verse 3 gives the positive side in language that recalls that of Amos 5.6,14-15: **Seek the LORD, all you humble of the land, who do his commands**: the expression **Seek the LORD** means "worship and obey the LORD." The way in which this can be done is shown in more detail in the third line, **seek righteousness, seek humility**. The phrase **humble of the land** is practically a technical term to describe the minority who remain faithful to the Lord. In some languages "**you humble people of the land**" will be rendered as "you people of the land who trust the Lord." In other languages the phrase will be translated as "all you who submit to the Lord," "you people of the land who put your hearts in the Lord," or " . . . who keep your hearts resting in the Lord." The proof of those people's dependence on the Lord is that they **do his commands**, even though the majority of the people ignore or reject them. These are the people Jesus spoke about in the Beatitudes, especially in Matthew 5.3,5,6. In some languages the clauses in this sentence may be ordered in a different way: "All you people of the land who trust in the Lord and obey the Lord's commands, you must worship him."

Seek righteousness, seek humility: this part of the verse in Hebrew is somewhat parallel to the first part, with repetition of the words **seek** and **humble/humility**. TEV expands to "**Do what is right, and humble yourselves before the Lord**." One may also say "Do right (correct) things, and keep your hearts humble (low) before the Lord" or "Do the things which the Lord wants you to do, and do not be proud (have swollen hearts) before him."

Perhaps you may be hidden on the day of the wrath of the Lord: the prophet holds out some hope for the humble. **Perhaps** means that it is possible but not certain that the Lord will save them when his punishment falls upon his people (compare Amos 5.15). At any rate, no one can claim salvation as a right.

The word translated **be hidden** is a figure of speech which is not sufficiently clear on its own in English, so TEV drops the figure and states the meaning in nonfigurative language as "**escape punishment**." Most other modern English translations use some form of the word "shelter" which gives both the idea of hiding and that of protection (JB, NAB, NEB, NIV, NJV). If translators can find a term with these implications in their own language, it will be suitable here, but if they cannot, then it is best to use nonfigurative language, as TEV does.

The day of the wrath of the Lord refers to the same event as "the (great) day of the Lord" in 1.7,14 and makes it even clearer that this will be a day of judgment. In English this longer expression is a little clumsy, and TEV expresses it in more natural terms as "on the day when the Lord shows his anger." It is also possible to translate this last sentence as "perhaps you will escape on the day when the Lord punishes mankind" or "perhaps you will not be punished by the Lord on the day when he punishes all people."

SECTION 2: THE DOOM OF ISRAEL'S NEIGHBORS
(Chapter 2.4-15)

2.4-15

RSV	TEV
	The Doom of the Nations around Israel
4 For Gaza shall be deserted, and Ashkelon shall become a desolation; Ashdod's people shall be driven out at noon, and Ekron shall be uprooted.	4 No one will be left in the city of Gaza. Ashkelon will be deserted. The people of Ashdod will be driven out in half a day, and the people of Ekron will be driven from their city. 5 You Philistines are doomed, you people who live along the coast. The LORD has passed sentence on you. He will destroy you, and not one of you

THE DOOM OF ISRAEL'S NEIGHBORS　　　　　　　　　　　　　　　　Zeph 2.4-15

5　Woe to you inhabitants of the seacoast,
　　　you nation of the Cherethites!
　　The word of the LORD is against you,
　　　O Canaan, land of the Philistines;
　　　and I will destroy you till no inhabitant
　　　　is left.
6　And you, O seacoast, shall be pastures,
　　　meadows for shepherds
　　　and folds for flocks.
7　The seacoast shall become the possession
　　　　of the remnant of the house of Judah,
　　　on which they shall pasture,
　　　and in the houses of Ashkelon
　　　they shall lie down at evening.
　　For the LORD their God will be mindful
　　　　of them
　　　and restore their fortunes.

8　"I have heard the taunts of Moab
　　　and the revilings of the Ammonites,
　　how they have taunted my people
　　　and made boasts against their territory.
9　Therefore, as I live," says the LORD of
　　　　hosts,
　　　the God of Israel,
　　"Moab shall become like Sodom,
　　　and the Ammonites like Gomorrah,
　　a land possessed by nettles and salt pits,
　　　and a waste for ever.
　　The remnant of my people shall plunder
　　　　them,
　　　and the survivors of my nation shall
　　　　possess them."
10　This shall be their lot in return for their
　　　　pride,
　　　because they scoffed and boasted
　　　against the people of the LORD of
　　　　hosts.
11　The LORD will be terrible against them;
　　　yea, he will famish all the gods of the
　　　　earth,
　　and to him shall bow down,
　　　each in its place,
　　　all the lands of the nations.

12　You also, O Ethiopians,
　　　shall be slain by my sword.

13　And he will stretch out his hand against
　　　　the north,
　　　and destroy Assyria;
　　and he will make Nineveh a desolation,
　　　a dry waste like the desert.
14　Herds shall lie down in the midst of her,
　　　all the beasts of the field;
　　the vulture and the hedgehog
　　　shall lodge in her capitals;
　　the owl shall hoot in the window,
　　　the raven croak on the threshold;
　　for her cedar work will be laid bare.
15　This is the exultant city
　　　that dwelt secure,
　　that said to herself, "I am and there is
　　　　none else."
　　What a desolation she has become,
　　　a lair for wild beasts!
　　Everyone who passes by her
　　　hisses and shakes his fist.

will be left. 6 Your land by the sea will become open fields with shepherds' huts and sheep pens. 7 The people of Judah who survive will occupy your land. They will pasture their flocks there and sleep in the houses of Ashkelon. The LORD their God will be with them and make them prosper again.

8 The LORD Almighty says, "I have heard the people of Moab and Ammon insulting and taunting my people, and boasting that they would seize their land. 9 As surely as I am the living LORD, the God of Israel, I swear that Moab and Ammon are going to be destroyed like Sodom and Gomorrah. They will become a place of salt pits and everlasting ruin, overgrown with weeds. Those of my people who survive will plunder them and take their land."

10 That is how the people of Moab and Ammon will be punished for their pride and arrogance and for insulting the people of the LORD Almighty. 11 The LORD will terrify them. He will reduce the gods of the earth to nothing, and then every nation will worship him, each in its own land.

12 The LORD will also put the people of Sudan to death.

13 The LORD will use his power to destroy Assyria. He will make the city of Nineveh a deserted ruin, a waterless desert. 14 It will be a place where flocks, herds, and animals of every kind will lie down. Owls will live among its ruins and hoot from the windows. Crows will caw on the doorsteps. The cedar wood of her buildings will be stripped away. 15 That is what will happen to the city that is so proud of its own power and thinks it is safe. Its people think that their city is the greatest in the world. What a desolate place it will become, a place where wild animals will rest! Everyone who passes by will shrink back in horror.

In this section the outlook widens, and Zephaniah announces details of the Lord's judgment on various foreign nations. These are the Philistines in the west (verses 5-7), the Moabites and Ammonites in the east (verses 8-11), the Ethiopians in the south (verse 12), and the Assyrians in the north (verses 13-15). These nations thus represent heathen people surrounding Judah on all sides, and also peoples who are both near (Philistines, Moabites and Ammonites) and far away (Ethiopians, Assyrians). The sovereignty of the Lord extends over all of them. Philistia, Moab, and Ammon may be located on TEV maps of "The United Israelite Kingdom"; Assyria may be located on maps of "The Ancient World" or "The Assyrian Empire" in American editions of TEV, or on the map of "The World of Genesis" in British editions. The British map also shows "Cush," the name sometimes translated "Ethiopia" (see comments on verse 12).

SECTION HEADING: "**The Doom of the Nations around Israel.**" This may need to be expanded into a full sentence such as "The LORD will punish the nations around Israel" or "The LORD will punish foreign nations." Translators who prefer to follow Ball's analysis will not have the section heading here but at 2.8.

2.4

RSV

For Gaza shall be deserted,
  and Ashkelon shall become a
    desolation;
Ashdod's people shall be driven
    out at noon,
  and Ekron shall be uprooted.

TEV

No one will be left in the city of Gaza. Ashkelon will be deserted. The people of Ashdod will be driven out in half a day,[d] and the people of Ekron will be driven from their city.

[d] in half a day; *or* by a surprise attack at noontime.

There were five major cities belonging to the Philistines, and four of them are mentioned here as deserving the Lord's punishment. The fifth one, Gath, had already been destroyed by the Assyrian king Sargon II in 711 B.C. The four cities may be located on the map "The United Israelite Kingdom" in TEV.

There is a play on the sounds in Hebrew between the name '*azzah* **Gaza** and the word '*azubah* **deserted**. This kind of wordplay was quite common in Hebrew in solemn situations (see especially Micah 1.10-16), but it would not be appropriate in English even if it could be copied. It will rarely be possible for other languages to copy such wordplays, and translators should not attempt to do so unless it is a common custom in their language. **Deserted** means "not having any inhabitants," and this is put in simple terms in TEV as "**No one will be left in the city of Gaza.**" Since **Gaza** is not one of the best known place names in scripture, TEV identifies it as a "**city**," and many translators will do well to include a similar descriptive word.

Ashkelon shall become a desolation is a statement parallel in meaning to the statement about Gaza. TEV expresses it more naturally as "**Ashkelon will be deserted.**" If repetition is not good style in the receptor language, the translator may prefer to put these two sentences into one and say "There will be no people left in the cities of Gaza and Ashkelon" or "The cities of Gaza and Ashkelon will be empty of people (have no people remaining)."

The third city mentioned is **Ashdod**. The Hebrew says literally that its **people shall be driven out at noon**. This has two possible meanings, one of which is given in the TEV text and the other in the footnote. **Noon** was the hottest time of day, when people were resting, so "a surprise attack at noontime" (TEV footnote) would be likely to catch them unprepared and lead to a quick defeat. The other meaning is that the attack on the city will be over by noon. This is the more probable meaning and has some parallels in archaeological inscriptions. It is expressed in the TEV text as "**The people of Ashdod will be driven out in half a day.**" **At noon** (TEV "half a day") may be expressed in certain languages as "before the sun reaches its highest point."

Ekron shall be uprooted: again there is a similarity of sound in Hebrew between **Ekron** and the verb **uprooted**. Since the fourth statement is parallel in meaning to the third, **uprooted** refers to the people rather than the buildings. Thus TEV translates "**the people of Ekron will be driven from their city.**" In languages which do not use the passive, one may express this sentence as "Their enemies will drive out the people of Ashdod in half a day, and force the people of Ekron to leave their city."

The four cities are mentioned in geographical order from south to north. This may perhaps reflect attacks by the Scythian cavalry as they swept northward along the coastal plain on their withdrawal from Egypt.

2.5

RSV	TEV
Woe to you inhabitants of the seacoast, you nation of the Cherethites! The word of the LORD is against you, O Canaan, land of the Philistines; and I will destroy you till no inhabitant is left.	You Philistines are doomed, you people who live along the coast. The LORD has passed sentence on you. He will destroy you, and not one of you will be left.

Woe to you inhabitants of the seacoast, you nation of the Cherethites! TEV puts the two parts of the sentence in the opposite order so as to identify the people by name ("**Philistines**") before giving the description of where they live. The **Cherethites** were a clan among the Philistines and here stand for the whole nation, which TEV calls by its better-known name. It was from among the **Cherethites** that some of King David's bodyguard had been drawn (2 Sam 8.18). The Philistine area was the southern part of the coast of Palestine, to the west and southwest of Judah.

This sentence in Hebrew has the form of an exclamation, which is kept in RSV. TEV changes this to a statement, which is more natural in English. Translators should use whatever form is appropriate to the situation in their own language. In some languages translators may wish to restructure this first sentence and say "People of Philistia, you who live along the edge of the sea, you are doomed!" For other ways to translate **Woe** ("doomed"), see the comments on Nahum 3.1 or Habakkuk 2.6.

The word of the LORD is against you: this means "The LORD's verdict (or, decision) about you is unfavorable." TEV has made the sentence more personal, with the Lord as subject: **"The LORD has passed sentence on you."** The expression **"passed sentence"** has legal overtones in English which are not present in the Hebrew but which fit the setting quite well. **"Passed sentence"** may also be rendered "has condemned you," "decided how you will be punished," or "decided how he will punish you."

Since the Philistines have been mentioned by name in the earlier part of the verse, TEV does not repeat the name here. Thus the RSV expression **Canaan, land of the Philistines** is all included in the "you" of TEV. Nowhere else in the Old Testament is the land described in this way, and some modern English versions make a change in the traditional Hebrew text here (see JB, NAB, NEB). However, the Philistine areas are included within Canaan in Joshua 13.2, and so it seems unnecessary to make any change. The **Philistines** probably came originally from Crete (see NAB for this verse, and compare Amos 9.7), but linguistically and culturally they were largely assimilated to the Canaanites.

I will destroy you till no inhabitant is left: the verdict which the Lord has passed is in the first person in Hebrew, but TEV puts it into the third person to bring it into line with the rest of the paragraph, and so to improve the English style. Thus TEV has "He will destroy you, and not one of you will be left." One may also join these two clauses and say "He will destroy every single one of you." For other ways to translate **destroy**, see the comments on Nahum 1.9.

2.6   RSV   TEV

    And you, O seacoast, shall be pastures,
      meadows for shepherds
      and folds for flocks.

Your land by the sea will become open fields with shepherds' huts and sheep pens.

And you, O seacoast, shall be pastures: the Philistine cities will be so completely destroyed that animals will graze on their sites. In English it sounds odd to address the **seacoast** directly, and so TEV restructures in order to continue addressing the Philistines who lived there. This gives the more natural sentence "Your land by the sea will become open fields." This can also be rendered " . . . will become bush (forest)" or " . . . will become land where sheep graze."

Meadows for shepherds and folds for flocks: the word translated **meadows** is of uncertain meaning. These fields or meadows are of course places with abundant grass rather than plowed fields for growing crops. NEB and TEV translate **meadows** as "huts." The Septuagint translator apparently read this word at an earlier point in the sentence, instead of **seacoast**, and understood it as a proper name, Crete. This tradition is followed by NAB and NEB. The overall meaning of the verse is much the same either way. **Folds** or "sheep pens" (TEV) are the enclosed areas where sheep can be kept safe at night.

2.7   RSV   TEV

    The seacoast shall become the possession
      of the remnant of the house of Judah,

The people of Judah who survive will occupy your land. They will pasture their flocks there and sleep in the houses of Ashkelon. The LORD their

THE DOOM OF ISRAEL'S NEIGHBORS Zeph 2.8

> on which they shall pasture,
> and in the houses of Ashkelon
> they shall lie down at evening.
> For the LORD their God will be
> mindful of them
> and restore their fortunes.

> God will be with them and make them prosper again.

The Hebrew text is rather wordy and repetitive, as reflected in RSV, but TEV shortens it somewhat to make the English style more natural. **The seacoast shall become the possession of** becomes "will occupy your land," and **the remnant of the house of Judah** becomes "The people of Judah who survive." The shorter forms of TEV will be a more satisfactory translation model for most translators. However, in some languages it will be helpful to translate as "The people of Judah who do not die" or "The people of Judah who escape judgment."

"Occupy" (**shall become the possession**) may be rendered as "take over" or "take control of," or the whole sentence may be restructured as "your land will belong to the people of Judah . . . ," or even "the people of Judah . . . will take possession of your land." There is no suggestion of military force here. The people of Judah will be able to take the land because there will be no Philistines left.

The remnant of the house of Judah probably refers to the people who have passed through the judgment described in 1.4-16. **The remnant** may also be translated as "those who do not die" or "those who are still alive." The former Philistine land will be so uninhabited that the people of Judah will be able to **pasture** their flocks of sheep and goats there. In the deserted **houses of Ashkelon**, the shepherds will **lie down at evening**, or as TEV puts it more briefly, "sleep." Some translators will need to designate Ashkelon as a city.

The reason for this growth of territory and power among the people of Judah is that **The LORD their God will be mindful of them and restore their fortunes**. The Hebrew verb translated **will be mindful of them** is literally "shall visit them" (KJV), which often carries overtones of punishment. Here, however, it clearly refers to blessing. TEV says simply "**will be with them**." In some languages this will be translated as "be good to them" or even "treat them well."

The expression rendered **restore their fortunes** usually refers to the return from captivity in Babylon and perhaps has the same overtones here, though it sometimes has a more general meaning, as in Job 42.10. TEV translates with a general meaning as "**make them prosper again**." In languages which do not have a general word for prosperity, it will be necessary to indicate whether **restore their fortunes** refers to "material prosperity," or "health, happiness," and so on. The former is more likely in this context.

2.8   RSV   TEV

> "I have heard the taunts of Moab
> and the revilings of the Ammonites,
> how they have taunted my people
> and made boasts against their
> territory.

> The LORD Almighty says, "I have heard the people of Moab and Ammon insulting and taunting my people, and boasting that they would seize their land.

Translators who are following Ball's analysis will have a section heading here rather than at 2.4.

The opening words in TEV, "**The LORD Almighty says,**" actually occur in verse 9 in the Hebrew, but TEV places them here at the start of the paragraph, where they identify the speaker before the direct speech begins.

<u>**I have heard the taunts of Moab and the revilings of the Ammonites, how they have taunted my people**</u>: as can be seen from this literal translation, the Hebrew sentence is expressed with parts parallel to each other. TEV drops this parallel structure and puts the sentence into an order more natural for English, "I have heard the people of Moab and Ammon insulting and taunting my people." Most translators will find this order more natural in their own languages. "Taunting" is similar to insulting. It refers to using contemptuous or sarcastic language which is intended to embarrass or hurt someone else.

"**The people of Moab and Ammon**" were Judah's neighbors on the east, across the River Jordan. They were both Semitic peoples, descendants of Abraham's nephew Lot, according to Genesis 19.30-38. Their relations with the people of Israel were usually hostile. Here the implication seems to be that hard words spoken against Israel as the Lord's people are in effect spoken against the Lord himself.

<u>**And made boasts against their territory**</u>: the probable meaning is that the Ammonites either advanced across the frontier (compare NEB "encroached on their frontiers") or threatened to do so. TEV understands the sentence in the second sense and translates it plainly as "**boasting that they would seize their land**" (compare GeCL). **Made boasts against** may be translated in a variety of ways; for example, "spoke big words saying that they would . . . " or "said that they were superior people and would . . . ." "Their" in the phrase "**their land**" refers to the people of Judah. "Seize" may also be rendered as "take by force."

Alternative translation models for the final sentence of this verse are "They used big words saying that they would take the land of the people of Judah by force" or "They used proud words, saying 'We will take your land by force.' "

2.9   RSV   TEV

    Therefore, as I live," says the LORD of hosts, the God of Israel,
"Moab shall become like Sodom, and the Ammonites like Gomorrah,
a land possessed by nettles and salt pits,
and a waste for ever.
The remnant of my people shall plunder them,
and the survivors of my nation shall possess them."

    As surely as I am the living LORD, the God of Israel, I swear that Moab and Ammon are going to be destroyed like Sodom and Gomorrah. They will become a place of salt pits and everlasting ruin, overgrown with weeds. Those of my people who survive will plunder them and take their land."

The verb of speaking, <u>**says the LORD of hosts**</u>, has been transferred to verse 8 in TEV, which is thus able to continue the direct quotation right through verse

THE DOOM OF ISRAEL'S NEIGHBORS   Zeph 2.9

9 without interruption. On ways to translate **LORD of hosts**, see the comments on Nahum 2.13.

Therefore, as I live is in Hebrew a formula used in introducing an oath. English has no standard form of language with an equivalent function, but other languages may well have such a form. If so, translators should think carefully about whether such a form will be appropriate when used of words coming from God. If it is, then it will be good to use it here. In this verse Yahweh is portrayed as a God who is alive and acts or does things for his people. This is in contrast to the dead gods of the pagans. The word "**swear**" in this context means "to make a strong promise" or " . . . a vow."

The God of Israel means "the God whom the people of Israel worship (or, serve)" or "the God who protects the people of Israel." In the present context the latter seems more probable.

Moab shall become like Sodom, and the Ammonites like Gomorrah: as in the previous verse, the Hebrew expresses this sentence with parallel parts. Again TEV drops the parallel structure and puts the sentence into an order more natural for English: "**I swear that Moab and Ammon are going to be destroyed like Sodom and Gomorrah.**" This is also the order which most translators will find more natural for their own languages. The phrase "**are going to be destroyed**" may also be translated as "I will destroy," or the whole clause may be rendered as "I will cause the people of Moab and Ammon to be killed" (see comments on Nahum 1.9).

Alternative translation models for the first part of this verse are:

> I am the LORD who is alive, the God who protects the people of Israel. So I make a solemn (strong) promise that I will cause the people of Moab and Ammon to be killed, like the people of Sodom and Gomorrah.

Or:

> I the LORD am alive, and I look after the people of Israel. Therefore I promise that . . . .

Sodom and **Gomorrah** were destroyed by the Lord in some kind of volcanic upheaval because of their great wickedness (Gen 19.23-29). Their fate became a proverbial example of utter destruction, and is used in this way many times in the Old Testament. It is particularly appropriate here because, although Lot was rescued from Sodom (Gen 19.12-22), his descendants, the people of Moab and Ammon, will be destroyed as completely as the people of Sodom and Gomorrah.

The phrase "**They will become**" can be rendered as "Their lands will become . . . ."

A land possessed by nettles and salt pits, and a waste for ever: the area around the Dead Sea, where Sodom and Gomorrah were located, is indeed very barren and sterile. For centuries it was customary to dig pits and allow them to fill with water from the Dead Sea. When this water evaporated, salt was left, and this was used commercially. Since nothing would grow in that area, **salt pits** were associated with "**everlasting ruin**" (TEV). The meaning here is that the whole territories of Moab and Ammon will become as barren as the area around the Dead Sea. In areas where salt pits are not known, one may translate "a land that is barren (or, not fertile)" or "a land where no food will grow." In the places where anything can grow, the land will not be cultivated but **possessed by nettles**. The word translated **nettles** probably refers to a particular species of plant. It cannot be identified with certainty today, and it is better for most translators to follow the example of TEV and use a generic term like "weeds," rather than substitute a specific weed known in their own area. The phrase **and a waste forever** can be rendered as "a place where crops will never be grown" or "where no one can ever grow crops again."

The remnant of my people shall plunder them, and the survivors of my nation shall possess them: once more TEV has dropped the parallel structure of the Hebrew in order to produce a natural sentence in English: "**Those of my people who survive will plunder them and take their land.**" Whereas the people of Moab and Ammon intended to seize the territory of Judah (verse 8), in fact the **survivors** of Judah will in the end **plunder them** and **possess** their land. The prophet here envisages those returned from exile expanding eastward across the Jordan, just as they would expand westward into the Philistine coastal plain in verse 7. **Plunder** can be rendered in many languages as "take (someone's) possessions by force." For **survivors** see the comments on "remnant" in verse 7 of this chapter.

The direct words of the LORD which began at verse 8 end at the end of verse 9, and in many languages it will be helpful to mark this in some way.

An alternative translation model for the latter half of this verse is:

" . . . Their lands will become a place full of salt pits where no one will ever grow crops again. Only weeds will grow there. Those of my people who do not die will take the possessions of the people of Moab and Ammon by force and take away their land." This is what the LORD says.

2.10   RSV   TEV

This shall be their lot in return   That is how the people of Moab
    for their pride,   and Ammon will be punished for their
because they scoffed and   pride and arrogance and for insulting
    boasted   the people of the LORD Almighty.
against the people of the LORD
    of hosts.

This verse is a comment by the prophet, and translators may make this explicit if necessary. It summarizes the fate announced in the two previous verses.

This shall be their lot: here the word **lot** means "fate" or "destiny." TEV renders as "**That is how . . . will be punished.**" In languages which do not use the passive, this may be rendered as "that is how the LORD will punish . . . ."

The phrase **for their pride** may be also expressed as "because they are proud." TEV has used the word "**arrogance**" to show what this pride involved. These arrogant people always looked down on others and tried to run their lives. Other English words with similar meanings are "domineering" or "overbearing."

The terms here translated **scoffed and boasted** are the same Hebrew words as those translated "taunted" and "made boasts" in verse 8. As in verse 8, insults **against the people of the LORD of hosts** are seen as practically the same as insults against the Lord himself.

Another possible translation model for this verse is:

That is how the LORD Almighty will punish the people of Moab and Ammon because they are proud and arrogant, and because they have insulted his people.

2.11

RSV

The LORD will be terrible against them;
yea, he will famish all the gods of the earth,
and to him shall bow down,
each in its place,
all the lands of the nations.

TEV

The LORD will terrify them. He will reduce the gods of the earth to nothing, and then every nation will worship him, each in its own land.

Because the people of Moab and Ammon have, in effect, insulted the Lord (verse 10), **The LORD will be terrible against them**. In particular he will show his superiority over **all the gods of the earth**. The phrase **will be terrible against them** (TEV "will terrify them") may be rendered as "will make them very afraid." In some languages the idea of "terrify" can be expressed idiomatically; for example, "cause their hearts to fall" or "cause their hearts to shrink."

Yea, he will famish all the gods of the earth: it is not clear why RSV has used the word **yea**, which is intended to carry emphasis. The Hebrew word usually means "when" (as in NAB, BJ, JB, and NIV) or "for" (as in Mft and NEB). Several modern versions (TEV, TOB, FrCL, GeCL) simply omit it here. The verb translated **famish** literally means "to make thin." The prophet seems to envisage that, with a lack of people to offer them sacrificial food, the false gods of the heathen nations, including of course the gods of Moab and Ammon, will waste away and in this way come "to nothing" (TEV). **Famish all the gods of the earth** may be translated as "make the gods of the world (or, the spirits that people worship) so small that nothing is left of them."

Nations everywhere will then see how futile the worship of false gods is, and as a result all of them will **bow down** to worship the Lord. **Each in its place** (TEV "each in its own land") means that the people of other nations will worship the Lord in their own countries and will not need to go to Jerusalem. In Hebrew the subject of the verb **bow down** is **all the lands of the nations**. Since **lands** cannot **bow down**, it is clear that **the lands** stands for their inhabitants. TEV drops the figure of speech and states the nonfigurative meaning as "**every nation will worship him, each in its own land.**" Of course in certain languages translators will need to make "people" explicit and say "the people of every nation will worship him in their own lands."

2.12

RSV

You also, O Ethiopians,
shall be slain by my sword.

TEV

The LORD will also put the people of Sudan to death.

This verse deals with a distant nation to the south, called in Hebrew "Cushites" (NAB, NEB, NIV). The area occupied by these people was the Upper Nile, which included most of the country now called Sudan as well as part of modern Ethiopia. TEV therefore translates **"the people of Sudan"** rather than the more traditional <u>Ethiopians</u> (KJV, RSV, JB). In this verse "Cushites" may stand for Egyptians, since, during the years of the twenty-fifth dynasty (715-663 B.C.), the throne of Egypt had been occupied by Cushites. Their power had ended over thirty years before the time of this prophecy, but it is possible, as mentioned in the comments on 1.1, that Zephaniah himself had some ancestral link with the people of Cush, and perhaps it was this that led him to use that name here, even if he intended to refer to Egypt. See also comments on Nahum 3.9.

Another possibility is that "Cushites" represent a typical large and remote nation on the border of the known world. If this is the correct meaning, the effect is to emphasize the great power of the Lord, which reaches even to the most distant places.

These <u>Ethiopians</u>, or **"people of Sudan,"** will also undergo the punishment of the Lord. They will be <u>slain by my sword</u>. Mention of the particular weapon sounds very old-fashioned in English, and TEV therefore uses a more general term, **"put ... to death."** However, this refers to death in warfare, so an alternative translation model is "The LORD will cause enemy soldiers to kill the people of Sudan." Translators should use whatever expression is natural in their own language.

2.13 RSV   TEV

And he will stretch out his hand against the north, and destroy Assyria; and he will make Nineveh a desolation, a dry waste like the desert.

The LORD will use his power to destroy Assyria. He will make the city of Nineveh a deserted ruin, a waterless desert.

After dealing with nations to the west, east, and south, the prophet turns finally to **Assyria**, the enemy to **the north**. Actually, Assyria was northeast of Judah, but the roads did not run direct between the two places, and so Assyrian invaders always approached from the north along the easiest route. For this reason the Assyrians were considered fit to represent the northern direction.

<u>Assyria</u> had been the major power in the Near East for over a century. Its armies were well known, greatly feared, and bitterly hated by the smaller nations for their savage cruelty. In a sense the Assyrians stand for every enemy of God's people, and thus it was very appropriate for the prophet to mention them at the climax of his list of enemy nations.

In the first part of the verse, the Hebrew uses a figure of speech which is translated literally in RSV as <u>he will stretch out his hand against the north, and destroy Assyria</u> (compare 1.4). The pronoun **he** refers to the Lord, last mentioned in the Hebrew in verse 11, and so TEV makes this explicit by repeating "The LORD." The meaning of the metaphor **stretch out his hand against** is expressed in nonfigurative language in TEV as "use his power." Some translators will wish to follow TEV's example, but many will be able to retain the Hebrew figure of speech in their own language at this point. Another translation model is "The LORD will take action to destroy Assyria." The terms **north** and <u>Assyria</u> really both refer to the same place, and to avoid any confusion TEV has translated both terms by the one word "Assyria." It is quite possible for many translators to keep both terms but avoid ambiguity, by saying "Assyria in the north" or "the people who live in the north, namely, the Assyrians." It may be helpful also to be more specific and say "the country of Assyria in the north."

In the second part of the verse, the prophet turns to Assyria's capital, **Nineveh**. TEV adds a generic term to identify the name and says "**the city of Nineveh**." It was situated on the river Tigris and had been founded by Nimrod, according to the tradition of Genesis 10.8-11. In Zephaniah's day it was a large and famous city (compare Jonah 1.2; 3.2; 4.11) and the center of a vast empire. Zephaniah proclaims that it will become **a desolation** (RSV), which is expressed more concretely in TEV as "**a deserted ruin**." **A desolation** or "**a deserted ruin**" may also be expressed as "a ruin where no humans live." In the days of its greatness, Nineveh was well supplied with water from the river Tigris by a series of canals, but the prophet declares that it will become **a dry waste like the desert**, or as TEV puts it more briefly, "**a waterless desert**."

In point of historical fact, Nineveh was captured by the Medes and Babylonians in 612 B.C., so Zephaniah probably lived to see his prophecy fulfilled. The Book of Nahum records the joy shown by those who had suffered from Assyrian imperialism at the news of the fall of Nineveh. The city was destroyed so completely that, when the Greek traveler Xenophon visited its site in 401 B.C., he could find no trace of it.

2.14   RSV   TEV

RSV	TEV
Herds shall lie down in the midst of her, all the beasts of the field;[d] the vulture[e] and the hedgehog shall lodge in her capitals; the owl[f] shall hoot in the window, the raven[g] croak on the threshold; for her cedar work will be laid bare.	It will be a place where flocks, herds, and animals of every kind will lie down. Owls will live among its ruins and hoot from the windows. Crows[e] will caw on the doorsteps. The cedar wood of her buildings will be stripped away. [e] *Some ancient translations* Crows; *Hebrew* Desolation.

[d] Tg Compare Gk: Heb *nation*
[e] The meaning of the Hebrew word is uncertain
[f] Cn: Heb *a voice*
[g] Gk Vg: Heb *desolation*

This verse describes in detail the condition of Nineveh after its fall. It is similar in theme to the descriptions of Ashkelon in verse 7, and of Moab and Ammon in verse 9. There are several textual problems in the verse, and some of the Hebrew words used are of uncertain meaning.

The first clause is relatively simple: **Herds shall lie down in the midst of her**. The Hebrew word which is translated **herds** refers to a group of domestic animals of any kind, whether cattle, sheep, or goats, or a mixture of these. The English word **herds** applies mainly to cattle, and the normal collective term in English for sheep and goats is "flocks" (compare JB, NEB). So in order to include both types of animal, TEV uses both the term **"flocks"** and the term **"herds"** (compare NIV).

All the beasts of the field: the Hebrew text actually says "all the beasts of the nations," as in KJV and RV, and RSV is here following the Aramaic translation, called the Targum (compare NEB), rather than the Hebrew. It is possible that the Hebrew text originally contained a form *gay'* rather than the form *goy*, which is in our present Hebrew texts. The form *gay'* means "valley" and is the term assumed to be correct by the translators of NAB ("hollows") and JB ("valley").

Even if the Hebrew *goy* is correct and carries the meaning "nations," what does the expression "all the beasts of the nations" mean? HOTTP suggests "all the beasts living in flocks (or, herds)," but this meaning is not found in any major translation. Many scholars believe that "nations" is used here in the sense of "species," as in Proverbs 30.25, and that the whole phrase means "all beasts of every kind" (Lehrman), or as TEV expresses it, **"animals of every kind."** Compare Deissler, Mft, BJ, TOB, NIV, NJV, FrCL. This makes perfectly acceptable sense in the context, and translators are recommended to follow it.

The vulture and the hedgehog shall lodge in her capitals: in this setting **capitals** are the top parts of the columns which supported the roofs of the fine buildings of Nineveh. The prophet is here assuming that the buildings are destroyed and the columns thrown to the ground so that various creatures could **lodge** among them, or take shelter during the night. TEV translates **capitals** by the more general term **"ruins."**

The main problem here is that the names of the creatures mentioned are very uncertain in meaning. The first term is *qa'ath*, which is translated **vulture** (RSV), "cormorant" (KJV), "pelican" (RV, JB), "jackdaw" (BJ, NJV), "screech owl" (NAB), "horned owl" (NEB), and "desert owl" (NIV). All that can be said for certain is that the *qa'ath* is found in a list of unclean birds in Leviticus 11.18 and Deuteronomy 14.17. It is also mentioned as inhabiting deserted places in Psalm 102.6 and Isaiah 34.11. This seems to make it unlikely that a water bird like the cormorant or pelican is intended, or a scavenger like the **vulture**. On the whole, some kind of owl seems to fit the context best, and if a receptor language has a general word for owl, it will be good to use that rather than give a more exact term that denotes a particular species of owl. If owls do not exist in a particular culture, one may refer to some kind of predatory night bird which gives a hooting or screeching sound.

The second uncertain word is *qippod*, which is translated **hedgehog** (RSV, BJ), "bittern" (KJV), "heron" (JB), "porcupine" (RV), "desert owl" (NAB), "ruffed bustard" (NEB), "screech owl" (NIV), and "owl" (NJV). The word also occurs in Isaiah 14.23, but its context there does not give much help in identifying the creature intended. The ancient translations support the interpretation of *qippod* as **hedgehog** or porcupine, but this meaning does not seem to fit the context of Zephaniah 2.14 very well. Also, as with *qa'ath*, it seems unlikely that a water bird is intended, and again some kind of owl seems to be the most probable creature. TEV accepts this understanding and translates both *qa'ath* and *qippod* by the single generic term **"owls."** In English this fits well, as English speakers readily associate owls with ruined or deserted buildings. If some other bird has a similar association in other languages, it may be best to use the name of that bird. The translator must always remember that, in a passage like this, the prophet is writing poetically to create an impression of ruin and desolation. He is not writing a scientific account of the wild life of a ruined city, and if we translate this passage as if it were a scientific text book, we are mistranslating it. The effect of this can be seen for instance in the NEB rendering "ruffed bustard." This may perhaps be a correct identification of the creature intended, but most English speakers have never heard of such a bird. Its name means nothing to them and has no emotional impact, except perhaps amusement. This is not what Zephaniah intended.

In the third sentence of the verse, RSV has **the owl shall hoot in the window, the raven croak on the threshold**. The problems here are the words underlying **owl** and **raven**. In the first case the Hebrew has the word *qol*, which means "voice" (KJV, RV). RSV has accepted a suggestion to emend the text to say instead *kos*, which means **owl**. Mft, BJ, JB, NEB, and NJV do the same. This fits the context but is hardly necessary, since the word "voice" applied to the call of the birds mentioned in the previous sentence makes perfectly good sense. This can be seen in NAB's "Their call shall resound from the window," and NIV's "Their calls will echo through the windows" (compare HOTTP). TEV follows this interpretation but combines the first part of this sentence with the previous sentence and says **"Owls will live among its ruins and hoot from its windows."** The word **hoot** in English is used especially of the cry an owl makes, and if translators have a term in their own languages which is closely linked with the birds named in the earlier part of the verse, it will be good to use it here (see comments on the translation of "owl" above).

The second bird in the sentence is called **the raven** in RSV. The Hebrew text actually has the word *choreb*, which means "desolation" (KJV, RV; compare HOTTP). The Septuagint, the ancient Greek translation, evidently read a different Hebrew word, *'oreb*, which means **raven** or "crow." This possibility is followed by most modern translations (RSV, Mft, BJ, JB, NAB, NJV) and is to be recommended. TEV also follows the Greek and translates **"Crows will caw on the doorsteps."** The words **croak** and "caw" are used in English especially of the cry of birds like crows and ravens, and translators may be able to use a similar specific term in their own languages. In some languages it will be necessary to refer to some sort of black bird that has a raucous cry. In areas where houses do not have a **threshold**, or "doorsteps," a more generic word like "doorway" will be suitable (compare NAB, NIV).

For her cedar work will be laid bare: the last sentence of the verse is somewhat separate from the earlier sentences and speaks about the ruin of the splendid buildings of Nineveh. Some scholars believe that the underlying Hebrew words have arisen by confusion with the opening words of verse 15, which contain some similar letters, and that they should be dropped. Some modern versions (Mft, JB, NAB, NEB) therefore omit this sentence. Other scholars divide up the Hebrew letters slightly differently to give the meaning "the cedar has disappeared." This interpretation seems to be behind the TEV rendering **"The cedar wood of the buildings will be stripped away."** Note that TEV has made two small points explicit. First, it has stated that **"cedar"** is **"wood,"** and second, it has stated that this wood was used in the city's **"buildings."** Many translators will wish to follow this example, especially in cultures where cedar and its uses are not well known. In certain languages translators may wish to render this clause as "For they will strip the cedar wood from her buildings," "they" being unknown people (compare HOTTP). It is also possible to say "For enemies will strip . . . ," because the pronoun "they" might be misunderstood to refer to the animals and birds mentioned earlier in the verse.

Zeph 2.14 THE DOOM OF ISRAEL'S NEIGHBORS

The hard and long-lasting wood of the <u>cedar</u> tree was highly valued for use in luxurious buildings. It was used for instance in the building of Solomon's temple (1 Kgs 6.9, 10) and palace (1 Kgs 7.3, 7). When the buildings of Nineveh were destroyed, it was natural that people would take away the expensive cedar timbers to use again elsewhere. This interpretation therefore seems to fit the context well and is recommended to translators.

An alternative translation model for this verse is:

> She (the city of Nineveh) will be a place where domesticated and wild animals of all kinds will lie down. Owls (predatory night birds) will live among the ruins and make hooting sounds from the windows. Black birds (crows) will make cawing sounds on the doorsteps. People will strip away the cedar wood from her buildings.

2.15

RSV	TEV
This is the exultant city that dwelt secure, that said to herself, "I am and there is none else." What a desolation she has become, a lair for wild beasts! Everyone who passes by her hisses and shakes his fist.	That is what will happen to the city that is so proud of its own power and thinks it is safe. Its people think that their city is the greatest in the world. What a desolate place it will become, a place where wild animals will rest! Everyone who passes by will shrink back in horror.

This verse summarizes the fate of Nineveh. **This is the exultant city**: the meaning is given somewhat more fully in TEV as "That is what will happen to the city that is so proud of its own power." The words **that dwelt secure** are also expressed in more detail in TEV as "and thinks it is safe," that is, safe from enemy attack.

That said to herself, "I am and there is none else": the city is made to speak as though it were a person, and the words spoken are quoted directly. In a case like this the city stands for its inhabitants. TEV drops the figure of speech and turns the quotation into indirect speech, saying "**Its people think that their city is the greatest in the world.**"

The third part of the verse is an exclamation which repeats the main points of the two previous verses. **What a desolation she has become** echoes the second half of verse 13, and **a lair for wild beasts!** echoes verse 14. The verbs are probably to be understood as "prophetic perfects," in which the prophet speaks about things which have not yet happened as though they were already past. Several modern translations retain past tenses (RSV, NAB, TOB, NIV), but TEV uses the future, "will become . . . will rest," to make clearer that this is a prediction about the future (compare FrCL, GeCL). The words **desolation** or "desolate" are difficult to translate in many languages. Another way to express the clause is "It will become a complete ruin."

In the last part of the verse, the prophet states the reaction of those who see the city in its ruined state. **Everyone who passes by her hisses and shakes his fist**. These were gestures of horror, scorn, and revulsion (compare, for instance, 1 Kgs

9.8; Lam 2.15; Micah 6.16), and TEV gives their plain meaning with "**Everyone who passes by will shrink back in horror**." If the gestures of hissing and shaking the fist carry the right meaning in the receptor culture, a literal translation is possible here. However, in certain cultures other gestures or bodily movements such as pointing a finger or shaking the head may be used to signify horror or scorn. Translators may mention such gestures as long as they do not involve anything incompatible with Biblical culture. If no such solution is possible, then translators will do better to follow the example of TEV and give the plain meaning without mentioning the actual gestures.

Possible restructurings of the whole verse are:

> That is what will happen to the buildings of the city because its people are proud of their power and think they are safe (from danger). They consider that their city is the greatest in the world, but it will become a complete ruin where wild animals live. Everyone who passes by will show how scornful they are, and how much they detest this city.

Or:

> The people of this city are so proud that they think nothing can harm them. They say to themselves, "Our city is greater than all others." But that city will fall and will become utterly desolate. Only wild animals will live there, and everyone who passes by will show their scorn and horror.

SECTION 3: JERUSALEM'S DOOM AND REDEMPTION
(Chapter 3.1-20)

Chapter 3

3.1-13

RSV

TEV
Jerusalem's Sin and Redemption

1 Woe to her that is rebellious and defiled,
   the oppressing city!
2 She listens to no voice,
   she accepts no correction.
She does not trust in the LORD,
   she does not draw near to her God.

3 Her officials within her
   are roaring lions;
her judges are evening wolves
   that leave nothing till the morning.
4 Her prophets are wanton,
   faithless men;
her priests profane what is sacred,
   they do violence to the law.
5 The LORD within her is righteous,
   he does no wrong;
every morning he shows forth his justice,
   each dawn he does not fail;
but the unjust knows no shame.

6 "I have cut off nations;
   their battlements are in ruins;
I have laid waste their streets
   so that none walks in them;
their cities have been made desolate,
   without a man, without an inhabitant.
7 I said, 'Surely she will fear me,
   she will accept correction;
she will not lose sight
   of all that I have enjoined upon her.'
But all the more they were eager
   to make all their deeds corrupt."

8 "Therefore wait for me," says the LORD,
   "for the day when I arise as a witness.
For my decision is to gather nations,
   to assemble kingdoms,
to pour out upon them my indignation,
   all the heat of my anger;
for in the fire of my jealous wrath
   all the earth shall be consumed.

9 "Yea, at that time I will change the
   speech of the peoples
   to a pure speech,
that all of them may call on the name of
   the LORD

1 Jerusalem is doomed, that corrupt, rebellious city that oppresses its own people. 2 It has not listened to the LORD or accepted his discipline. It has not put its trust in the LORD or asked for his help. 3 Its officials are like roaring lions; its judges are like hungry wolves, too greedy to leave a bone until morning. 4 The prophets are irresponsible and treacherous; the priests defile what is sacred, and twist the law of God to their own advantage. 5 But the LORD is still in the city; he does what is right and never what is wrong. Every morning without fail, he brings justice to his people. And yet the unrighteous people there keep on doing wrong and are not ashamed.

6 The LORD says, "I have wiped out whole nations; I have destroyed their cities and left their walls and towers in ruins. The cities are deserted; the streets are empty—no one is left. 7 I thought that then my people would have reverence for me and accept my discipline, that they would never forget the lesson I taught them. But soon they were behaving as badly as ever.

8 "Just wait," the LORD says. "Wait for the day when I rise to accuse the nations. I have made up my mind to gather nations and kingdoms in order to let them feel the force of my anger. The whole earth will be destroyed by the fire of my fury.

9 "Then I will change the people of the nations, and they will pray to me alone and not to other gods. They will all obey me. 10 Even from distant Sudan my scattered people will bring offerings to me. 11 At that time you, my people, will no longer need to be ashamed that you rebelled against me. I will remove everyone who is proud and arrogant, and you will never again rebel against me on my sacred hill. 12 I will leave there a humble and lowly people, who will come to me for help. 13 The people of Israel who survive will do no wrong to anyone, tell no lies, nor try to deceive. They will be prosperous and secure, afraid of no one."

Jerusalem's sin and redemption Zeph 3.1

<pre>
        and serve him with one accord.
10   From beyond the rivers of Ethiopia
          my suppliants, the daughter of my
              dispersed ones,
          shall bring my offering.

11   "On that day you shall not be put to
              shame
          because of the deeds by which you have
              rebelled against me;
          for then I will remove from your midst
              your proudly exultant ones,
          and you shall no longer be haughty
              in my holy mountain.
12   For I will leave in the midst of you
          a people humble and lowly.
       They shall seek refuge in the name of the
              LORD,
13   those who are left in Israel;
       they shall do no wrong
          and utter no lies,
       nor shall there be found in their mouth
          a deceitful tongue.
       For they shall pasture and lie down,
          and none shall make them afraid."
</pre>

This section has two main divisions in the TEV text, comprising verses 1-13 and 14-20. There is a separate section heading at verse 14, and verses 14-20 are set out as poetry. Within verses 1-13 different translations and commentaries have various ways of dividing the text into paragraphs. Most modern versions start new paragraphs at verses 6, 8, 9, and 11, and this division is recommended for most translators to follow. The first paragraph (verses 1-5) denounces the sins of Jerusalem, and the second (verses 6-7) speaks of her failure to learn from the example of the fate of other cities. The third paragraph (verse 8) speaks again of the universal day of judgment (compare 1.2-3,17-18), and the fourth (verses 9-10) deals with the renewal of the gentile nations after the judgment. The last paragraph (verses 11-13) describes the characteristics of the people of Israel who survive the judgment.

SECTION HEADING: "**Jerusalem's Sin and Redemption.**" This section heading will sound more natural in many languages if it is expressed with verbs rather than nouns, and with the participants made explicit: "The people of Jerusalem have sinned, but the LORD promises to redeem them." Since this is rather long, some translators may prefer to break it into two parts and say here only "The people of Jerusalem have sinned." Then "The LORD promises to redeem them" can be a separate heading at verse 9 (compare FrCL, GeCL). Translators who follow Ball's analysis will prefer a heading here such as "The LORD will judge his enemies in Jerusalem." They may also wish to place another section heading at 3.9, such as "The LORD will bless those who obey him."

3.1	RSV	TEV
	Woe to her that is rebellious and defiled, the oppressing city!	**Jerusalem is doomed, that corrupt, rebellious city that oppresses its own people.**

The city to which this chapter is addressed is not actually named until verse 14, but the content of the accusations made against her, especially in verse 4, makes it clear that the city is Jerusalem. This is generally agreed among commentators, and TEV makes it explicit at the beginning of the paragraph by saying "**Jerusalem is doomed**" (compare FrCL). The words "**is doomed**" translate a Hebrew word that means **Woe to** (RSV). This sounds old fashioned in English, and TEV has therefore restructured it into a more natural sentence pattern. Some translators may have a term equivalent to **Woe to** in current use in their own language, and they may therefore be able to remain closer to the Hebrew structure. In many languages one may say "Jerusalem will be destroyed," "The Lord will destroy Jerusalem," or "Enemies will destroy Jerusalem" (see comments on Nahum 3.1).

For comments on how to translate "city," see Nahum 3.1. The city is described in Hebrew by three terms which were understood in various ways in ancient translations and commentaries. However, there is general agreement among modern translators and commentators about their meaning, as may be seen from RSV and TEV. The city is **rebellious**, that is, disobedient to the Lord (compare verse 3); **defiled** by the sinful actions of its people; and **oppressing**, which means, as TEV makes clear, that the leadership "**oppresses its own people**" (compare verses 3 and 4). Note that in TEV the order of the first two terms reverses that of the Hebrew, which is kept by RSV. It is not clear why this change has been made, but presumably the TEV translators felt that it resulted in better English style. Translators should be alert to the possibility that such small adjustments may improve the style in their own languages so long as they do not alter the meaning. In many languages it will be necessary to make the participants in the various actions explicit.

An alternative translation model is as follows: "Jerusalem will be destroyed. It is a city full of rebellious and evil people whose leaders oppress their own people."

3.2

RSV	TEV

She listens to no voice,
  she accepts no correction.
She does not trust in the Lord,
  she does not draw near to her
    God.
	It has not listened to the Lord or accepted his discipline. It has not put its trust in the Lord or asked for his help.

This verse consists of four negative clauses describing how the city has failed in its responsibility to God. RSV translates with four separate clauses, each with its own negative, while TEV links the clauses into two pairs with only one negative in each pair. Translators should use whatever structures are appropriate to their own language.

In all four clauses the subject is literally **She**, referring to the city. Here, as often elsewhere, the city stands for its inhabitants, and some translators will need to make this explicit and say "The people of Jerusalem."

She listens to no voice: the **voice** is that of the Lord, or perhaps that of prophets speaking on his behalf, and TEV makes this explicit by saying "**It has not listened to the Lord**."

She accepts no correction: the **correction** also comes from the Lord, and so TEV again makes this clear by translating "**or accepted his discipline**." This is a favorite expression in Jeremiah—see especially Jeremiah 7.28. **Correction** or

Jerusalem's sin and redemption Zeph 3.3

"**discipline**" here means instruction in right conduct and rebuke of wrong conduct. Another possible rendering is "it (RSV **she**) would not let the LORD discipline it." However, in many languages it will be necessary to say "they (the people of Jerusalem) would not let the LORD discipline them."

She does not trust in the LORD refers not just to intellectual belief but to active reliance on the Lord in daily affairs. In some languages an idiomatic expression such as "place heart in" may be helpful here.

The fourth clause says literally **she does not draw near to her God**, referring probably to the inner attitude of those who attended worship in the Temple, or perhaps to their failure to attend at all (compare 1.5-6). The purpose of drawing near to God is to demonstrate trust in him by asking for his help. TEV makes this clear by translating "**or asked for his help.**" Another way of phrasing this clause is "or asked him to help them." Note that in RSV **the LORD** and **her God** are parallel with each other, but TEV does not use both expressions. After mentioning "**the LORD**" in the third clause, it simply refers to "**him**" in the fourth. Translators should follow the natural usage of their own language in matters like this.

3.3   RSV   TEV

Her officials within her   Its officials are like roaring lions; its
  are roaring lions;   judges are like hungry wolves, too
her judges are evening wolves   greedy to leave a bone until morning.
  that leave nothing till the
  morning.

The Hebrew here uses metaphor to describe the **officials** of Jerusalem as **lions** and **wolves**. RSV and most other modern translations retain the metaphor, but TEV turns it into a simile by saying "**like roaring lions**" and "**like hungry wolves.**" Translators will need to decide which figure of speech is more appropriate in their own language. In areas where lions, wolves, or other fierce wild animals like hyenas are known, the meaning may be quite clear if the translator uses a metaphor. However, in areas where such animals are not well known, it will probably be better to follow the example of TEV and thus to make the comparison more explicit. If translators have made the participants (inhabitants of Jerusalem) explicit in the previous two verses, it will be good to begin this verse with the words, "The officials of Jerusalem . . . ," in order to distinguish between the people in general in verse 2 and the leaders in verse 3.

Even if a simile is used, the TEV statement, "**Its officials are like roaring lions,**" does not make explicit the point of the comparison, which is of course the way in which the officials use their power to oppress the ordinary people. Some translators may need to state this clearly and say something like "Its officials are as greedy as roaring lions." Compare GeCL "Its leading men are lions greedy for prey," which keeps a metaphor but makes the point of the comparison explicit.

The second part of the verse does contain some indication of the point of the comparison: **her judges are evening wolves that leave nothing till the morning** (TEV "**its judges are like hungry wolves, too greedy to leave a bone until morning**"). However, there are other problems in this part of the verse. The word translated "**hungry**" in TEV is literally **evening**. The evening was the time when wolves went out to hunt for food, and so a wolf encountered in the evening was more likely to be hungry and therefore dangerous. The meaning of **evening wolves** is therefore another figure of speech embedded within the metaphor. TEV drops this second figure and expresses its meaning in plain language as "**hungry wolves.**" Compare FrCL "wolves which hunt in the evening," and see Habakkuk 1.8 for a note on the translation of **wolves**.

Some scholars consider the expression **evening wolves** to be rather difficult and suggest changing the Hebrew word *'ereb* "evening" to *'arab* "Arabia" (compare the ancient Greek translation) or to *'arabah* "the plain." This last suggestion lies behind the NEB "wolves of the plain" (compare BJ). However, the Hebrew makes good sense as it stands and is followed by the majority of modern English versions (compare also HOTTP). Translators are therefore recommended to follow it.

They leave nothing till the morning: the last part of the verse is literally "they do not gnaw in the morning." The word "gnaw" implies "bones" as an object, and the most probable meaning of the clause in its context is "they eat up everything they can catch straight away in the evening, and do not leave any over until next day." This understanding seems to be represented both in RSV and more explicitly in TEV, "**too greedy to leave a bone until morning.**" By using the word "greedy" TEV brings out the point of comparison in this second picture.

Some translations take the phrase **till the morning** to mean "since the morning." In this case the effect is to emphasize how hungry the wolves are by the evening, and therefore fierce and greedy. This interpretation is followed by JB "that have had nothing to gnaw that morning."

In areas where lions, wolves, and other fierce animals are unknown, it may be necessary for translators to combine the two pictures into one and use more general language. In such a situation a translation model for the verse may be "Its officials and judges are as cruel and greedy as fierce wild animals, which eat all their food at once and do not keep any till next day."

3.4   RSV   TEV

> Her prophets are wanton,
>   faithless men;
> her priests profane what is sacred,
> they do violence to the law.

> The prophets are irresponsible and treacherous; the priests defile what is sacred, and twist the law of God to their own advantage.

This verse continues the attack on the Jerusalem leaders and mentions in particular the **prophets** (compare Micah 2.11; 3.5-7) and **priests** (compare Hos 4.6-9; 6.9; Micah 3.11). Two statements are made about each group. The **prophets** are **wanton** and **faithless**. The word here translated **wanton** elsewhere means either "unstable" (Gen 49.4) or "reckless" (Judges 9.4). Some translations assume the latter meaning here, apply it to recklessness in speech, and render "braggarts" (JB), "insolent" (NAB), or "arrogant" (NIV). Both RSV and TEV seem to prefer the former meaning, which TEV renders as "**irresponsible.**" The second term, **faithless**, may in this context mean "giving false messages that do not come from the LORD" (compare JB "impostors," NEB "no true prophets"); or it may mean "not to be trusted," that is, "**treacherous**" (TEV, NAB, NIV), which is the usual meaning of the Hebrew term.

Jerusalem's sin and redemption   Zeph 3.5

One of the tasks of the **priests** was to distinguish between those things set apart for God's use and those in common use (Lev 10.10; Hag 2.10-13). Zephaniah here accuses them of failing to do this (compare Ezek 22.26). Rather they **profane what is sacred** and treat it as though it were for general use. It is possible that **what is sacred** refers to "the sanctuary" (NEB, NIV, GeCL), that is, the Temple, but probably a more general meaning is intended, as understood by RSV, JB, NAB, TEV, and FrCL. **Profane** in this context means "to make impure" in a religious sense. Some languages have technical words for "defilement" in this sense. In other languages the idea of "religious contamination" may be useful. **Sacred** may be expressed in many languages as "things dedicated to the LORD." Some languages will express the clause **profane what is sacred** as "use things dedicated to the LORD for common (ordinary) purposes."

The second accusation against the priests is that **they do violence to the law**. This means either that they break the law, or that in their duty of interpreting it, they give interpretations favorable to people who can afford to pay them (compare Micah 3.11). This is the understanding behind the TEV statement that they "twist the law of God to their own advantage." **The law** here refers primarily to the laws given through Moses. Translation models are "they openly break the law" or "they interpret the law so that they themselves make gains they have no right to."

3.5

RSV	TEV
The LORD within her is righteous, he does no wrong; every morning he shows forth his justice, each dawn he does not fail; but the unjust knows no shame.	But the LORD is still in the city; he does what is right and never what is wrong. Every morning without fail, he brings justice to his people. And yet the unrighteous people there keep on doing wrong and are not ashamed.

In the first four verses of this chapter RSV has never identified the city as Jerusalem, and TEV has named the city only once. For many translators it will be helpful to say " . . . in Jerusalem" in the first sentence or at some other point in the verse.

Despite the failures of the leading men, the Lord himself "is still in the city" (TEV). His presence **within her** is contrasted with that of the "officials within her" (verse 3). Whereas they acted wickedly, the Lord **is righteous, he does no wrong**. TEV expresses this in a structure which brings out more sharply the contrast between the positive and negative sides of the statement: "He does what is right and never what is wrong."

The next part of the verse consists in Hebrew of two clauses with partially overlapping meaning: **every morning he shows forth his justice, each dawn he does not fail**. TEV compresses these two clauses into one and avoids repetition by saying "every morning without fail, he brings justice to his people." In languages which use repetitive structures, the more literal version of RSV may be a satisfactory translation base. However, many translators will prefer to avoid repetition, and they will find useful guidance in the example of TEV.

The words **every morning** here echo "till the morning" of verse 3 and again heighten the contrast between the cruelty of the leaders and the faithfulness of the Lord. If a literal translation of **every morning** would imply the exclusion of the rest of the day, then one may translate as "every day." The focus is on the constancy of God's justice.

The clause **He shows forth his justice** may also be rendered as "He treats his people with justice," "He uses justice in his relations with his people," or "He shows what it means to behave justly."

He does not fail (TEV "without fail") means he does it "constantly" or "never missing a day." Some languages will handle this idea of "constantly" through reduplication of some sort; for example, "every every morning."

The final words of the verse seem to have no close connection with the earlier part, and this, together with the variety of translations in the ancient versions, has led some scholars to suggest that they should be deleted (compare NAB, NEB margin). However, the words in Hebrew make sense, and there is no textual reason to omit them. RSV **but the unjust knows no shame** is expanded in TEV to "**And yet the unrighteous people there keep on doing wrong and are not ashamed.**" They continue with their evil conduct despite every evidence of the Lord's goodness to his people mentioned in the earlier part of the verse. **Unjust** or "unrighteous" refers to the people mentioned in verses 3-4, and in many languages may be translated as "evil people" or "wicked people."

3.6

RSV	TEV

"I have cut off nations;
   their battlements are in ruins;
I have laid waste their streets
   so that none walks in them;
their cities have been made desolate,
   without a man, without an inhabitant.
	The LORD says, "I have wiped out whole nations; I have destroyed their cities and left their walls and towers in ruins. The cities are deserted; the streets are empty—no one is left.

From the beginning of verse 6 through to the end of verse 13, the speaker is the Lord. In the Hebrew the direct speech begins with no introduction, but TEV avoids this abruptness by naming the speaker in the opening words, "**The LORD says**" (compare FrCL, GeCL).

Verse 5 stated how the people of Jerusalem had failed to learn from the Lord's faithfulness to them. Verses 6 and 7 develop this idea from a different point of view and state that they also failed to learn from the example of how the Lord punished other nations. Compare Amos 4.4-12.

I have cut off nations: for the use of **cut off** in Hebrew, see comments on 1.3. RSV and NIV give a literal translation, but NAB gives the meaning in plain language with "destroyed." JB, NEB and TEV replace the Hebrew figure with an equivalent figure which is natural in English, and say "**I have wiped out**." Translators who cannot use the Hebrew figure in their own language may do well to follow this example and look for an equivalent figure in their own language. In certain languages translators may express this phrase as "I have killed all the people of the nations" or "I have caused all the people of the nations to be killed."

Nations refers to gentile peoples. NEB here follows the Septuagint in reading "the proud," but there is no need to do this.

Jerusalem's sin and redemption Zeph 3.7

In the rest of the verse, the Lord's words deal with two results of his action, the destruction of towns and the departure of their inhabitants. For the first result, RSV gives as usual a literal translation: **their battlements are in ruins; I have laid waste their streets**. This puts specific statements about **their battlements** and **their streets** before the more general statement **their cities have been made desolate**. TEV reorders the components of meaning to give the more general statement "I have destroyed their cities" before the more specific one "and left their walls and towers in ruins." The words "walls and towers" explain in simple language the meaning of the more difficult term **battlements**. See comments on "lofty battlements" under 1.16.

TEV adopts the same procedure in handling the second topic also, and thus puts the general statement "The cities are deserted" before the more detailed ones "the streets are empty—no one is left." The last clause "no one is left" translates the two Hebrew phrases rendered in RSV as **without a man, without an inhabitant** and avoids the repetition which is not natural in English. But in some languages repetition is unavoidable. "The cities are deserted" will be translated in these languages as "The cities are without people" or "There are no people living in the cities." An alternative translation model for the latter part of the verse is "There are no people in the cities. No one walks in the streets. Everyone is gone."

3.7   RSV   TEV

I said, 'Surely she will fear me,   I thought that then my people would
    she will accept correction;   have reverence for me and accept my
she will not lose sight[h]   discipline, that they would never for-
    of all that I have enjoined   get[f] the lesson I taught them. But soon
    upon her.'   they were behaving as badly as ever.
But all the more they were eager
    to make all their deeds cor-   [f] *Some ancient translations* they would
    rupt."   never forget; *Hebrew* their dwelling
                                                 would not be cut off.
[h] Gk Syr: Heb *and her dwelling will
not be cut off*

This verse shows the intended purpose of the Lord's actions in verse 6 and the actual result, which was quite different from what was desired.

Verse 7 opens with the words **I said** and then gives a quotation within the main quotation that runs from verse 6 to verse 13. TEV interprets **I said** to mean "I said to myself" (compare TOB, FrCL) and translates as "I thought" (compare GeCL). Then it continues by turning the words quoted into indirect speech. Translators may use direct or indirect speech according to the normal patterns of their own language.

In the first two clauses RSV uses the third person pronoun **she** where BJ, JB, NAB, TOB, and NIV use the second person "you." The Hebrew actually has second person feminine forms in these two clauses (addressing the city, which is feminine in Hebrew) but third person forms in the third and fourth clauses. Such a change of person is somewhat awkward in English. It is not clear whether the RSV translators changed the Hebrew text, or whether they made the alteration to third person on translational grounds. Translators should use whichever form best fits the overall paragraph structure in their own language. Note that by using indirect speech TEV avoids this problem.

Surely (TEV "**then**") refers back to the words of the Lord in verse 6. Many translators will need to say, for example, "Because of this I thought that my people . . . ." The Lord's intention was that his own people, on seeing the punishment of gentile nations, would **fear me** and **accept correction**. The words "**have reverence for**" (TEV) give the meaning in this context of the word translated **fear** in RSV and most other modern English versions. The main component of meaning of **fear** in ordinary usage is "to be afraid of," whereas the sense intended here is rather that of "respect." The expression **accept correction** is the same expression which occurred in verse 2, and its recurrence here helps to tie these paragraphs together.

In the next part of the verse, most modern versions follow the Septuagint in rendering **not lose sight** or something of similar meaning such as "remember." Compare BJ, NAB, JB, NEB, TEV, NJV, GeCL. This understanding depends on reading the Hebrew word *meʿonah* "her dwellings" with different vowels as *meʿeneha* "from her eyes." The Hebrew is retained by TOB and NIV as it stands (compare HOTTP), but the Septuagint understanding as found in the majority of modern versions fits the context better, and translators are recommended to follow it.

All that I have enjoined upon her: the Hebrew verb translated **enjoined** is a word of wide meaning. The basic sense is "to visit" (compare NAB), either with the intention of punishing (compare JB, NIV, NJV) or of giving responsibility or instruction (compare Mft, NEB). RSV **enjoined** has the idea of responsibility. TEV has the idea of instruction and expresses it in simple terms as "**the lesson I taught them.**"

But all the more they were eager to make all their deeds corrupt: the final sentence shows the reaction of the people to the lessons the Lord had tried to teach them. Literally it says "but they rose early and corrupted all their doings" (RV). The combination of the verb translated "rise early" with another verb is a favorite expression of Jeremiah (for example, Jer 7.13,25; 11.7; 25.3,4). It usually means "to do something persistently or eagerly," and this is the sense here. The words **eager** or "eagerly" are used in RSV, NAB, NIV, and NJV, but TEV seems to miss this element of meaning. It apparently takes the idea of rising early to refer to time and translates "**But soon they were behaving as badly as ever.**" An alternative translation model can be "But they were just as eager as before to do all sorts of wicked things."

3.8   RSV   TEV

"Therefore wait for me," says the LORD,
"for the day when I arise as a witness.
For my decision is to gather nations,
    to assemble kingdoms,
    to pour out upon them my indignation,
    all the heat of my anger;

"Just wait," the LORD says. "Wait for the day when I rise to accuse the nations. I have made up my mind to gather nations and kingdoms in order to let them feel the force of my anger. The whole earth will be destroyed by the fire of my fury.

Jerusalem's sin and redemption   Zeph 3.8

> for in the fire of my jealous wrath
> all the earth shall be consumed.

This verse goes more closely with those that follow than with those that precede. It turns again to the theme of universal judgment found earlier in 1.2-3,17-18. The persons addressed here are not stated clearly but are referred to in the second person plural. In the light of the note of hope sounded in verses 9-13, many scholars think that verse 8 is addressed to the minority of people in Jerusalem who remain faithful to the Lord (compare 2.3). Jerusalem would of course be involved in a universal judgment, but those of her people who continued to trust the Lord would still have cause to hope for blessing in the end. See especially verse 11.

The opening word of the verse, **Therefore**, normally refers back to what has gone before. In this case it is not clear exactly how the sins of the people of Jerusalem in verses 1-7 are linked with the Lord's universal judgment. TEV omits any exact equivalent.

The word **wait** often has overtones of waiting for help from the Lord (for example Isa 8.17; 64.4), but here it carries rather the idea of waiting for disaster. The word **day** also reinforces this idea (compare 1.7-10,14-16). TEV's expression "just wait" is very idiomatic. Another possible translation model is "You must wait for the day."

In using the words **as a witness**, RSV, in common with BJ, JB, NAB, NEB, TOB, TEV, NIV, and NJV, is following the ancient Greek and Syriac translations rather than the Hebrew, though only BJ, JB, NIV, and NJV acknowledge this in a footnote. The Hebrew actually has "rise up to the prey" (KJV, RV, GeCL). In a context of judgment and punishment like this, the overall difference in meaning between these alternatives is not very great. However, the meaning given by the ancient translations seems to fit the context better and also matches other places in the Old Testament where the Lord is spoken of **as a witness** to give evidence of people's crimes. See for instance Jeremiah 29.23; Micah 1.2; Malachi 3.5. **As a witness** may also be rendered as "to give evidence against" or "to accuse" (TEV). TEV also makes it explicit that the people to be accused are "the nations," though in Hebrew they are not mentioned until the next sentence.

The central part of the verse uses parallel expressions to emphasize its point (**to gather nations** and **to assemble kingdoms; my indignation** and **all the heat of my anger**). TEV avoids this repetition and expresses the meaning in more natural English as "I have made up my mind to gather nations and kingdoms in order to let them feel the force of my anger." Note that the Hebrew figure **to pour out upon them my indignation** is replaced in TEV by another figure, "to let them feel the force of my anger." Translators will have to decide for themselves whether they can use the Hebrew figure, or whether they should replace it by a figure similar in meaning in their own language. If neither is possible, the sense can be stated in nonfigurative language as "they will experience my great anger" or "I will make them know that I am very angry with them."

The last clause of this verse is repeated from 1.18 with only a change of pronoun. See the comments made there.

| 3.9 | RSV | TEV |

"Yea, at that time I will change
the speech of the peoples
to a pure speech,
that all of them may call on the
name of the LORD
and serve him with one accord.

"Then I will change the people of the nations, and they will pray to me alone and not to other gods. They will all obey me.

The paragraph which consists of verses 9-13 contrasts with the earlier part of the chapter and sounds a note of hope for restoration after the judgment of the Lord is completed. Some translators may wish to place a separate section heading here, as mentioned in the comments on the previous section heading at verse 1.

Verse 9 speaks of the conversion of the heathen nations, presumably as a result of the punishment described in the previous verse. **Yea, at that time I will change the speech of the peoples to a pure speech**: the opening clause says literally "Yes, I will then give the peoples lips that are clean" (JB). "Lips" stands for **speech** and is so translated in RSV. Lips or **speech** were made unclean primarily by the worship of false gods (compare Psa 16.4; Isa 6.5), so when they are made clean or **pure** again, the result is that the people will **call upon the name of the LORD, and serve him with one accord**. To **call upon the name of the LORD** means to pray to and worship him, and so TEV translates "they will pray to me alone and not to other gods." RSV follows the Hebrew in having God speak of himself in the third person as **the LORD**. This is very awkward in English, so TEV maintains the first person throughout the verse and translates as "me." Many other languages will need to do the same.

The phrase translated **with one accord** is literally "with one shoulder" and is probably derived from the practice of yoking oxen together for plowing. NIV translates with a comparable English expression as "shoulder to shoulder." TEV drops the figure of speech and translates the whole clause in nonfigurative language as "They will all obey me."

| 3.10 | RSV | TEV |

From beyond the rivers of Ethiopia
my suppliants, the daughter of
my dispersed ones,
shall bring my offering.

Even from distant Sudan my scattered people will bring offerings to me.

The word "Cush" (NEB, NIV), translated **Ethiopia** in RSV, refers to the Upper Nile region, which included most of modern "Sudan" (TEV) and part of Ethiopia. The expression **beyond the rivers of Ethiopia** emphasizes that this area was at the borders of the known world, so TEV renders "distant Sudan." See also comments on 1.1; 2.12; and Nahum 3.9. "Sudan" may not be very "**distant**" from the locations of some modern Bible translators, but it was distant from the point of view of someone living in Judah, and the translator must represent this viewpoint. "**Distant Sudan**" may also be expressed as "Sudan which is very far away" or "The country of Sudan which is . . . ."

Jerusalem's sin and redemption   Zeph 3.11

The difficulties in this verse arise from the phrases rendered **my suppliants, the daughter of my dispersed ones** in RSV. The Hebrew word translated **my suppliants** comes from a well-known verb meaning "pray, entreat, worship," but the form of it occurring here is found nowhere else. The meaning is clear enough, but it is not so easy to decide who the **suppliants** are. They seem to be explained by the next phrase, **the daughter of my dispersed ones**. This is again an expression that occurs nowhere else in the Old Testament, and for this reason some scholars have suggested changing it (see for instance Mft and NAB), while others omit.it, following the Septuagint (BJ, JB). Most modern English versions retain the phrase and understand **my suppliants** and **the daughter of my dispersed ones** to refer to Jews scattered outside the promised land, in this case in Ethiopia (Sudan).

The meaning of the verse is then that those Jews living in Ethiopia (Sudan) will pray to the Lord and bring offerings to him. This is the meaning expressed in TEV: "**Even from distant Sudan my scattered people will bring offerings to me.**" However, TEV seems to have omitted the element of meaning carried by the words **my suppliants**, so a more complete translation may be " . . . my scattered people will pray to me and bring me offerings." "**My scattered people**" may be expressed as "my people who are living in far off places."

The difficulty with this interpretation is that verse 10 is then speaking of a different group of people from verse 9, where converted heathen were the subject. If the phrase **the daughter of my dispersed ones** is omitted with BJ and JB, then **my suppliants** will refer to the same group of converted heathen as verse 9.

Another approach to the problem is found in the RV margin. This takes **my suppliants, the daughter of my dispersed ones** as object rather than subject of the verb **bring**. The whole verse is then translated "From beyond the rivers of Ethiopia shall they bring my suppliants, the daughter of my dispersed, for an offering unto me." Thus the converted heathen are regarded as showing their new respect for the Lord by returning to their homeland those of his people who lived among them. Compare GeCL.

None of these possibilities is without difficulty, but the majority of modern English versions (RSV, NEB, TEV, NIV) adopt the first one, and translators are recommended to do the same. If they do take the first approach mentioned above, the clause **bring my offering** may also be expressed in some languages as "bring things (objects) to offer to me." Another translation model, then, for this verse is "My people who are living in far-off lands will come even from distant Sudan, to pray to me and bring things to offer to me."

3.11	RSV	TEV
	"On that day you shall not be put to shame because of the deeds by which you have rebelled against me; for then I will remove from your midst your proudly exultant ones,	At that time you, my people, will no longer need be ashamed that you rebelled against me. I will remove everyone who is proud and arrogant, and you will never again rebel against me on my sacred hill.[g] [g] SACRED HILL: *Mount Zion (see Zion in Word List)*.

and you shall no longer be
haughty
in my holy mountain.

The opening words **On that day** (compare 1.9; 3.16) refer to the period when the Lord's punishment is carried out and the time immediately following, rather than to a particular day. TEV accordingly translates by a more general term, "**At that time.**"

The verbs have a second person singular feminine subject, which is the city of Jerusalem, or as the paragraph goes on to explain, the few remaining people in the city who trust the Lord. TEV makes it clear at this point that the subject is different from the previous verses by saying "**you, my people.**"

The exact sense here of the verb rendered **you shall not be put to shame** is uncertain. RSV together with NEB and NIV seems to understand it to mean "you will no longer need to suffer shame and punishment for your wicked deeds." This will be because the wicked people will have been removed, as the rest of the verse states. An alternative possibility is that, because the people responsible for the wicked deeds are no longer there, the righteous people who remain will no longer need to feel ashamed of what had happened in the past. This understanding is somewhat less convincing but is represented in TEV's wording, "**you ... will no longer need to be ashamed**" (compare FrCL, GeCL). TEV's "**You, my people**" may be expressed in many languages as "You, who are my people." The concept of **shame** may be translated in many languages idiomatically as "lose face" (Mandarin, Thai, Lao, and others) or even "lose face lose eye" (Thai).

The reason for the **shame** which the people had either suffered or felt was the wicked deeds of the leaders (verses 3-4), which showed that they had **rebelled against** the Lord. The word **rebelled** emphasizes deliberate rejection of the Lord's commands. In certain languages it will be necessary to make the underlying meaning explicit and say "you refused to obey my commands."

In certain languages it will be necessary to expand the clause **I will remove from your midst** to "I will remove (take away) all of you who ... " or "I will remove every person from Jerusalem (or, from among you) who ...." Those leaders who had rebelled the Lord **will remove** from among his people as part of his judgment. They are described as **proudly exultant,** the same phrase as is used in Isaiah 13.3 to describe conquering soldiers who are confident in their own power. TEV uses more natural English in translating as "**everyone who is proud and arrogant.**" See 2.10 for comments on how to translate "**arrogant.**" In languages where it is difficult to find two words with similar meaning like "**proud**" and "**arrogant,**" it may be necessary to say "very proud." Pride is regarded as the basic human sin, and when the leaders are taken away, no one else will **be haughty in my holy mountain**. The word translated **be haughty** implies an open show of contempt for God. This effect is conveyed in various ways in modern English translations such as "you will cease to strut" (JB) and "never again shall you flaunt your pride" (NEB). The religious aspect of the pride is underlined by the words **in my holy mountain**, that is, the hill where the Lord's Temple stood. Human pride exhibited in such a place was an intentional insult to the Lord, and so TEV translates "**you will never again rebel against me on my sacred hill.**" "**On my sacred hill**" may be translated "on the hill where my sacred (holy) house stands." See verse 4 for comments on ways to translate "**sacred**" or **holy**.

Jerusalem's sin and redemption Zeph 3.13

3.12 RSV   TEV

> For I will leave in the midst of   I will leave there a humble and lowly
> you   people, who will come to me for help.
> a people humble and lowly.
> They shall seek refuge in the
> name of the LORD,

Earlier the Lord's righteous presence in the city (verse 5) was contrasted with the presence of the evil leaders. In a similar way here, the presence of the Lord's righteous people in the city is contrasted with the removal of the evil leaders in verse 11.

The word translated <u>**I will leave**</u> is a form of the root often translated "remnant." It is applied to the minority of people who trust in the Lord and obey him, and who will consequently survive the period of his judgment. In some languages it will be helpful to translate <u>**I will leave in the midst of you**</u> as "I will leave in my city (Jerusalem)" or "In Jerusalem I will leave . . . ."

These people in Jerusalem are described as **humble and lowly**. The word used here for **humble** is not the same as that used in 2.3. There the term referred primarily to those who humbled themselves in obedience to the Lord. Here the term implies rather those who have been humbled and humiliated (made to lose face) by the oppression and judgment through which they have passed.

The **lowly** are originally simply the poor people (NEB here translates "poor"). Since the majority of those who remained true to the Lord came from the ranks of the poor and weak rather than those of the rich and powerful, the term "poor" gradually came to mean "faithful to the Lord" and "obedient to his commands." Its use in passages like this one helps to explain the use of similar terms by Jesus in such passages as Matthew 5.3,5. In languages where it is difficult to find two words with similar meaning like **humble and lowly**, it may be necessary to say "very humble" or "have lost much face."

The characteristic feature of these **humble and lowly** people is that <u>**they shall seek refuge in the name of the LORD**</u>. The **name of the LORD** stands for his person and qualities. To **seek refuge** is a metaphor which is expressed in nonfigurative language in TEV as **"come to me for help."** (This last phrase is included in verse 13 in JB and NEB.)

3.13 RSV   TEV

> those who are left in Israel;   The people of Israel who survive will
> they shall do no wrong   do no wrong to anyone, tell no lies,
> and utter no lies,   nor try to deceive. They will be pros-
> nor shall there be found in their   perous and secure, afraid of no one."
> mouth
> a deceitful tongue.
> For they shall pasture and lie
> down,
> and none shall make them
> afraid."

The first phrase of this verse, **those who are left in Israel**, is taken with the last part of verse 12 by several modern versions (RSV, BJ, JB, NAB, NEB, GeCL). They understand it either to be the subject of the verb "seek" (BJ, JB, NEB) or to refer back to the pronoun "they," which itself refers back to the "humble and lowly" in the earlier part of verse 12 (RSV, NAB). The parallelism of the Hebrew text suggests that these words are indeed better taken with verse 12. However, others such as TOB, TEV, NIV, NJV, and FrCL take this phrase with the verb which follows it. Thus TEV renders **"The people of Israel who survive will do no wrong to anyone."** Since the same group of people, the minority who obey the Lord, is in view throughout verses 12 and 13, the difference is more one of emphasis than of meaning. For comments on **those who are left**, see notes on "remnant" in Zephaniah 2.7.

Further marks of this faithful minority are that they **utter no lies, nor shall there be found in their mouth a deceitful tongue**. This last expression is a figure of speech called metonymy. Most translators will need to express its meaning in nonfigurative language. TEV offers a model by saying that they will **"tell no lies, nor try to deceive."** NEB replaces the Hebrew figure of speech with an English one and says "no words of deceit shall pass their lips." Some translators may be able to find a suitable idiomatic expression in their own language.

As a result of the new character of the remaining inhabitants of Jerusalem, they will enjoy security and peace. This is expressed by means of a picture taken from sheep-farming: **They shall pasture and lie down, and none shall make them afraid**. Only when sheep are safe and undisturbed will they "graze and rest" (JB). At any sign of danger they scatter in all directions. In areas where sheep are well known, the translator can probably keep the Hebrew metaphor, but where sheep are not known, it will probably be better to express the meaning in nonfigurative language, as TEV does with **"They will be prosperous and secure, afraid of no one."** The description of sheep at rest as a picture of security is quite common in the Old Testament. Compare Psalm 23.1-3; Isaiah 17.2; Micah 7.14. In this context it refers to safety. Another possible restructuring of the last part of the verse is "They will be like sheep which graze in safety. They will rest and no one will make them afraid."

3.14-20

RSV	TEV
	A Song of Joy
14 Sing aloud, O daughter of Zion; shout, O Israel! Rejoice and exult with all your heart, O daughter of Jerusalem!	14 Sing and shout for joy, people of Israel! Rejoice with all your heart, Jerusalem!
15 The LORD has taken away the judgments against you, he has cast out your enemies. The King of Israel, the LORD, is in your midst; you shall fear evil no more.	15 The LORD has stopped your punishment; he has removed all your enemies. The LORD, the king of Israel, is with you; there is no reason now to be afraid.
16 On that day it shall be said to Jerusalem: "Do not fear, O Zion; let not your hands grow weak.	16 The time is coming when they will say to Jerusalem, "Do not be afraid, city of Zion! Do not let your hands hang limp!
17 The LORD your God is in your midst, a warrior who gives victory; he will rejoice over you with gladness, he will renew you in his love; he will exult over you with loud singing	17 The LORD your God is with you; his power gives you victory. The LORD will take delight in you, and in his love he will give you new life. He will sing and be joyful over you,
	18 as joyful as people at a festival." The LORD says,

A song of joy Zeph 3.14

18 as on a day of festival.
"I will remove disaster from you,
    so that you will not bear reproach for
      it.
19 Behold, at that time I will deal
    with all your oppressors.
And I will save the lame
    and gather the outcast,
and I will change their shame into praise
    and renown in all the earth.
20 At that time I will bring you home,
    at the time when I gather you together;
yea, I will make you renowned and praised
    among all the peoples of the earth,
when I restore your fortunes
    before your eyes," says the LORD.
	"I have ended the threat of doom
	    and taken away your disgrace.
	19 The time is coming!
	I will punish your oppressors;
	    I will rescue all the lame
	    and bring the exiles home.
	I will turn their shame to honor,
	    and all the world will praise them.
	20 The time is coming!
	I will bring your scattered people home;
	    I will make you famous throughout the
	      world
	    and make you prosperous once again."
	The LORD has spoken.

The book of Zephaniah concludes with a paragraph different in tone from the whole of the rest of the book. The faithful minority have passed through the punishment of the nation. The prophet now calls upon them to rejoice in the ending of that punishment and in the new sense of the Lord's presence and protection that followed. This paragraph is similar in outlook to such passages as Isaiah 52.7-10; 54.1-8; Zechariah 2.10; 9.9.

The paragraph falls into two main parts. From verse 14 up to and including the first phrase of verse 18 is a message of encouragement to the nation from the mouth of the prophet. The rest is a message of promise from the mouth of the Lord himself.

SECTION HEADING: "**A Song of Joy.**" For many translators this may be a suitable translation base as it is. However, if a fuller form of expression is needed, one can say "The people receive a joyful message" or "The prophet encourages the people."

In keeping with its use of the word "Song" in the section heading, TEV sets out this section as poetry. There is no need for translators to follow this example unless it will be particularly meaningful in their own language.

3.14	RSV	TEV

	**Sing aloud, O daughter of Zion;
	    shout, O Israel!
	Rejoice and exult with all your
	    heart,
	O daughter of Jerusalem!**
		**Sing and shout for joy, people of
		    Israel!
		Rejoice with all your heart,
		    Jerusalem!**

In Hebrew this verse consists of two lines parallel with each other in thought but not in structure. The first line in Hebrew is translated as the first two lines of RSV; it is itself composed of two parts parallel with each other in both thought and structure. Each part contains an imperative verb and a vocative, as shown in RSV's literal translation: <u>**Sing aloud, O daughter of Zion; shout, O Israel!**</u>

The expression <u>**daughter of Zion**</u> refers to the community of people faithful to the Lord and is quite common in the Old Testament. It means the same here as <u>**Israel**</u>, and so TEV combines the two parts of this line into one and says "**Sing and shout for joy, people of Israel!**" This sentence may also be rendered as "Sing and shout to show that you are joyful . . . " or "You people of Israel, sing and shout to show your joy."

The second line of the Hebrew is translated as the last two lines of RSV; it expresses the same thought but uses two verbal phrases with only one vocative, **Rejoice and exult with all your heart, O daughter of Jerusalem!** TEV combines the two verbs **rejoice** and **exult** and simply says "**Rejoice with all your heart.**" The **heart** is here the source of the emotions, the very center of one's personality, and in situations where some other organ is regarded as having this function, the translator should be free to use some other term, such as liver or throat.

The vocative **daughter of Jerusalem** refers to the small group of faithful Israelites who live in Jerusalem. TEV translates as "**Jerusalem**," since in this context it is already clear that the city stands for its inhabitants. However, in certain languages where one does not normally speak or talk to a city, it will be helpful to say "people of Jerusalem."

3.15

RSV

The LORD has taken away the judgments against you,
he has cast out your enemies.
The King of Israel, the LORD, is in your midst;
you shall fear evil no more.

TEV

The LORD has stopped your punishment;
he has removed all your enemies.
The LORD, the king of Israel, is with you;
there is no reason now to be afraid.

This verse gives the reason why the people were commanded in verse 14 to rejoice. The Hebrew verbs here are in the past (the so-called "prophetic perfect"), but they really refer to events which are still future. The prophet sees these future events as so certain to happen that he describes them as if they were already past. In some languages it may not be possible to speak of the future as though it were past, and in such cases it is perfectly acceptable to use future tenses here. In fact, from verse 16 on, the reference is quite explicitly to the future, and in the light of this, it may be wiser for many translators to use the future in verse 15 also.

Verse 15 consists of two sentences, each with two parts. In the first sentence the two parts are fairly closely parallel with each other: **The LORD has taken away the judgments against you, he has cast out your enemies**.

The **judgments against you** refers to the condemnation of the city for the evil behavior of the leaders (1.4-9; 3.1-7), and to the resulting punishment. TEV makes this clearer by saying "**The LORD has stopped your punishment.**" However, in some languages it will be necessary to say "The LORD has stopped punishing you." The **judgments** or "**punishment**" were of course carried out by the foreign nations who attacked Judah, and the second half of the sentence explains that the **judgments** were stopped by the disappearance of the **enemies** who were inflicting them. The Hebrew verb used here is mildly figurative. JB comes close to the literal meaning in saying "he has driven your enemies away." Some English translations use more obviously figurative expressions: **he has cast out your enemies** (RSV); "he has swept away your foes" (NEB). If a translator can find a figure of speech like these which is natural in his language, this will be a good place to use it. But if not, then he can follow the example of TEV and express the

A song of joy Zeph 3.16

meaning in nonfigurative language: "he has removed all your enemies" (see Nahum 1.8 for ways to translate **enemies**).

The second sentence gives the opposite side of the picture: not only are the enemies removed, but the Lord is present. **The King of Israel, the LORD, is in your midst**: the idea of the Lord as king is found quite frequently in the Old Testament. See for instance Isaiah 6.5; 44.6; Obadiah 21. The actual kings of Israel and Judah often fell far short of the ideal of kingship (compare 1 Sam 8.10-18); nevertheless the prophets could still use the concept of kingship to express the Lord's relationship to his people in the future restored community. **Is in your midst** means "is among you" (NEB) or just "**is with you**" (TEV, NIV), or even "lives among you."

One of the main tasks of a king was to protect the people and fight their battles (compare 1 Sam 8.20). The actual kings often failed to do so, but when **the LORD** is present as **the King of Israel**, he will protect his people perfectly, and so they **shall fear evil no more**. **Evil** in this context does not refer to sin, but rather to "trouble" (Mft), "disaster" (NEB), "harm" (NIV), or "misfortune" (NJV). TEV does not express any object but says "**there is no reason now to be afraid.**" This clause may also be expressed as "Because of this, you do not need to be afraid any more," or even "Because of this, no one can harm you any more. So do not be afraid."

3.16	RSV	TEV
	On that day it shall be said to Jerusalem: "Do not fear, O Zion; let not your hands grow weak.	The time is coming when they will say to Jerusalem, "Do not be afraid, city of Zion! Do not let your hands hang limp!

The opening words **On that day** mark explicitly that the prophet is speaking about the future (compare 1.9,10; 3.11). TEV translates with a more general expression, "The time is coming." As in verse 11, this refers to the period following the punishment that the Lord will bring on his people. When **that day** comes, the message to the people of Jerusalem will be one of encouragement and no longer of threat.

The Hebrew uses a passive form, **it shall be said to Jerusalem**, which avoids stating who brings the message that follows. In languages which have no passive forms, translators may wish to follow the example of TEV and state the subject in an indefinite way: "**they will say to Jerusalem.**" **Jerusalem** here, as often elsewhere, stands for "the inhabitants of Jerusalem," and some translators may need to make this explicit.

The message begins **Do not fear, O Zion**. As in the previous sentence, the city stands for its inhabitants. The use of the name **Zion** here puts emphasis on Jerusalem as a religious center, since **Zion** was the name for the area which included the temple.

The last part of the verse, **Do not let your hands grow weak**, speaks in traditional language of one of the effects of fear, especially on a soldier who should be gripping his weapons. (Compare 2 Sam 4.1 [KJV]; 2 Chr 15.7; Isa 13.7; Jer 6.24.) If the meaning of this expression will not be clear, a translator can follow the example of NAB and translate in nonfigurative language as "be not discouraged."

3.17-18   RSV   TEV

17   The LORD your God is in your   17   The LORD your God is with you;
         midst,   his power gives you victory.
     a warrior who gives victory;   The LORD will take delight in
     he will rejoice over you with   you,
         gladness,   and in his love he will give you
     he will renew you^i in his love;   new life.^h
     he will exult over you with loud   He will sing and be joyful over
         singing   you,
18   as on a day of festival.^j   18   as joyful as people at a festi-
     "I will remove disaster^k from   val."
         you,   The LORD says,
     so that you will not bear re-   "I have ended the threat of doom
         proach for it.   and taken away your disgrace.^i

^i Gk Syr: Heb *he will be silent*   ^h *Some ancient translations* give you
^j Gk Syr: Heb obscure   new life; *Hebrew* be silent.
^k Cn: Heb *they were*   ^i *Verse 18 in Hebrew is unclear.*

The verse opens by giving the reason for the people of Jerusalem to take courage. The language is similar to that of verse 15: **The LORD, your God, is in your midst**. For other ways of expressing this, see the comments on verse 15.

The next phrase pictures the effect of the Lord's presence with his people in terms of battle: he is **a warrior who gives victory**. In verse 15 the description of the Lord as a king spoke of how he would defend his people. Here the picture is one of attack rather than defense, and TEV gives the meaning without picture language as "**his power gives you victory.**" The word translated **warrior** is used of human warriors, such as David's "mighty men" (2 Sam 23.8), and is also used elsewhere to describe the Lord's help to his people (Isa 42.13; Jer 20.11). In languages where it may sound strange to use such a term to speak about God, it may be better to follow the example of TEV and use plain language. It is also possible to restructure the clause slightly and say "you will be victorious through his power" or "you will overcome through his power."

The rest of the verse speaks of the Lord's attitude toward his people. The first clause states that **he will rejoice over you with gladness**. This is somewhat repetitive, and TEV expresses its meaning more simply with "**The LORD will take delight in you.**" The clause "take delight in you" is difficult to translate in many languages. Perhaps one can say "He will be very happy with you."

The second clause says in Hebrew "he will be silent in his love" (RV margin; compare HOTTP). Various attempts have been made to find a meaning for this, but none are convincing, and the mention of silence here clashes with the **loud singing** in the next clause (compare "Sing aloud . . . shout" in verse 14). Accordingly most modern translations follow the ancient Septuagint and Syriac versions and translate as **he will renew you in his love** or something very similar. TEV accepts this and expresses the meaning more fully as "**in his love he will give you new life.**" Some commentators see in these two clauses a picture of a

A song of joy Zeph 3.17-18

bridegroom rejoicing in his bride (Eaton, Murphy). Such a picture of the relationship between the Lord and his people is found elsewhere in scripture (compare Isa 62.5; 2 Cor 11.2; Rev 21.2), and it will not be out of place here to use in translation terms which may have sexual overtones. In many languages **in his love** may be expressed as "because he loves you."

He will exult over you with loud singing: the last clause of verse 17 repeats and summarizes the main point of the message which began in verse 16. The term translated **loud singing** is a form of the same root which was translated "Sing aloud" in verse 14. Its recurrence here may serve to mark verses 14-17 as a unit in the Hebrew text. TEV repeats the word "sing" from verse 14 and translates the whole clause "**He will sing and be joyful over you.**" Another possible rendering is "You will make his heart full of joy, and he will sing loudly." Certain languages have special words for the joy that parents, relatives, or lovers have for the object of their love. Such a word should be used for "joy" here.

Most modern translations follow the Septuagint and take the first phrase of verse 18 with verse 17 as the concluding words of the message begun in verse 16 (RSV, BJ, JB, NAB, NEB, TEV, FrCL, GeCL). Except for NEB, they also follow the text of the Greek and Syriac versions and translate **as on a day of festival** (RSV, JB) or something similar. TEV makes explicit both the participants and the ground of comparison with a festival by saying "**as joyful as people at a festival.**" An alternative translation model is "as people are full of joy (have joyful hearts) when celebrating a festival."

Those translations which do not take the first phrase of verse 18 with verse 17 still differ in their handling of it. KJV and RV understand the Hebrew words to mean "them that sorrow for the solemn assembly" (RV) and take them as the object of the verb that follows in the next line in Hebrew, "I will gather." The whole clause "I will gather them that sorrow for the solemn assembly" appears to be interpreted as a promise that the Lord will bring back to Jerusalem those people who were in exile—those who were thus sorrowing because they could no longer take part in the religious festivals of Judah. This interpretation is also found in GeCL and in the NIV footnote. The word translated "sorrow" in RV can also be translated "are removed from" (RV margin, and apparently TOB), but this translation seems to offer the same overall interpretation as the previous one—a promise of restoration from exile.

A bigger difference of meaning appears if the word "gather" is understood in the sense of "gather together for removal" (as one might gather weeds) rather than "gather things (or people) that have been (unfortunately) scattered." This is the understanding of NIV, which translates "The sorrows for the appointed feasts I will remove from you."

The words that follow the verb translated "gather" also present difficulties. As they stand they mean "who were of thee" (RV) and seem to refer to the people sorrowing in exile. The word translated "of thee" in RV can mean "from thee" and is taken in this way by TOB, with the sense "far from you," referring again to the people who were in exile far away in Jerusalem. NIV takes the word "from you" with the preceding verb "remove," and understands the verb "were" to go with the last part of the sentence.

The other modern versions, those which followed the Septuagint by taking the first two words of verse 18 with verse 17, also follow it in reading **disaster** or something similar in meaning instead of the verb "they were." They then take this word with the verb "gather" (understood in the sense of "gather for removal") and translate as **I will remove disaster from you** (RSV, compare NAB) or "I have taken away your misfortune" (JB). TEV adopts this understanding but surprisingly expresses it in rather high-level language as "**I have ended the threat of doom.**" In many languages this clause may be rendered as "I will not let you be harmed again." Note that TEV has also made it explicit that with these words there begins a new speech by the Lord. In the Hebrew the speaker is not stated until the end of verse 20, but to avoid confusion TEV introduces the speech with the words "**The LORD says**" here in verse 18.

The final clause of the verse, which consists of three words in Hebrew, has also been understood in different ways. KJV translates "to whom the reproach of it was a burden." RV reverses the subject and complement and so translates "to whom the burden upon her was a reproach." In both versions the words "to whom" are printed in italics, indicating that they are not found in the Hebrew. The meaning of KJV and RV seems to be that the burden of having her children in exile was a reproach to the city of Jerusalem.

Some modern scholars wish to follow the ancient Syriac translation and read "upon you" for the "upon her" of RV. NIV appears to do this in rendering "they are a burden and a reproach to you," with an alternative in a footnote, "your reproach is a burden to you."

A number of modern versions take the word translated "burden" in KJV, RV and NIV as a verb rather than a noun, having the meaning of "bear." Thus RSV renders **so that you will not bear reproach for it**, and JB "no longer need you bear the disgrace of it." TEV follows this interpretation but expresses it in a form that fits the syntax of the previous clause: "**I have . . . taken away your disgrace.**" "Your disgrace" may be expressed as "your great shame" or "your humiliation." The whole sentence may be restructured as "and will not let you be ashamed any more," or more idiomatically in certain languages, "and will not let you lose face again."

Such are the difficulties in this verse that the TEV footnote "*Verse 18 in Hebrew is unclear*" can only be described as a masterpiece of understatement. However, despite the problems of detail, it is still evident that the verse is, in its main thrust, appropriate to its context, and is a continuation of the theme of promise and encouragement. It is impossible to give firm advice about the best understanding of this verse, but since RSV and TEV are similar in their approach, translators may as well follow them. An alternative way of expressing the verse is "The LORD says, 'I will take away your troubles, and no one will reproach you (scorn you) again because of them.' " An interpretation of verse 18 different from that of RSV or TEV may be found in HOTTP. However, this interpretation is not represented in any modern English translation and does not fit the context very readily, so it must be viewed with some reserve.

3.19	RSV	TEV
	Behold, at that time I will deal with all your oppressors. And I will save the lame and gather the outcast, and I will change their shame into praise and renown in all the earth.	The time is coming! I will punish your oppressors; I will rescue all the lame and bring the exiles home. I will turn their shame to honor, and all the world will praise them.

A song of joy Zeph 3.20

The verse begins in Hebrew with the exclamation translated **Behold** in RSV. Since this is no longer used in modern spoken English, other versions have tried to convey the same effect of catching attention, but by different means. Thus NAB begins with "Yes," and NEB has "see" later in the sentence. TEV does not use a separate word but rather uses punctuation to achieve the same effect. It makes a separate sentence of the phrase **at that time** and adds an exclamation mark "**The time is coming!**"

The statement **I will deal with all your oppressors** has an overtone of threat (compare Ezek 20.44), and this is made explicit in TEV as "**I will punish your oppressors**" (compare JB). **Your oppressors** may be expressed as "those who oppress you" or "those who treat you cruelly."

The next two clauses use the figure of a shepherd caring for sheep, to express what the Lord will do for his people: **I will save the lame and gather the outcast**. The language is closely similar to that used in Micah 4.6-7. The word translated **outcast** in RSV is often used to refer to the people who were in exile, and TEV makes this clear by saying "I will . . . bring the exiles home." However, the word translated **lame** in RSV is the same in TEV. This means that TEV retains the figure of speech in one clause and drops it in the other. It may be better for translators either to expand these two clauses and give both the figures and their meanings, or else to drop the figures and state the meanings in nonfigurative language. A translation model of the former can be "I will rescue the people who are as helpless as lame sheep, and will bring home those who, like scattered sheep, have been driven into exile." For those who wish to state the meaning in nonfigurative language, a model can be "I will rescue the people who are helpless, and bring home those who have been driven into exile."

I will change their shame into praise and renown in all the earth: the last clause promises that the people will have a new reputation to match their new status. Because of their exile, they had been mocked and scorned by other nations (compare Obadiah 10-14), but once restored by the Lord, they will have **praise and renown in all the earth**. TEV turns this into two clauses and says "**I will turn their shame to honor, and all the world will praise them.**" In certain languages it will be necessary to rephrase these final clauses and say "I will make people honor them so that they will no longer be ashamed."

The word translated **their shame** in RSV makes the sentence a little awkward grammatically in Hebrew. Some scholars think that it is wrong and should be replaced by some words from verse 20 which are somewhat similar in spelling. These words are translated "when I restore your fortunes" in RSV. This view is adopted in BJ, JB, and NAB, and thus JB for instance has here "when I restore their fortunes." However, the Hebrew text can be understood as it stands, and there is no need for translators to make this alteration.

3.20	RSV	TEV
	At that time I will bring you home, at the time when I gather you together; yea, I will make you renowned and praised	The time is coming! I will bring your scattered people home; I will make you famous throughout the world and make you prosperous once again."

> among all the peoples of the earth,
> when I restore your fortunes before your eyes," says the LORD.

> The LORD has spoken.

This verse repeats the sense of the second half of verse 19 and expands it slightly. Although the Hebrew does not in this case begin with the word translated "Behold" in verse 19, TEV again makes an emphatic separate sentence of **"The time is coming!"**

The two clauses **I will bring you home, at the time when I gather you together** are joined into one in TEV as "I will bring your scattered people home." One may also translate "I will bring home your people who are living in many lands."

The next clause is closest in wording to verse 19, as is clear from RSV, **yea, I will make you renowned and praised among all the peoples of the earth**. TEV expresses this in more modern and natural language as **"I will make you famous throughout the world."** Some translators may need to state the participants more explicitly and say something like "I will cause people all over the world to praise you." The opening word **yea** simply adds emphasis. One can also say "I will indeed make you famous."

The last clause of the speech by the Lord, which began in verse 18, is translated **when I restore your fortunes before your eyes** in RSV. The expression **restore ... fortunes** has already occurred in 2.7. It refers to the time of the return from exile but includes more than just the return itself (compare Job 42.10). TEV expresses the wider meaning with **"make you prosperous once again"** (see comment on "restore their fortunes" in Zeph 2.7). TEV appears to have no equivalent to RSV **before your eyes**. This means that the change in the people's fortunes was to take place within the lifetime of the generation to which the prophet was speaking (compare Jer 16.9; 51.24). Other modern versions render "before your very eyes" (NAB, NIV), or in plain language "and you shall see it" (NEB). Presumably the omission in TEV is an accident, and translators ought not to follow the example of TEV at this point.

The direct speech of verses 18-20 is closed with the words **says the LORD**. TEV makes this a separate sentence and gives it a perfect tense form more suitable to the concluding words of a book: **"The LORD has spoken."** Translators should be sure that the expression they use here points backward to the words which have preceded.

Bibliography

TEXTS

Biblia Hebraica. 7th edition. 1951. Edited by Rudolph Kittel. Stuttgart: Württembergische Bibelanstalt.

Biblia Hebraica Stuttgartensia. 1966/77, 1983. Edited by K. Elliger and W. Rudolph. Stuttgart: Deutsche Bibelgesellschaft.

Septuaginta: Id est Vetus Testamentum graece iuxta LXX interpretes. 1935. Edited by Alfred Rahlfs. Stuttgart: Württembergische Bibelanstalt. (Cited as Septuagint.)

Biblia Sacra: Iuxta Vulgatam Versionem. 1983. Edited by Robert Weber. Stuttgart: Deutsche Bibelgesellschaft. (Cited as Vulgate.)

VERSIONS

The Bible: A New Translation. 1926. James Moffatt, translator. London: Hodder & Stoughton. (Cited as Mft.)

La Bible de Jérusalem. 1973. Paris: Éditions du Cerf. (Cited as BJ.)

La Bible en français courant. 1982. Paris: Société biblique française. (Cited as FrCL.)

Good News Bible: The Bible in Today's English Version. 1976, 1979. New York: American Bible Society. (Cited as TEV.)

Die Bibel in heutigem Deutsch: Die Gute Nachricht des Alten und Neuen Testaments. 1982. Stuttgart: Deutsche Bibelgesellschaft. (Cited as GeCL.)

The Holy Bible (Authorized or King James Version). 1611. (Cited as KJV.)

The Holy Bible: New International Version. 1978. New York: New York International Bible Society. (Cited as NIV.)

The Holy Bible (Revised Version.) 1885. (Cited as RV.)

BIBLIOGRAPHY

The Holy Bible: Revised Standard Version. 1952, 1971, 1973. New York: Division of Christian Education of the National Council of the Churches of Christ in the United States of America. (Cited as RSV.)

The Jerusalem Bible. 1966. London: Darton, Longman, & Todd; and New York: Doubleday. (Cited as JB.)

The New American Bible. 1970. New York: P.J. Kenedy & Sons. (Cited as NAB.)

The New English Bible. 1961, 1970. London: Oxford University Press; and Cambridge: Cambridge University Press. (Cited as NEB.)

The Prophets: A new translaton of the Holy Scriptures according to the Masoretic text. 1978. Philadelphia: The Jewish Publication Society of America. (Cited as New Jewish Version, or NJV.)

La Sainte Bible: Nouvelle version Segond révisée. 1981. Paris: Alliance biblique universelle.

Traduction Oecuménique de la Bible. 1975. Paris: Société biblique française et Éditions du Cerf. (Cited as TOB.)

COMMENTARIES AND ARTICLES

Ball, Ivan J., Jr. 1987, "The Rhetorical Shape of Zephaniah." In: *Perspectives on Language and Text*, Edgar W. Conrad and Edward G. Newing, eds., pages 155-165. Winona Lake, Indiana: Eisenbrauns.

Clark, David J., "Of birds and beasts: Zephaniah 2.14." *The Bible Translator* 34 (1983): 243-6.

———. "Wine on the lees (Zeph 1.12 and Jer 48.11)." *The Bible Translator* 32 (1981): 241-3.

Deissler, A. 1964. "Sophonie." In: *La Sainte Bible*, Vol. 8, Part 1. Paris: Letouzey & Ané.

Delcor, M. 1964. "Nahum, Habacuc." In: *La Sainte Bible*, Vol. 8, Part 1. Paris: Letouzey & Ané.

Driver, S.R. 1906. *The Minor Prophets, Nahum, Habakkuk, Zephaniah, Haggai, Zechariah, Malachi* (The Century Bible). Edinburgh: T.C. & E.C. Jack.

Elliger, Karl. 1982. *Das Buch der zwölf Kleinen Propheten*. Vol. 2, *Die Propheten Nahum, Habakuk, Zephanja, Haggai, Sacharja, Maleachi*. Göttingen: Vandenhoeck & Ruprecht.

Gailey, J.H. 1962. *Micah to Malachi* (Layman's Bible Commentaries). London: SCM Press.

Lehrman, S.M. 1948. "Habakkuk." In: *The Twelve Prophets* (Soncino Books of the Bible). London, Jerusalem, New York: The Soncino Press.

———. 1948. "Nahum." In: *The Twelve Prophets* (Soncino Books of the Bible). London, Jerusalem, New York: The Soncino Press.

———. 1948. "Zephaniah." In: *The Twelve Prophets* (Soncino Books of the Bible). London, Jerusalem, New York: The Soncino Press.

McKane, William. 1974. "Observations on the tiqqûnê sôperîm." In: *On Language, Culture and Religion: In Honor of Eugene A. Nida*. Matthew Black and William A. Smalley, eds. The Hague, Paris: Mouton.

Murphy, Richard T.A. 1968. "Zephaniah, Nahum, Habakkuk." In: *The Jerome Biblical Commentary*. Englewood Cliffs: Prentice-Hall.

Nute, A.G. 1979. "Habakkuk." In: *A Bible Commentary for Today*. Glasgow: Pickering & Inglis.

Reid, Victor A.S. 1979. "Zephaniah." In: *A Bible Commentary for Today*. Glasgow: Pickering & Inglis.

Smith, George Adam. 1928. *The Book of the Twelve Prophets: Commonly Called the Minor*. Vol. 2, *Zephaniah, Nahum, Habakkuk, Obadiah, Haggai, Zechariah, Malachi, Joel, Jonah*. London: Hodder & Stoughton.

Smith, J.M.P., W.H. Ward, and J.A. Bewer. 1911. *A Critical and Exegetical Commentary on Micah, Zephaniah, Nahum, Habakkuk, Obadiah and Joel* (International Critical Commentary). Edinburgh: T. & T. Clark.

Smith, Ralph L. 1984. *Micah-Malachi* (Word Biblical Commentary). Waco: Word Books.

Taylor, Charles L., Jr. 1956. "The Book of Nahum." In: *The Interpreter's Bible*, Vol. 6. New York and Nashville: Abingdon Press.

———. 1956. "The Book of Habakkuk." In: *The Interpreter's Bible*, Vol. 6. New York and Nashville: Abingdon Press.

———. 1956. "The Book of Zephaniah." In: *The Interpreter's Bible*, Vol. 6. New York and Nashville: Abingdon Press.

Thompson, John A. "Translation of the Words for Locust." *The Bible Translator* 25 (1974): 405-411.

Watts, John D.W. 1975. *The Books of Joel, Obadiah, Jonah, Nahum, Habakkuk and Zephaniah* (Cambridge Bible Commentary). Cambridge: Cambridge University Press.

DICTIONARIES, GRAMMARS, AND HELPS

Achtemeier, Paul J., ed. 1985. *Harper's Bible Dictionary*. San Francisco: Harper & Row.

Barthélemy, Dominique, A.R. Hulst, Norbert Lohfink, W.D. McHardy, H.P. Rüger, and James A. Sanders. 1980. *Preliminary and Interim Report on the Hebrew Old Testament Text Project*, Vol 5. New York: United Bible Societies.

Brown, Francis, S.R. Driver, and Charles A. Briggs. 1968. *A Hebrew and English Lexicon of the Old Testament*. London: Oxford University Press.

Buttrick, G.A., ed. 1962. *The Interpreter's Dictionary of the Bible*. 4 Vols. New York and Nashville: Abingdon Press.

Cowley, A.E., ed. 1910. *Gesenius' Hebrew Grammar: As Edited and Enlarged by the Late E. Kautzsch*. Second English edition. Oxford: The University Press.

Fauna and Flora of the Bible. 1972. London: United Bible Societies.

Orr, James, ed. 1960. *The International Standard Bible Encyclopaedia*. 5 Vols. Grand Rapids: Eerdmans.

Glossary

This Glossary contains terms which are technical from an exegetical or a linguistic viewpoint. Other terms not defined here may be referred to in a Bible dictionary.

ACROSTIC refers to a style of writing lines, usually poetic lines, in such a way that the first letter of every line will combine with the other first letters to form the letters of the alphabet in their order, or else to form a phrase or a message.

ACTIVE. See VOICE.

ADJECTIVE is a word which limits, describes, or qualifies a noun. In English, "red," "tall," "beautiful," and "important" are adjectives.

AGENT is that which accomplishes the action in a sentence or clause, regardless of whether the grammatical construction is active or passive. In "John struck Bill" (active) and "Bill was struck by John" (passive), the agent in either case is John.

AMBIGUOUS (AMBIGUITY) describes a word or phrase which in a specific context may have two or more different meanings. For example, "Bill did not leave because John came" could mean either (1) "the coming of John prevented Bill from leaving" or (2) "the coming of John was not the cause of Bill's leaving." It is often the case that what is ambiguous in written form is not ambiguous when actually spoken, since features of intonation and slight pauses usually make clear which of two or more meanings is intended. Furthermore, even in written discourse, the entire context normally serves to indicate which meaning is intended by the writer.

ANALYSIS is the process of determining what are the various units which enter into any complex structure and describing how these units are related to one another.

ANCIENT VERSIONS. See VERSIONS.

ANTECEDENT describes a person or thing which precedes or exists prior to something or someone else. In grammar, an antecedent is the word, phrase, or clause to which a pronoun refers.

APPOSITION is the placing of two expressions together so that they both refer to the same object, event, or concept; for example, "my friend, Mr. Smith."

CAUSATIVE (CAUSAL) relates to events and indicates that someone or something caused something to happen, rather than that the person or thing did it directly. In "John ran the horse," the verb "ran" is a causative, since it was not John who ran, but rather it was John who caused the horse to run.

CHIASMUS is a reversal of the order of words or phrases in an otherwise parallel construction. For example: "(1) I / (2) was shapen / (3) in iniquity // (3) in sin / (2) did my mother conceive / (1) me."

CLAUSE is a grammatical construction, normally consisting of a subject and a predicate.

COLLECTIVE refers to a number of things (or persons) considered as a whole. In English, a collective noun is considered to be singular or plural, more or less on the basis of traditional usage; for example, "The crowd is (the people are) becoming angry."

COMMON LANGUAGE TRANSLATION is one that uses only that portion of the total resources of a language that is understood and accepted by all as good usage. Excluded are features peculiar to a dialect, substandard or vulgar language, and technical or highly literary language not understood by all.

COMPLEMENT is a word or phrase which grammatically completes another word or phrase. The term is used particularly of expressions which specify time, place, manner, means, etc.

CONDITIONAL refers to a clause or phrase which expresses or implies a condition, in English usually introduced by "if."

CONSONANTS are symbols representing those speech sounds which are produced by obstructing, blocking, or restricting the free passage of air from the lungs through the mouth. They were originally the only spoken sounds recorded in the Hebrew system of writing; VOWELS were added later as marks associated with the CONSONANTS. See also VOWELS.

CONSTRUCTION. See STRUCTURE.

CONTEXT is that which precedes and/or follows any part of a discourse. For example, the context of a word or phrase in Scripture would be the other words and phrases associated with it in the sentence, paragraph, section, and even the entire book in which it occurs. The context of a term often affects its meaning, so that a word does not mean exactly the same thing in one context that it does in another context.

CULTURE (CULTURAL) is the sum total of the beliefs, patterns of behavior, and sets of interpersonal relations of any group of people. A culture is passed on from one generation to another, but undergoes development or gradual change.

DEUTEROCANONICAL BOOKS is another term for the apocryphal books (Apocrypha), writings included in the Septuagint and Vulgate but excluded from the Jewish and Protestant books of the Old Testament.

DIRECT DISCOURSE, DIRECT QUOTATION, DIRECT SPEECH. See DISCOURSE.

DISCOURSE is the connected and continuous communication of thought by means of language, whether spoken or written. The way in which the elements of a discourse are arranged is called DISCOURSE STRUCTURE. DIRECT DISCOURSE (or, DIRECT QUOTATION, DIRECT SPEECH) is the reproduction of the actual words of one person quoted and included in the discourse of another person; for example, "He declared 'I will have nothing to do with this man.'" INDIRECT DISCOURSE (or, INDIRECT QUOTATION, INDIRECT SPEECH) is the reporting of the words of one person within the discourse of another person, but in an altered grammatical form rather than as an exact quotation; for example, "He said he would have nothing to do with that man."

DUAL is a grammatical form in Hebrew involving two items rather than either singular or plural items. The form is often used for things that occur in pairs, such as "horns" or "eyes," but sometimes it is applied to things that clearly do not occur in pairs, as in the Hebrew word for "Egypt."

EMENDATION (EMEND) is the process of substituting what appears to be a better form of the text for one which is judged to be incorrect.

EMPHASIS (EMPHATIC) is the special importance given to an element in a discourse, sometimes indicated by the choice of words or by position in the sentence. For example, in "Never will I eat pork again," "Never" is given emphasis by placing it at the beginning of the sentence.

EUPHEMISM is a mild or indirect term used in the place of another term which is felt to be impolite, distasteful, or vulgar; for example, "to pass away" is a euphemism for "to die."

EXCLUSIVE first person plural excludes the person(s) addressed. That is, a speaker may use "we" to refer to himself and his companions, while specifically excluding the person(s) to whom he is speaking. See INCLUSIVE.

EXEGESIS is the process of determining the meaning of a text (or is the result of this process), normally in terms of "who said what to whom under what circumstances and with what intent." A correct exegesis is indispensable before a passage can be translated correctly.

EXPLICIT refers to information which is expressed in the words of a discourse. This is in contrast to implicit information. See IMPLICIT.

FEMININE is one of the Hebrew genders. See GENDER.

FIGURE, FIGURE OF SPEECH, or FIGURATIVE EXPRESSION involves the use of words in other than their literal or ordinary sense, in order to bring out some aspect of meaning by means of comparison or association. For example, "raindrops dancing on the street," or "his speech was like thunder." METAPHORS and SIMILES are figures of speech.

FIRST PERSON. See PERSON.

FUTURE TENSE. See TENSE.

GENDER is a grammatical category of Hebrew nouns and pronouns consisting of two subclasses (called "masculine" and FEMININE), which determine agreement with and selection of other words or grammatical forms.

GENERIC has reference to a general class or kind of objects, events, or abstracts; it is the opposite of SPECIFIC. For example, the term "animal" is generic in relation to "dog," which is a specific kind of animal. However, "dog" is generic in relation to the more specific term "poodle."

GOAL is the person or thing which receives or undergoes the action of a verb. Grammatically, the goal may be the subject of a passive construction ("John was hit," in which "John" is the goal of "hit"), or of certain intransitives ("the door shut"), or it may be the direct object of a transitive verb ("[something] hit John").

GRAMMATICAL refers to GRAMMAR, which includes the selection and arrangement of words in phrases, clauses, and sentences.

HEBREW is the language in which the Old Testament was written. It belongs to the SEMITIC family of languages. By the time of Christ, many Jewish people no longer used Hebrew as their common language.

IDEOPHONE is a vocal expression, often one that does not fit into the usual grammatical pattern of a language, yet expresses such things as an emotion, a quality, or a movement, and may sometimes mark or emphasize a feature of discourse. The sound is often intended to resemble or describe a feature of that which the ideophone represents. Ideophones are especially common in African languages, where their use and definition vary greatly.

IDIOM (or IDIOMATIC EXPRESSION) is a combination of terms whose meanings cannot be understood by adding up the meanings of the parts. "To hang one's head," "to have a green thumb," and "behind the eightball" are American English idioms. Idioms almost always lose their meaning or convey a wrong meaning when translated literally from one language to another.

IMPERATIVE refers to forms of a verb which indicate commands or requests. In "Go and do likewise," the verbs "Go" and "do" are imperatives. In most languages imperatives are confined to the grammatical second person; but some languages have corresponding forms for the first and third persons. These are usually expressed in English by the use of "may" or "let"; for example, "May we not have to beg!" or "Let them work harder!"

IMPLICIT (IMPLIED) refers to information that is not formally represented in a discourse, since it is assumed that it is already known to the receptor, or evident from the meaning of the words in question. For example, the phrase "the other son" carries with it the implicit information that there is a son in addition to the one mentioned. This is in contrast to **EXPLICIT** information, which is expressly stated in a discourse. See **EXPLICIT**.

INCLUSIVE first person plural includes both the speaker and the one(s) to whom that person is speaking. See **EXCLUSIVE**.

INDIRECT SPEECH, INDIRECT DISCOURSE. See **DISCOURSE**.

INTERPRETATION of a text is the exegesis of it. See **EXEGESIS**.

IRONY (IRONIC, IRONICAL) is a sarcastic or humorous manner of discourse in which what is said is intended to express its opposite; for example, "That was a smart thing to do!" when intended to convey the meaning, "That was a stupid thing to do!"

LINGUISTIC refers to language, especially the formal structure of language.

LITERAL means the ordinary or primary meaning of a term or expression, in contrast with a figurative meaning. A **LITERAL TRANSLATION** is one which represents the exact words and word order of the source language; such a translation is frequently unnatural or awkward in the receptor language.

MANUSCRIPTS are books, documents, or letters written or copied by hand. A **SCRIBE** is one who copies a manuscript. Thousands of manuscript copies of various Old and New Testament books still exist, but none of the original manuscripts. See **TEXT**.

MASORETIC TEXT is the form of the text of the Hebrew Old Testament established by Hebrew scholars around the eighth and ninth centuries A.D.

METAPHOR is likening one object, event, or state to another by speaking of it as if it were the other; for example, "flowers dancing in the breeze." Metaphors are the most commonly used figures of speech and are often so subtle that a speaker or writer is not conscious of the fact that he is using figurative language. See **SIMILE**.

METONYM is a figure of speech in which the name of one thing is replaced by the name of another thing which is associated with it in some way. For example, in "the pen is mightier than the sword," the words "pen" and "sword" symbolize and replace "written words" and "war."

NONFIGURATIVE. See **FIGURE, FIGURATIVE**.

NOUN is a word that names a person, place, thing, or idea, and often serves to specify a subject or topic of discussion.

OBJECT of a verb is the goal of an event or action specified by the verb. In "John hit the ball," the object of "hit" is "ball."

GLOSSARY

PARALLEL, PARALLELISM, generally refers to some similarity in the content and/or form of a construction; for example, "The man was blind, and he could not see." The structures that correspond to each other in the two statements are said to be parallel.

PARTICIPLE is a verbal adjective, that is, a word which retains some of the characteristics of a verb while functioning as an adjective. In "singing children" and "painted house," "singing" and "painted" are participles.

PASSIVE. See **VOICE.**

PAST TENSE. See **TENSE.**

PERFECT TENSE is a set of verb forms which indicate an action completed before the time of speaking or writing. For example, in "John has finished his task," "has finished" is in the perfect tense. See also **TENSE.**

PERSON, as a grammatical term, refers to the speaker, the person spoken to, or the person or thing spoken about. **FIRST PERSON** is the person(s) speaking (such as "I," "me," "my," "mine," "we," "us," "our," or "ours"). **SECOND PERSON** is the person(s) or thing(s) spoken to (such as "thou," "thee," "thy," "thine," "ye," "you," "your," or "yours"). **THIRD PERSON** is the person(s) or thing(s) spoken about (such as "he," "she," "it," "his," "her," "them," or "their"). The examples here given are all pronouns, but in many languages the verb forms have affixes which indicate first, second, or third person and also indicate whether they are **SINGULAR** or **PLURAL.**

PERSONIFY is to refer to an inanimate object or an abstract idea in terms that give it a personal or a human nature; as in "Wisdom is calling out," referring to wisdom as if it were a person.

PHRASE is a grammatical construction of two or more words, but less than a complete clause or a sentence. A phrase is usually given a name according to its structure in a sentence, such as "noun phrase," "verb phrase," or "prepositional phrase."

PLAY ON WORDS. See **WORDPLAY.**

PLURAL refers to the form of a word which indicates more than one. See **SINGULAR.**

POSSESSIVE refers to a grammatical relationship in which one noun or pronoun is said to "possess" another ("John's car," "his son," "their destruction").

PREDICATE is the part of a clause which contrasts with or supplements the subject. The **SUBJECT** is the topic of the clause, and the **PREDICATE** is what is said about the subject. For example, in "The small boy ran swiftly," the subject is "The small boy," and the predicate is "ran swiftly." See **SUBJECT.**

GLOSSARY

PREPOSITION is a word (usually a particle) whose function is to indicate the relation of a noun or pronoun to another noun, pronoun, verb, or adjective. Some English prepositions are "for," "from," "in," "to," and "with."

PREPOSITIONAL refers to **PREPOSITIONS**. A prepositional phrase or expression is one governed by a preposition. "For his benefit" and "to a certain city" are prepositional phrases.

PRESENT TENSE. See **TENSE**.

PROPHETIC PERFECT refers to a Hebrew use of the perfect tense, in which a prophet speaks of a future event as though it had already happened. See also **PERFECT TENSE**.

PRONOUNS are words which are used in place of nouns, such as "he," "him," "his," "she," "we," "them," "who," "which," "this," or "these."

READ, READING, frequently refers to the interpretation of the written form of a text, especially under the following conditions: if the available text appears to be defective; or if differing versions of the same text are available; or if two or more different sets of vowels will fit the consonants in languages such as Hebrew, in which only the consonants are written. See also **TEXT, TEXTUAL**.

RECEPTOR is the person(s) receiving a message. The **RECEPTOR LANGUAGE** is the language into which a translation is made. For example, in a translation from Hebrew into German, Hebrew is the source language and German is the receptor language. The **RECEPTOR CULTURE** is the culture of the people who speak the receptor language.

REFERENT is the thing(s) or person(s) referred to by a pronoun, phrase, or clause.

RELATIVE CLAUSE is a dependent clause which describes the object to which it refers. In "the man whom you saw," the clause "whom you saw" is relative because it relates to and describes "man."

RENDER means translate or express in a language different from the original.

RENDERING is the manner in which a specific passage is translated from one language to another.

RESTRUCTURE. See **STRUCTURE**.

RHETORICAL QUESTION is an expression which is put in the form of a question but which is not intended to ask for information. Rhetorical questions are usually employed for the sake of emphasis.

ROOT is the minimal base of a derived or inflected word. For example, "friend" is the root of "friendliness."

SARCASM (SARCASTIC) is an ironical and frequently contemptuous manner of discourse in which what is said is intended to express its opposite; for example, "What a brilliant idea!" when intended to convey the meaning, "What a ridiculous idea!"

SCRIBE, SCRIBAL. See **MANUSCRIPT**.

SECOND PERSON. See **PERSON**.

SEMITIC LANGUAGES are those which belong to a large family of languages spoken primarily by many people who live in western Asia and North Africa. Hebrew, Aramaic, and Arabic are Semitic languages.

SENTENCE is a grammatical construction composed of one or more clauses and capable of standing alone.

SEPTUAGINT is a translation of the Hebrew Old Testament into Greek, made some two hundred years before Christ. It is often abbreviated as LXX.

SIMILE (pronounced SIM-i-lee) is a **FIGURE OF SPEECH** which describes one event or object by comparing it to another, using "like," "as," or some other word to mark or signal the comparison. For example, "She runs like a deer," "He is as straight as an arrow." Similes are less subtle than metaphors in that metaphors do not mark the comparison with words such as "like" or "as." See **METAPHOR**.

SINGULAR refers to the form of a word which indicates one thing or person, in contrast to **PLURAL**, which indicates more than one. See **PLURAL**.

SPECIFIC refers to the opposite of general, generic. See **GENERIC**.

STRUCTURE is the systematic arrangement of the elements of language, including the ways in which words combine into phrases, phrases into clauses, clauses into sentences, and sentences into larger units of discourse. Because this process may be compared to the building of a house or bridge, such words as **STRUCTURE** and **CONSTRUCTION** are used in reference to it. To separate and rearrange the various components of a sentence or other unit of discourse in the translation process is to **RESTRUCTURE** it.

STYLE is a particular or a characteristic manner in discourse. Each language has certain distinctive **STYLISTIC** features which cannot be reproduced literally in another language. Within any language, certain groups of speakers may have their characteristic discourse styles, and among individual speakers and writers, each has his own style. Various **STYLISTIC DEVICES** are used for the purpose of achieving a more pleasing style. For example, synonyms are sometimes used to avoid the monotonous repetition of the same words, or the normal order of clauses and phrases may be altered for the sake of emphasis.

SUBJECT is one of the major divisions of a clause, the other being the predicate. In "The small boy walked to school," "The small boy" is the subject.

Typically the subject is a noun phrase. It should not be confused with the semantic **AGENT**. See **PREDICATE**.

SUFFIX is a letter or one or more syllables added to the end of a word, to modify the meaning in some manner. For example, "-s" suffixed to "tree" changes the word from singular to plural, "trees," while "-ing" suffixed to "sing" changes the verb to a participle, "singing."

SYMBOL is a form, whether linguistic or nonlinguistic, which is arbitrarily and conventionally associated with a particular meaning. For example, the word "cross" is a linguistic symbol, referring to a particular object. Similarly, within the Christian tradition, the cross as an object is a symbol for the death of Jesus.

SYNONYMS are words which are different in form but similar in meaning, such as "boy" and "lad." Expressions which have essentially the same meaning are said to be **SYNONYMOUS**. No two words are completely synonymous.

SYNTAX is the selection and arrangement of words in phrases, clauses, and sentences.

TENSE is usually a form of a verb which indicates time relative to a discourse or some event in a discourse. The most common forms of tense are past, present, and future.

TEXT, TEXTUAL refers to the various Greek and Hebrew manuscripts of the Scriptures. A **TEXTUAL READING** is the form in which words occur in a particular manuscript (or group of manuscripts), especially where it differs from others. **TEXTUAL EVIDENCE** is the cumulative evidence for a particular reading. **TEXTUAL PROBLEMS** arise when it is difficult to reconcile or to account for conflicting readings. **TEXTUAL VARIANTS** are readings of the same passage that differ in one or more details. See also **MANUSCRIPTS** and **READ, READING**.

THIRD PERSON. See **PERSON**.

TRANSLATION is the reproduction in a receptor language of the closest natural equivalent of a message in the source language, first, in terms of meaning, and second, in terms of style.

VERBS are a grammatical class of words which express existence, action, or occurrence, such as "be," "become," "run," or "think."

VERBAL has two meanings. (1) It may refer to expressions consisting of words, sometimes in distinction to forms of communication which do not employ words ("sign language," for example). (2) It may refer to word forms which are derived from verbs. For example, "coming" and "engaged" may be called verbals, and participles are called verbal adjectives.

GLOSSARY

VERSIONS are translations. The ancient, or early, versions are translations of the Bible, or of portions of the Bible, made in early times; for example, the Greek Septuagint, the ancient Syriac, or the Vulgate versions.

VOCATIVE indicates that a word or phrase is used for referring to a person or persons spoken to. In "Brother, please come here," the word "Brother" is a vocative.

VOICE in grammar is the relation of the action expressed by a verb to the participants in the action. In English and many other languages, the **ACTIVE VOICE** indicates that the subject performs the action ("John hit the man"), while the **PASSIVE VOICE** indicates that the subject is being acted upon ("The man was hit").

VOWELS are symbols representing the sound of the vocal cords, produced by unobstructed air passing from the lungs though the mouth. They were not originally included in the Hebrew system of writing; they were added later as marks associated with the consonants. See also **CONSONANTS**.

VULGATE is the Latin version of the Bible translated and/or edited originally by Saint Jerome. It has been traditionally the official version of the Roman Catholic Church.

WORDPLAY (**PLAY ON WORDS**) in a discourse is the use of the similarity in the sounds of different words to produce a special effect.

Index

This index includes concepts, key words, and terms for which the Handbook contains a discussion useful for translators.

adonai 138
anger 7, 11
anointed 129
arrogance, arrogant 174, 194
arrows 125, 126, 131

Babylonians 66, 75
bars 55
battering ram 31
battlements 159, 189
behold 21, 38, 104, 203
Belial 17, 22
belly 133
birds of the air 147
blood 100, 103
bloody 41
body 133
bonds 19

call upon 192
captivity 51
Chaldeans 66, 75
chargers 29
chariot, chariots 29, 30, 124
city, cities 41, 100, 159, 184
correction 184
cup 107
Cush 50, 121, 143, 144, 175, 176, 192
cut off 18, 20, 22, 147, 188
    cutting off 102

daughter
    daughter of Jerusalem 198
    daughter of Zion 197
day 191, 194, 199
    day of the LORD 151, 157, 166
deep 127
den 36

discipline 184
dismay 32
draw water 55
dream 4, 68

eagle 77
earth 100
emperor 61
enjoined 190
Ethiopia 50, 121, 144, 176, 192
evening wolves 76, 186
everlasting 82
exile 51

faithful 92
faithless 84
fear 115, 190
fig trees 53
fish of the sea 147
flock 137
fold, folds 137, 170
fortress, fortresses 53, 79
forts 55
fury 11, 158

gates 54
gird your loins 26
glory 27, 105, 107, 118
GOD 138
gods 20
grasshopper 58
graven image 20
guilty 80

harlot 43, 44
head 130, 131
heart 35, 198
herd 137
hinds 138

INDEX

holy 82, 84
horsemen 77
horses 124
host, hosts 38
    host of the heavens 149
    Lord of hosts 38
house 100, 101, 153
humble 166, 195

idol 110
image
    graven image 20
    metal image 110
    molten image 20
incense 86
iniquity 103

jealous 6
judgments 198
justice 188

king 61, 144
knowledge 105

lamps 156
lees 156
leopards 76
lion, lions 36, 37, 185
locust 57, 58
loins 26, 35
look 21
Lord, LORD
    adonai 138
    LORD Almighty 38
    LORD of hosts 38
lot, lots 52, 174
lowly 195

majesty 27
mantelet 31
men 160
merchants 59, 155
molten image 20
mountains 10

name 149, 195
nation, nations 164, 189
net 86

oath 173
officials 152

oracle 3, 68

pagans 152
pens 170
pestilence 119
plague 119
pledges 97
plunder 28, 34, 41, 42, 174
    plunderers 28
poor 132
pride 174
princes 60
profane 187
promised 22
prophet 68
prostitute 43, 44
pure
    purer 84

rampart 49
rebelled 194
refuge 53
remnant 171, 195
restore . . . fortunes 171, 204
righteous 84, 92
    righteousness 166
roofs 149

sacred 187
salvation 129
save 129
scribes 60
seek 165
seine 86
Selah 118
shafts 131
shame 102, 106, 108, 194
shameless 164
Sheol 94
shepherds 61
Shigionoth 115
soul 92
stagger 107
stalls 137
stretch out
    stretch out his hand 176
    stretch out my hand 148
stronghold 12
Sudan 50, 121, 143, 144, 175, 176, 192
swear 149, 173

sword 38, 56, 176

tablets 90
taunt 96
    taunting 172
tents 122
terror 32
threshold 152, 179
tower 89
traders 155
treacherous 84
trust 185

vines 136
vineyards 157

violence 70, 78, 100, 108, 153, 187
vision 4, 68, 90
vows 22

wall 49
watchtower 89
whore 43, 44
wind 80
woe 41, 97, 184
wolves 76, 185
    evening wolves 76, 186
world 100
wrath 158, 161

yoke 19

Printed in the United States of America